Competing with Integrity in International Business

COMPETING WITH INTEGRITY IN INTERNATIONAL BUSINESS

RICHARD T. DE GEORGE

NEW YORK   OXFORD
OXFORD UNIVERSITY PRESS
1993

Oxford University Press

Oxford   New York   Toronto
Delhi   Bombay   Calcutta   Madras   Karachi
Kuala Lumpur   Singapore   Hong Kong   Tokyo
Nairobi   Dar es Salaam   Cape Town
Melbourne   Auckland   Madrid

and associated companies in
Berlin   Ibadan

Copyright © 1993 by Richard T. De George

Published by Oxford University Press, Inc.
200 Madison Avenue, New York, New York 10016

Oxford is a registered trademark of Oxford University Press

Library of Congress Cataloging-in-Publication Data
De George, Richard T.
Competing with integrity in international business
Richard T. De George.
p. cm.   Includes bibliographical references and index.
ISBN 0-19-508225-7
ISBN 0-19-508226-5 (pbk.)
1. International business enterprises—Moral and ethical aspects.
2. Business ethics.   I. Title.
HD2755.5.D42   1993   338.8′8—dc20   92-39089

1 3 5 7 9 8 6 4 2

Printed in the United States of America
on acid-free paper

Preface

Business is global. Large corporations no longer operate within the confines of a single nation. They routinely cross borders in search of resources, labor, and markets. American multinational corporations are American in origin and in central control, but truly international as functioning enterprises.

The development of international and global business has proceeded faster than traditional institutions have been able to keep up with. The ordinary restraints of law that keep competition fair have national roots. A comparable system of international ground rules lags far behind the international activity of corporations. In such a situation how is a company of integrity to act? This question, to which some companies respond with perplexity and others not at all, is the topic of this book.

In dealing with this question, I develop three themes. The first is that business—national or international—can be no more ethical than the persons who run the firms. Companies that act with integrity are a function of individuals within them who act with integrity. Top managers are the crucial players. Unless they exemplify integrity, demand it of their employees, and support it throughout the firm, the company cannot—and so will not—act with integrity. Acting with integrity requires moral imagination and courage, as well as recognition of the fact that so acting is sometimes costly. Nonetheless, personal integrity is not enough.

The second theme is the need to adopt the techniques of ethical displacement in approaching many issues in international business. Ethical issues and dilemmas are not always resolvable at the level at which they appear. For this reason concern with corporate structures and policies is essential. Individuals are constrained by the organization, structures, and policies of the companies for which they work. These may either reinforce their intention to act with integrity or thwart it. The same is true at each level—that of the firm, the industry, the nation, or the international community. Firms that wish to act with integrity may find themselves impelled to follow unfair industry practices or may find their actions constrained by them. The story can be recapitulated at the level of industries and nations, and finally at the global level. Solutions must be sought at the appropriate level.

The third theme is the urgent need for adequate background institutions to constrain tendencies toward unfairness by the market, the free-enterprise system, and perceived self-interest on all levels. The purpose of such institutions is to promote fair conditions of competition and to offset the power of multinational corporations and banks with comparably strong international and global social, political, and economic forces.

After arguing in the first two chapters for the possibility of and the need for both ethical norms and constraining international background institutions—laws, customs, nongovernmental organizations, and unions—in Chapter 3 I propose seven specific guidelines that apply to American multinationals operating in less developed countries. These are built primarily on a widely accepted principle: do no direct intentional harm. Chapter 4 considers the application of these guidelines to five different kinds of industries, each of which requires a different analysis.

In chapter 5 I argue for three additional norms that apply to dangerous industries, based on an examination of the Union Carbide Bhopal case. The purpose of that analysis is to show how the guidelines can be extended.

Chapter 6 explicitly develops the technique of ethical displacement and illustrates it by examining bribery in the international context. It develops the notions of moral imagination and moral courage, so necessary for a company of integrity.

Business ethics has most often closed its eyes to the fact that business sometimes operates in corrupt environments. How is a company of integrity to behave in such an environment? Chapter 7 attempts to answer that question by developing ten strategies such corporations may legitimately adopt in defending their interests. It then exemplifies those strategies in different kinds of corrupt contexts in which multinationals may operate.

The changes in Central and Eastern Europe since 1989 raise new possibilities and new temptations for American multinationals. Chapter 8 deals with these, while Chapter 9 investigates, from an ethical perpsective, the growing tensions between Japanese and American business interests, and the challenges posed by the emerging European Community.

The final chapter goes beyond rules to develop notions of ethical ideals and corporate virtue and to discuss their place in corporate culture in an international context.

Ethical issues in international busines are not of concern only to specialists in business ethics. Such issues arise as an integral part of everyday questions that must be decided by those in business. Hence, discussions and analyses of these issues should be intelligible and accessible to those in business and to the general public. To meet this requirement I have avoided technical terms and philosophical jargon to the extent possible. Those not interested in the philosophical disputes surrounding some issues can ignore the footnotes without loss. Those who wish to pursue a topic further or who wish some guidance to the literature on certain philosophically contentious points will find help in the notes.

Managers of multinationals who are interested in acting with integrity on the international scene can refer to this book to guide them through some of the perplexing problems they face, to answer some of the objections critics raise, and to find examples of what some companies have already done along these lines. The norms, discussions, guidelines, and strategies can help members of the interested and the critical public sort through complicated issues in order to assess the actions of multinationals from an ethical point of view before imposing ethical censure. The book can also serve as an aid in developing model codes and in discussing appropriate national legislation or international agreements. Finally it may serve as a guide for students approaching international business, sensitizing them to some of the problems they may face in their careers.

No single work that attempts to deal with the whole scope of ethical issues in international business can expect to provide the last word. I hope that this initial effort will stimulate a much needed continuing discussion.

I wrote the first draft of this book while I was on sabbatical from the University of Kansas and while a Resident at the Rockefeller Foundation Bellagio Study and Conference Center. I am pleased to acknowledge the support of both the University and the Foundation.

Lawrence, Kan.   R. T. DeG.
November 1992

Contents

Competing with Integrity in International Business

1

Integrity in International Business: A Contradiction in Terms?

An American businessman was transferred to Italy from the home office in Connecticut. On his first assignment, on a warm July day, he accompanied a shipment of several trucks loaded with butter from Switzerland to the company's plant in Milan. When the trucks reached the Italian border, they were waved to the side of the road. There they stood as the customs inspectors passed other vehicles through. It soon became apparent to the businessman that the absence of a small payment to the customs officials was delaying his shipment. But as a proper American he refused to offer such a payment. Several hours later he noticed melted butter beginning to seep out a crack below the rear door of one of the trucks.

Another American manager was transferred to the company's auto manufacturing plant in South Africa. Although the company in the United States prided itself on its anti-discrimination policy and on the way it treated its employees, the manager soon saw that blacks were systematically discriminated against in many ways in the South African plant, even though the company claimed not to enforce the apartheid laws.

When a business-person is faced with situations such as these, is integrity in international business possible or is it a contradiction in terms—comparable to military intelligence or an inexpensive hospital stay? Can a multinational corporation compete successfully in international markets while living up to its own highest standards of ethical integrity? After all, profit is the corporation's aim, competition is often fierce, and not all the players abide by the same rules.

Globalization is the major business strategy for the 1990s. A global company internalizes the worldwide division of labor and stands ready to move its operations as necessary to take advantage of lower wages, of attractive interest and tax rates, and of available resources. Such companies loosen their national roots and identification, and assume a global stance. In the first wave of internationalization, American multinational companies were clearly *American* companies operating abroad. In the second wave they sought to be "good citizens" of each of the countries in which they located. In the third wave, they are increasingly global and owe primary allegiance to no particular nation. American workers have no special claim on the jobs such companies make available; and their owners are as likely to be non-American as American. Although we can still speak of Ford, General Motors, IBM, Hewlett-Packard, and Johnson & Johnson as American corporations, the sense in which they are American is becoming more and more tenuous.

In such a situation American laws and restraints become less and less confining, as do the laws of any other nation. If it is too heavily taxed, or if wage levels or the cost of operating are too high, a company can simply move all or part of its operations to more fertile ground. As the corporate ability to escape national constraints increases, the need for multinational and global restraints becomes more pressing. And in the absence of such restraints, corporate self-restraint—corporate integrity—becomes more important.

Americans now accept as legitimate discussions about business ethics in the United States, even though such talk has not yet greatly changed the way business is done. In 1987–1988, commentators on the insider trading scandals often attempted to excuse Wall Street from any obligation to change its ways by instead blaming the business schools for not teaching business ethics[1]—as if Ivan Boesky or David Levine would never have engaged in their vastly lucrative (and illegal) activities if they had only taken a course in business ethics.[2] Newly adopted ethical codes have enabled some firms to clothe themselves in moral trappings, while changing little or nothing in their structures or practices.

In many firms, raising ethical issues used to be taboo; now it is legitimate. The media have recognized the importance of ethics in business and have helped foster it. *Financial World* dedicated an issue to business ethics;[3] the *Wall Street Journal,* the *Christian Science Monitor,* and the *Boston Globe* have featured business ethics articles. Some corporations—Boeing, among others— have introduced ethical hotlines and ombudsmen, enabling workers to get answers to ethical problems they face on the job or to report sexual harassment or other perceived injustices without fear of negative repercussions. Major corporations, such as McDonnell Douglas and GTE, have introduced in-house ethics education programs.[4] According to one survey, 93 percent of responding Fortune 500 firms have adopted corporate ethical codes.[5] At least some of those firms are genuinely interested in acting ethically.

Nor has interest in business ethics been confined to the United States. The United Kingdom, Brazil, Belgium, France, Italy, Germany, Spain, Switzerland, and Japan have all evinced interest in business ethics through centers, journals, and conferences. The European Business Ethics Network[6] provides a forum where business leaders and academics can discuss ethical issues in business in the broad European context.

Still, the Myth of Amoral Business—the belief that morality has no role to play in business or business decisions—persists on the national level and dominates the thinking and perceptions of most people on the international level.[7] This myth is worth exploring, since it hides more than it reveals.

On the international level, the Myth of Amoral Business expresses the belief that multinationals generally do not bother about ethics in their international dealings. The belief is not that they always act unethically, but that they proceed amorally: they ignore the ethical dimension of their actions. Since they are in the business of making money, not of doing good, why should anyone expect them to act differently? And according to the myth, if any company were to consider ethics seriously, it would probably operate at such a competitive disadvantage that it would soon go out of business. The pervading attitude is exemplified by the remark: "They're an ethical firm, so we have the competitive edge."

Internationally, the Myth of Amoral Business correctly describes the attitude of many people inside and outside multinationals. But it is only part of the story; the myth conceals the other part.

Multinationals have received a great deal of criticism during the past ten to fifteen years. Exxon's handling of the oil spill off of the Alaska coast is just one example. Early on, Exxon cavalierly declared that the oil spill had been cleaned up,[8] even though many beaches remained black and newly contaminated sea gulls could not flap their oil-soaked wings. The widespread critical reaction was expressed in ethical language, and Exxon's actions or its lack of adequate activity in the oil cleanup was characterized as unconscionable, uncaring, and despicable. The condemnation was made in moral terms, even leading some of its credit card customers to return their cards[9] with strong statements condemning the company's lack of adequate action.

This reaction would be unintelligible if the Myth of Amoral Business told the whole story. If no one believed that companies either did or should act in accordance with ethical principles, no one would apply ethical standards in evaluating Exxon's actions. Since ordinary people—as well as the news media and a number of governments—did apply ethical standards in evaluating Exxon's acts and omissions, they clearly believed it was proper to do so. Their ethical judgments were certainly intelligible. But if the myth of Amoral Business were correct, such judgments would be neither proper nor intelligible. The customers who sent back their credit cards and the many others who refused to purchase Exxon gasoline imposed moral sanctions on the company—another activity that would make no sense if Exxon could not or should not be expected to live up to any ethical norms.

The Myth of Amoral Business at most represents the belief that multinationals do not care about ethics or morality, that they concern themselves exclusively with profit, and that all else goes by the board. The myth obscures the fact that people do apply ethical criteria in judging international business. Those who believe the myth ignore the fact that people like themselves own, run, and work for the multinationals.

Integrity

Where and how does integrity enter this picture? Acting with integrity is the same as acting ethically or morally. Yet the word *integrity* does not have the same negative connotations that ethics does for many people; nor does it have the overtones of moralizing that the term *morality* often carries with it. Acting with integrity means both acting in accordance with one's highest self-accepted norms of behavior and imposing on oneself the norms demanded by ethics and morality. Since the word *integrity* implies self-imposed norms, a demand that companies act with integrity is more acceptable and less threatening to many multinationals than is a demand that they act ethically or morally—even though the two amount to the same demand.

At the heart of the multinational's concerns is competition. The stress of competition provides the major impetus for acting unethically or for violating the norms that prevail under ordinary conditions. Hence the importance of competing with integrity. In one sense "competing with integrity" means competing against others in a way consistent with one's own highest values. In a second sense, it captures the tension between integrity and competition: one competes against integrity, fights it, tries to avoid it for the sake of profit. Only a person or a firm of integrity competes with integrity in the first sense.

Integrity is an ethically charged term. Since it means living up to one's highest standards, and since these standards are self-imposed, acting with integrity emphasizes the autonomy of the firm and of the top managers. Managers of multinationals tolerate being preached at no better (and perhaps worse) than do others. Typically they are powerful people in their own domain; and although they may seek the expert advice or opinion of others in a variety of areas—perhaps even in the ethical domain—they consider it their right and obligation to make corporate decisions without being told what to do by others outside the firm.

The autonomy they claim is not only appropriate, it is also essential to ethical action. Firms and those who run them are responsible for what they do. They cannot avoid that responsibility, even though they might sometimes like to, and even though they may sometimes act as if they do not have the responsibility imputed to them—as did Exxon in response to the Alaska oil spill.

Although integrity requires norms to be self-imposed and self-accepted, they cannot be entirely arbitrary and self-serving. It is possible to talk about the integrity of acting in accordance with self-imposed norms that allow one to do whatever is necessary to achieve one's goals. But it is a misuse of the term to talk about the integrity of a Hitler who acted on his beliefs in order to achieve racial purity through genocide, or of a Mafia hitman who lives up to the code of his profession. Integrity requires norms not only to be self-imposed, but also to be ethically justifiable, proper, and integral to the self-imposed process of forming a whole with a set of positive values.

Acting with integrity involves more than simply acting as ethical or moral norms demand; such behavior constitutes the moral minimum. We can divide actions into those that are prohibited on the one hand, and those that are either required or permitted on the other hand. Consider a line dividing the two groups. Acting with integrity does not consist in testing how close one can come to committing a prohibited action while remaining on the permissible side of the line. Acting with integrity extends beyond satisfying the bare moral minimum; it involves acting in accordance with moral norms willingly, know-ingly, purposefully, and because one is in command of one's action. It requires one to make conscious choices so that one's actions accord with one's princi-ples. It often requires courage. How much more than the bare minimum is required? There is no way to answer this question prescriptively. But beyond what is required exists a sphere of actions that are morally praiseworthy though not required.[10] This sphere, which we might call the ideal, challenges the person or firm of integrity to do more than the minimum. And those with integrity will rise into that sphere at least to some extent.

No company that acts with integrity will exploit its workers or pay them less than subsistence wages. No company with integrity will fire its employees arbitrarily or without cause. Some companies go well beyond this requirement of fairness and adopt a policy of continuous employment. They are known for retaining their employees even in times of economic difficulty. Such willing-ness to go beyond basic moral requirements characterizes a company with integrity, and such actions build the company's positive reputation as a com-pany with integrity.

A firm that ignores ethics gains a competitive edge, claims the cynic. But a firm that acts with integrity need be no pushover: acting with integrity does not carry with it the overtones of naivete that acting ethically sometimes does. Competing with integrity does not imply either a reluctance to compete or an inability to compete aggressively. Integrity demands toughness, but not the simplistic toughness of a brute. In fact, it demands precisely the institutional discipline that often gives one a competitive edge. Competing with integrity is not synonymous with competing successfully, but it is by no means antithetical to it. Competing successfully with integrity is in fact the aim and the norm of individuals who compete with integrity.

Reputation and Integrity

A company's reputation is one of its most important assets—an asset that does not appear on its financial balance sheet. A reputation as a reliable, ethical company justifiably commands a premium from those who use the company's products or services. Employees take pride in working for a well-reputed com-pany, trust their futures to it, and assume that they will be treated fairly by it. Their loyalty to the company reflects the company's loyalty to them. Subcon-tractors and other firms prefer to do business with a firm known for its integrity, and they feel secure in doing so. Customers similarly prefer to deal with a firm they feel they can trust. Reputation is a result of continuous ethical action and of an ethical corporate culture. The reputation for being ethical depends not only on acting ethically but also on being perceived as acting ethically.[11]

The story of how Johnson & Johnson's credo and culture emboldened the leaders of the company's Tylenol division to order an immediate recall of the product after seven deaths were linked to it in Chicago in 1982 has almost passed into legend. They acted before the government forced a recall and before their PR department had a chance to paint a defensive picture. They acted despite the $100 million anticipated cost and the possible demise of their product.[12] They did so because they believed that their action would be backed up by the parent corporation. The company credo and culture fostered an atmosphere in which executives could and did act on principle.[13] The public reacted favorably to the company and its actions, and Tylenol was able to regain its former premier position in the market. Such stories are what reputations are made of.

IBM also has a reputation for acting on principle. Among other things, IBM is known for not paying or soliciting bribes. Some companies claim that one cannot do business in certain countries unless transactions take place under the table. But if IBM cannot conduct all its transactions above board in a particular market, it does not operate in that country. Having this reputation lessens the likelihood of its being approached for bribes and makes a negative response easy when it is approached.

Ethical action is compatible with profit and success. One might even claim that, to some extent, ethical action explains the success of IBM and Johnson & Johnson. Ethics without a good product and without good management will not make a company succeed. But without ethics a good product and smart management cannot guarantee a company's success.

A standard reply to the Johnson & Johnson and IBM stories is that it is easy for successful and profitable leaders in the field to be ethical. It is much harder for the many companies following the leader to be ethical, especially those losing money or barely making a profit. Although the reply is true, nothing important follows from it. The IBMs and the Johnson & Johnsons all started out small. If they had acted unethically then, they probably would not have achieved what they have. Certainly they would not have established the reputations they currently enjoy. A company cannot act unethically or amorally while it is young and marginal, and then suddenly become ethical when it becomes a leader and profitable. And it cannot earn a reputation for integrity if it has a history of behaving amorally or unethically.

What is true on the national level is true also on the international level. A company that behaves ethically in the United States tends to behave ethically abroad. But three difficulties face any company that operates abroad, and these difficulties are exacerbated if the company operates in developing countries. The first problem involves recognizing what is ethical in the often unfamiliar and unstructured conditions in which the company finds itself. The second involves being perceived as acting unethically, even though it acts ethically. The third relates to competing successfully against firms that do not act ethically.

Whose Ethics?

Competing ethically often raises the question: whose ethics? Competing with integrity avoids that question, since the ethics involved is clearly one's own.

Yet as simple as this sounds, it seems to beg the question of whose ethics an American multinational is to follow in foreign countries, where the ethical norms and ways of doing business may differ from those found in the United States. Are ethical norms universal or culture-bound?

As a first approach to answering this question we can look at three commonly held (but at least partly mistaken) positions. One is that ethical norms vary from place to place; hence, "when in Rome do as the Romans do"—that is, follow the local customs and rules of each country or culture. According to the "when in Rome" position, there exist no universal morality and no universal ethical rules. Its proponents implicitly say that, when operating abroad, one should ignore ethics altogether: one is not bound by the ethical rules of others, and conversely it is inappropriate to impose one's own rules on others. One should obey the enforced laws of each country when operating under its jurisdiction, but otherwise one should simply do what is best for one's business. To act otherwise is to impose one's views, standards, or norms imperialistically and unjustifiably on others.

A second view—the "righteous American" position—holds that American companies operating abroad are to be held to exactly the same rules of conduct that apply in the United States. Companies should obey the same standards of law, even if those standards are not mandated abroad. Implicitly proponents of this view claim that, since ethics requires American companies to adhere to the standards imposed by American law at home, if they wish to be ethical abroad, they must adhere to the American standards there as well. To fall below OSHA, FDA, or other U.S. regulations in one's operations abroad is to act unethically.

The third position—that of the "naive immoralist"—is that corporations from other countries and many self-styled global corporations do not follow any ethical rules. If American companies attempted to do so, they would be put at a competitive disadvantage. Hence, they need not follow ethical rules abroad. A variation of this position claims that putting oneself at such a competitive disadvantage undermines American business, and perhaps the American economy as a whole. Hence, obeying ethical rules in international business is either inappropriate or (to speak more strongly) immoral—since every company has a moral obligation to provide for the well-being of its employees, its stockholders, and its home country.

All three positions fail to prove their points; but individuals concerned with integrity in business want to know why. Moreover, each of the three positions does contain a certain amount of truth from which we can learn.

When in Rome

To the two cases with which we began this chapter, the "when in Rome" position gives an easy answer. Although that answer is not always wrong, it is too easy.

The "when in Rome" position holds that multinationals are either citizens or guests of the various countries in which they operate. Therefore in each location they should obey the country's laws and follow local customs. An American multinational has no right or obligation to promote laws against corruption or to foster labor unions or to promote other institutions governing the way business is done in the host country. That is a function of national governments. Multinationals should not try to second-guess their host countries but should respect the ability of those countries to govern themselves. Consequently, firms may ethically pursue their own advantage as long as they obey the laws and customs of the countries in which they operate.

If the "when in Rome" rationale stopped there, one could hardly fault the position. But its adherents go on to claim that there are no universal ethical norms; thus, an American company abroad has no obligation to abide by what it perceives to be the ethical norms at home, if they differ from the local norms.

If the "when in Rome" position is interpreted to mean that there is no universal morality and that no rules are accepted in fact in all civilized countries, it is simply false.[14] All countries hold that it is wrong for one person to kill another arbitrarily. Unless this were so, the lives of all foreigners (including all business people) would be at risk in any foreign country—which is clearly not the case. Nor is lying and stealing morally acceptable in any country. If these actions were morally acceptable, the society would soon fall into disarray and cease to exist. The differences between societies are not as extreme as the position maintains. At best, defenders of the position can claim that not all ethical rules are universally recognized, and that certain ethical rules may be recognized in one society but not in another. But even if we grant that significant ethical differences exist internationally, we still have a large number of ethical norms that are common to all civilized societies; and the "when in Rome" argument gives no grounds for violating these norms, even if they are violated more in the host country than at home.

This presumption frequently lies at the heart of the "when in Rome" claim. For example, it claims that, because more people engage in bribery in Italy than in the United States, therefore I may engage in bribery when in Italy. The conclusion in no way follows. The position conceals a double shift in its claims: the first is a shift from what ethical propriety demands in the one case (at home) to what people do, albeit unethically, in the other (in Rome); the second is a shift from what ethical propriety demands (at home) to what is easiest or most profitable to do (in Rome). Rarely do people who hold this position argue that one must adopt more stringent ethical rules abroad than at home if those are the ones found in Rome, or that one must follow the local customs even if they are more costly than those at home.

Because of differing circumstances, the application of the same ethical principles in different countries may yield different practices. The appropriate reaction is not to cast off ethics because some justifiable practices vary from place to place. The general obligation is to abide by what one believes are the ethical norms applicable to the case. If one's belief about the applicable ethical rules differs from the belief that prevails in the host country, then one's responsibility is to sort out the differences and to determine how properly to act. Disregarding ethics in these circumstances is like arguing that, if I add up the check in a restaurant and find that my total differs from the waiter's total, I don't have to pay any money because we disagree about the correct amount. I might wish that this were the case—especially when the bill is a large one—but my wishing does not make it so.

Yet there is more truth in the "when in Rome" position than many moralists are willing to admit. Customs do differ from country to country, as do laws, and firms are required to obey the established laws of the countries in which they operate. Otherwise, they are subject to the penalties prescribed for violation of the laws. If a company wishes to compete effectively within a country, it must meet the competition. If a company is to succeed abroad, it must know the local customs and comply with them. To this extent, when in Rome one should act as the Romans do.

Multinationals may legitimately claim that they are citizens of each of the countries in which they operate, and that the pattern of conduct adopted by a "good citizen" may vary somewhat from society to society. This is compatible with the general rule that one should abide by and obey all the just rules and laws of the country in which one operates. But how does one judge whether the rules or laws are "just"? Initially at least, the only answer consistent with integrity is that one must live up to one's own standards. A multinational with integrity must have standards.

However, there is an important difference between customs, mores, and law on the one hand and ethics on the other. Customs, mores, and law do vary from country to country, and a business that wishes to succeed must consider these differences and on the whole respect them. Yet despite the claims of some simplistic critics, basic morality does not vary from country to country, even though certain practices may be ethical in one country and not in another because of differing circumstances. Getting this subtle difference straight is the crux of the matter.

We can distinguish unethical actions from illegal ones and both of these from differing customs by looking at the extremes of this spectrum. No society can exist whose members are allowed to kill other members of the society arbitrarily. Such a society would be chaotic and short-lived. At the other end of the spectrum are customs that vary that are neither right nor wrong, ethical or unethical, in themselves. In the British Isles traffic moves on the left; in the United States it moves on the right. Neither driving on the right nor driving on the left is the ethically correct way to drive. But if you are in England, you had better drive on the left to avoid accidents and to get wherever you are going. Clearly not all differences are moral differences.

We cannot ignore the fact that different societies sometimes make different moral claims. But if the claims are truly contradictory, then only one of them can be correct. Often, however, the contradiction preserves an unresolved dispute about which side is right. In the past, countries that practiced slavery safeguarded that institution with laws; and many (if not all) of those that practiced slavery believed it was ethical to do so. If an American multinational were to operate in such a country today, could it ethically practice slavery under the "when in Rome" principle? After all, would it not be at a competitive disadvantage if it paid its workers while other firms did not? Who are we to say that people cannot be slaves in another country? Why must the ethics prevalent in the United States bind an American company abroad, when the ethics prevalent in the foreign country would be to its greater advantage? Surely these are specious questions.

An American company cannot ethically practice slavery, even if it is practiced in some host country. Slavery is ethically wrong, even if not all people recognize it as wrong. This is not just an American insight or belief: slavery is ethically wrong not because Americans believe it to be wrong, but because the practice fails to recognize human beings as human beings. It makes them chattels and fails to grant them the respect and dignity that all human beings have a right to enjoy.[15]

Most American companies would not balk at the statement that they could not ethically engage in slavery, even if it were practiced in the host country. If this is correct, then they must accept the principle that American companies may not ethically engage in some practices, even if those practices are legal in the host country. This is sufficient to controvert the principle of pure ethical relativity implied in the "when in Rome" position. American companies operating in Rome may not ethically do *whatever* the Romans do, if what the Romans do is recognized to be unethical by Americans and most others outside that country. Where there is a difference of ethical opinion, the American firm that wishes to act with integrity must act in accordance with its beliefs, even as it attempts to understand the ethical justification (if any) given for the practice in the host country; it cannot ethically change its beliefs merely to take advantage of less stringent practices in other countries.

Just as a company may not engage in slavery, neither may it engage in apartheid and other forms of non-competence-related discrimination. One cannot change one's ethics the way a chameleon changes color. Moreover, a company that tries to adopt one set of ethical norms here and another set there will tend not to act ethically, but to avoid ethical restraints to the greatest extent possible, playing off one side against the other. Acting with integrity means acting consistently with one's ethical principles or norms. The answer to the case of the American in South Africa, with which we began this chapter, therefore, is that the manager may not enforce the discrimination laws against blacks and must find some way to avoid such discrimination.

The issue of bribery is an interesting test of the "when in Rome" position. Typically proponents are quick to claim that bribery in this or that country is necessary if one is to compete successfully, and hence is a legitimate practice in which to engage, even if it is illegitimate in the United States.[16] The position moves too quickly both in claiming that bribery is customary in the country in question and in concluding that it is justifiable. Not only must a firm with integrity be willing to distinguish between what is customary and what is morally required, but it must also distinguish between what is customary and what is simply tolerated practice.

No society can adopt bribery as a universal practice, because by its nature bribery involves unfairness (harm to some and unearned benefit to others) and is practiced covertly. If bribery were the rule that everyone followed, it would cease to be bribery, and instead become a cost of doing a certain kind of business. Consider, for instance, the practice of tipping. In the United States it is customary to leave a tip for a waiter or waitress. But in some other countries tipping is not customary, and is considered demeaning and insulting. In itself tipping is neither ethical nor unethical. But tips now account for an important part of waiters' and waitresses' incomes in the United States. Not only is it customary to leave tips, but the practice is widely and openly practiced, even though not legally demanded, and it is a justifiable practice that one teaches one's children.

Now if in some country civil servants are known to earn part of their salary from small payments made by those who use their services, one can ensure better service by making such payments. Simply because Americans do not tip civil servants does not mean that it is wrong everywhere to do so. We can distinguish tipping from bribery, and should do so.

Are so-called "facilitating payments"[17] that induce civil servants to do their jobs closer to tipping than to bribery, and may they ethically be paid by a U.S. firm of integrity?

The line between acceptable and unacceptable payments is not always easy to draw. American and foreign laws provide some guidelines; ethical reasoning provides others. Ethical considerations prompt us to ask a number of questions. For instance, who (if anyone) gets hurt by the payment, and who benefits? Helping enrich the corrupt leaders of a country at the expense of their people is not ethically justifiable. Can the payments be declared on the company's books both in the country in question and in the United States? If not—and if the payment involves keeping dual sets of books, falsifying reports or tax statements, or some other subterfuge—it is ethically impermissible. How large is the sum involved, both absolutely and relative to the sale? Small reportable amounts are more likely to be a part of the ethically permissible cost of doing business than are large amounts, other things being equal. Does the payment take place after a bidding process or before? If after, can the payment be considered and recorded as a discount, and is the process open and known to all participants? If before, is the payment required to get consideration at all, or is it a guarantee of one's sale? The payment is not ethical if it subverts a fair bidding process. These and similar questions and considerations, if applied honestly, can help a firm distinguish justifiable from ethically unjustifiable payments. Unless the payment in question is truly a common practice that is openly accepted, it becomes ethically suspect.

In some cases a payment may be required but not ethically justifiable. If so, acting with integrity translates into not making a sale one could otherwise make. Acting with integrity is not always profitable, especially in the short run, but all companies draw the line somewhere in pursuing profit. A solid ethical foundation helps a company draw the line in a way that protects its integrity, its reputation, and the integrity of those who work for it.

Some American firms have learned that, if their products are good enough, they can compete without paying bribes in many countries; and in some countries they can find alternatives to paying bribes. Official complaints by groups of American companies have changed the practice of bribery in some countries,[18] and collective or industry-wide efforts have proved to be more effective than efforts by individual firms to oppose a pattern of bribery solicitation.

The "when in Rome" position does not bother to distinguish between unethical practices and ethically permissible customs that differ from those in the United States—a distinction that companies wishing to act with integrity must make. Often, those who profess the "when in Rome" position trade on differences in customs to do whatever is most profitable or otherwise advantageous for them. At its worst, the position becomes an excuse not to act on moral principle at all, and indeed to ignore ethics in all business actions. Since multinationals engage in trade across borders, they are not bound by the rules of any country when operating between countries. They can transfer prices as they wish on the open seas; they can charge more or less for products they buy from their foreign subsidiaries, as it suits them. Such practices, if not governed by the laws of either the host or the mother country, have no Rome to govern them. Integrity is all the more important when law does not apply.

The "when in Rome" position is partly correct and partly incorrect. Much confusion can be eliminated by sorting out the ethical issues from the issues of customs or law, and by keeping clear the distinction between ethical principles and matters of fact. Sorting out the issues will not solve all disputes or get rid of all confusion, but it is a necessary first step in solving or dissolving some of the ethical dilemmas that American firms face when operating abroad.

What of the melting butter case? The answer given by the "when in Rome" position—that the payment is justifiable—is correct, but not its reason. If this were a case of bribery, then the mere fact that it was widely practiced would not make it right. As presented, the case may either involve a customary payment that is legal, generally recognized, and accepted, or it is a case of extortion. In the latter instance, the great harm done to the cargo and the loss involved justifies the small payment involved, provided that the incident is reported and the company looks into ways of precluding such payments in the future.[19] If it is truly the custom to make such payments, then the action does not constitute the paying of a bribe (which would otherwise be unethical) that is somehow made right because it is widely practiced. Rather, it is a generally accepted payment that is made to get some minor official to do what he is supposed to do, and the initial failure to pay resulted from the American's not knowing local customs. In the case in point, the customs officer's job was to inspect and pass legitimate goods. The belated payment would induce him to do that job expeditiously; but it would not induce him to pass goods without inspecting them at all or to pass contraband goods. Such a transaction would constitute bribery and would be both unethical and illegal. The payment would not place the payee in some position of advantage vis-a-vis others. It would not undercut fair competition. It would not amount to a large sum. It would not require falsification of books, and would be reportable as a business expense. Hence, even though distasteful to the American, the payment if truly customary would not be unethical.

Not every payment of gratuities would be ethically justifiable. One that involved deceit, double bookkeeping, unfairness to others, corruption of high-level government officials, or other forms of wrongdoing would change the case and its outcome. The "when in Rome" position argues that even such payments are justifiable if widely practiced. That is a shortcoming of the "when in Rome" position.

The Righteous American

Arthur Kelly describes an American bank manager who was sent to Italy and was appalled to learn that the local branch's accounting department recommended grossly underreporting the bank's profits for income tax purposes.[20] The manager insisted that the bank report its earnings accurately, American-style. When he was called by the Italian Tax Department to the firm's tax hearing, he was told that his firm owed three times as much tax as it had paid, reflecting the department's standard assumption that each firm underreports its earnings by two-thirds. Despite his protests, the new assessment stood. Assuming that the case is accurately reported and that the same procedure will be followed the next year, how should the manager report his company's earnings the next time tax returns are due?

Individuals adhering to the "righteous American" position insist that the manager not underreport earnings, since that is not the American way.

The "righteous American" position maintains that American multinationals are American companies first and multinational companies second. Insofar as they are American companies they both represent the United States and benefit from the power, influence, and prestige of the American nation and the American government. The United States enters into treaties that enable American companies to operate abroad. The United States considers such companies American companies and takes an active interest in their welfare. Typically the American parent company controls the activities of its foreign subsidiaries, and the financial position of the parent company reflects the profits (and losses) of the subsidiary. Hence, this argument goes, American multinationals are not citizens of the various countries in which they operate. They are first and foremost American companies and are known and recognized as such wherever they operate. They must obey the laws of the countries in which they conduct business, provided that those laws are just by American standards. If a country enforces slavery or apartheid by law, that does not give an American multinational the right to engage in slavery or apartheid. Unlike citizens, who must emigrate and seek acceptance in another country, multinationals are like guests who are free to leave and return home.

The "righteous American" position thus claims that American standards of ethics are appropriate for American companies to follow in foreign countries. Furthermore, many critics of American multinationals claim not only that American companies should obey local laws and respect American ethical values, but also that they should operate in foreign countries—especially less developed ones—in the same ways as they do in the United States: they should pay comparable wages; they should enforce the same standards of worker protection; and they should recognize the same rights of workers and of consumers as they do in the United States. To do less is to take advantage of their strength and position and to exploit the host country's workers, consumers, environment, and nationhood in general.

In evaluating the "when in Rome" position we implicitly evaluated a portion of the "righteous American" position. The latter position correctly insists that, in cases of real moral disagreement, American firms must abide by their best lights. They cannot change their moral beliefs as they change the language in which their products are advertised.

The "righteous American" position also correctly points out that American companies are American. This fact is not lost on foreign countries in which American multinationals operate or seek to operate. Multinationals are different and are treated differently from local operations, even if they claim to be unexceptional enterprises operating according to local laws and customs.

Yet proponents of the "righteous American" position frequently go too far. Moral norms may apply universally and, in a case of conflicting views on the morality of a practice, one may be bound to follow one's own beliefs; but it does not follow from these facts that American firms must act in foreign countries just as they do in the United States. Although no firm is morally justified in exploiting its workers, American firms do not have to pay workers throughout the world what they pay American workers. The inexpensiveness of labor in other countries is a primary reason why American firms transfer some of their manufacturing abroad. If the rate of pay offered there is not exploitative, it amounts to using the comparative advantage offered by different locales—ideally to the benefit of the workers, the host country, and the multinational firm.

Nor do the regulations mandated by OSHA, the EPA, the FDA, or other American government agencies establish morally mandatory standards that American firms must follow in every country in which they operate. The general moral injunctions to do no harm and to respect the dignity of the human person operate across borders.[21] But such ethical norms should not be confused with U.S. government regulations that may attempt to implement them and give them specificity. This point can be made by comparing U.S. regulations with those of some Western European countries. The regulations concerning drug testing and the sale of specific drugs over the counter are not identical in the United States, the United Kingdom, and Germany. Each of these countries wishes to protect its people against fraud and against harmful drugs; yet their regulations differ to some extent. We have no basis for claiming that only the American regulations are morally correct. American regulators do not arrive at the standards they set by deduction from moral principles, but by a complex of scientific and political procedures within a framework that seeks to balance moral concern for human beings and their safety with perceived economic necessity.

Since American ways are not automatically the only ethical ways to act, we can argue that the American manager with whom we began this section need not report his company's earnings in Italy exactly as the company does in the United States. The reason is that the tax systems in the United States and Italy are different. The company's ethical obligation is to pay its fair share of taxes—not to pay three times as much. If the customary way to achieve this result is to underreport earnings initially and then to pay a multiple of the initially claimed amount of taxes due, that is the ethically proper approach to tax reporting. To an American, this sounds like an odd way to arrive at one's taxes; and it surely is. But if it is the way all firms in a given place arrive at their taxes, it constitutes the accepted procedure, notwithstanding the way the law is written. For the law also allows the tax assessor to do what he in fact does.

The process can be faulted for encouraging lying and for being inefficient, even if in the end people pay their fair share of taxes. But an individual's ethical obligation is to pay his fair share of taxes, and the method established by the government to achieve this end is the one he should follow, however arcane it is. In this case, the appropriate method to follow is the one actually practiced, not the one specified in the tax forms, which fails to account for the process of the tax interview and the actual practices that take place there. In reporting one's earnings, one is not understood to be reporting the actual amount but to be reporting a figure that will serve as the basis for later negotiations. The figure submitted by the business is thus not meant to deceive the tax assessor. Indeed, given the Italian tax practice, no one either is deceived or intends to deceive, whatever the appearances to outsiders may be.

To follow the officially stated procedure in filling out the Italian tax form when no one else does is to set a standard for oneself that the state does not expect its people to follow and that they in fact do not follow. Ethics does not require that one penalize oneself in this way. But the moralist might ask, does this not mean that one is ethically permitted to ignore the law and not pay one's fair share of taxes? The answer is no. Ethics requires each person or firm to pay his or its fair share of taxes. The question is how this is determined. If the fair tax is not determined by following the instructions of the written tax form, and if the stated requirements on the form are not enforced, then it is appropriate to determine how it is in fact determined and to act accordingly. There is no need to follow American ways simply because they are American.

It is simple arrogance to assume that American ways of acting are the only morally correct or permissible ways of conducting business.

The Naive Immoralist

An American manager in Colombia routinely pays off the local drug lord to guarantee that this plant will not be bombed and that none of his employees will be kidnapped. He argues that making such payments is ethically defensible because "everybody's doing it."[22]

The "naive immoralist" position asserts that, since companies from other countries do not follow any ethical norms, American companies do not have to follow any either. To do so would put them at a competitive disadvantage. The claim here is that, if others act unethically, we too may act unethically without deserving the reproach of others. Characteristically, the claim speaks of other companies' acting unethically, which implicitly accepts the appropriateness of an ethical judgment disapproving of their actions. Yet surely, if it is ethically appropriate to evaluate the actions of these other companies, their unethical actions cannot justify our acting unethically as well. If our neighbors all engage in slavery, that doesn't justify our engaging in slavery. We all know the difference between the claim that something is right and the claim that it is done. People may lie or cheat on their taxes or engage in deception; but the fact that many people do it does not make those actions right, nor does it justify our doing it. This justification does not work on the national level and it does not work on the international level either.

The short answer to the scenario of the American manager in Colombia is that, whether or not the action is justifiable, the rationale that "everyone is doing it" is ethically inadequate. In the first place, it is not the case that "everyone is doing it," since many companies refuse to engage in the practice in question, perhaps by not operating in the country or region in question. "Everyone is doing it" is usually a rationalization that focuses only on a select group of one's choosing, not on everyone. Second, even if everyone does do something, that is no justification for doing it, if the action harms others, violates their rights, or is for some other reason unethical. Third, the claim typically is made in defense of an action that is known otherwise to be unethical. A more accurate way to evaluate the action is not to suppose that everyone is doing it, but to ask what the results would be if everyone were in fact to do it.

This analysis of "everyone is doing it" also holds for the claim that all one's competitors are doing it, whether "it" consists of extorting kickbacks, paying bribes, engaging in misleading advertising, or cheating on taxes. The added claim that, unless American companies engaged in global competition behave as unethically as the competition from other countries allegedly behaves, the consequent failure of American business will hurt the American economy cannot be taken seriously. America's economy does not depend on bribery, deception, fraud, and harming others. If it did, not much could be said in its defense from an ethical point of view. Nor does any other healthy economy depend on such practices, since they are inimical to free enterprise, fair competition, efficiency, and increased productivity.

Nonetheless, implicit in the position is a difficult issue. Although it is untrue that companies from other countries do not follow any moral norms, some companies—both from one's own country and from elsewhere—do ignore ethical norms. How can a company that wishes to act with integrity compete with such companies? More generally, how is a company to act with integrity when confronted with a system that is corrupt or that allows corruption? Are the rules in such circumstances the same as those for operating in a more ethically sanitary environment? The answer is a long one that we shall postpone for a later chapter.

At this juncture, it suffices to note that all three positions are defective. Those that attempt to justify a multinational's ignoring ethical rules fail to reflect the fact that international business requires and presupposes certain moral norms, just as American business requires and presupposes them.

The Basic Moral Norms

Some general ethical norms apply to any business operating anywhere. These norms are universally applicable because they are necessary either for a society to function or for business transactions to take place. They are widely held, and everyone is expected to live by them and up to them; they are obvious, common-sensical, and available to all. If they were arcane or difficult or available only to an intellectual elite, they could not serve as basic norms governing all human interactions.

One such moral norm is the injunction against arbitrarily killing other members of the community to which one belongs. Without such an enforced rule, people could not interact in a society. To flourish, any society must enable its members to carry on everyday activities without constant fear for their lives. Without such an enforced rule, commerce between societies would not take place. This general rule does not prohibit all killing. There may be good reasons for killing one's fellow citizens—the most obvious being self-defense. Some societies believe that it is legitimate for the state to execute criminals; and some even justify (or once justified) ritual sacrifices to the gods. None of this vitiates the general injunction, which is also consistent with killing people in another community or society, if such extreme measures are justified by war or some other condition.

The prohibition against arbitrarily killing members of one's own society includes individuals with whom one is friendly or with whom one engages in commerce. If a society is not to exist in isolation, it must attempt to guarantee the safety of others who visit it, trade with it, or enter into alliances with it. Otherwise, these interactions can not take place, or they can take place only in exceptional circumstances. Clearly business today requires that each country recognize the basic rule of respecting the lives of those with whom its citizens and companies do business. If lives are threatened—as in civil or other war—commerce tapers off or comes to an end.

A second basic norm is truthfulness: the positive injunction is to tell the truth, and the reciprocal negative injunction is not to lie. Once again this is a commonplace. Human society is built on communication. If one could not for the most part believe other people, life would be reduced to a primitive level of constant mistrust and suspicion.

Cynics argue that, although truth telling in general is a requirement for society to function, portions of society can function successfully against this background without always telling the truth. Government and business are two candidates for wholesale exceptions. But clearly this could not be a rule. If it were known that government or business was not bound by the normal rules of truthfulness, no one would believe what they said, and their lying would not be effective. The purpose of a lie is to deceive, and if no one believes what some group says, no one will be deceived. A government or a business may attempt to fool others, but unless that entity itself receives reliable information and can believe what it is told, it cannot long function, much less function efficiently. The days of *caveat emptor* ("let the buyer beware") may have yielded short-term profits for some; but following such a norm, as well as lying in advertising, cannot lead to long-term stability.

The third basic moral norm is respect for property. This rule is also obvious, even though what is considered property and what respect for it means vary from society to society. Some societies that have the institution of private property have differing rules for its ownership, transferal, and use. All societies have some forms of common property, and some may hold all productive property in common. Some societies allow the private ownership of land; others do not. Some hold land in common; still others do not extend the concept of property to land at all. Despite these differences, every society has some concept of property, because human beings need goods—food, clothing, shelter—in order to survive; and rules that regulate the use and define the abuse of those goods are necessary for a society to continue.

In its general formulatoin, each of these three norms is universal: it applies to all peoples everywhere. That fact is compatible with each norm's being given somewhat different interpretations in different societies. Anyone doing business transculturally or internationally must determine how those general rules are applied in the particular cultures in which the business operates.

In addition to general norms of this type, certain other norms are required if any business is to function. Since business consists of transactions between individuals, the conditions that make such transactions possible lead to specific ethical rules for businesses. These are not exceptions to the general norms; they are additions to those norms and generally presuppose adherence to the broader and more fundamental norms.

Consider the two norms of honoring contracts and of exercising fairness in transactions. Since these norms involve transactions or interactions that are not required transculturally for survival, they are to some extent obligations that one can choose to accept or not. One can avoid the obligation of honoring a contract simply by declining to take part in one.

If one does enter into a contract, however, one is obliged to honor it. Presupposed is the understanding that both sides to a contract are bound to honor the contract if they have entered it with reasonable freedom—that is, without coercion. A coerced contract is generally not binding. But if one freely agrees to buy or sell a certain item at a certain price by a certain date, or if one borrows with the promise to repay at a certain rate of interest by a certain time, then the contract is binding. Part of the underlying meaning of making a contract is that one commits oneself to fulfilling its conditions. If that commitment is absent at the outset, then even if formal conditions of signing have been met, there is actually no contract but only the pretense of one. A contract ethically commits a person to act in the way agreed. Hence it is unethical to break a valid contract, even if there is no clear legal mechanism to enforce it. Unless both sides understood their mutual obligation to fulfill contracts, contracts would not be made. This is compatible with attempts to secure legal guarantees against reneging and failing to fulfill a contract. But these failures make sense only against a background in which the practice is recognized to involve the obligation to act as promised, and the failures are possible only because the rule is satisfactory fulfillment and compliance.

We can speak similarly about exercising fairness in business dealings. If there were not some minimum level of trust between buyer and seller on the international level, just as on the national level, business transactions would prove impossible. The requisite trust is built on the shared assumption that each party to the contract knows what the transaction involves, has a reasonable expectation of gaining something by it, and hence engages in it freely. Without fairness transactions would be forced or would be based on one side's taking advantage of the other. For example, one side could have an unfair advantage because of access to information that should be but is not available to the other. Such transactions do take place, but they cannot be the foundation of a lasting business relationship nor the assumed normal state of affairs. If they were, the transactions would tend not to take place and not to be continued.

The same is true of the market as a whole. Unless it is perceived as fair, only those who are forced to do so by adverse circumstances or who have no other alternatives will take part. It makes no sense to participate in the market unless one hopes to benefit from it. Lack of fairness undermines the system and works against the norm of efficiency so important to the workings of a free market. For people and businesses interested in acting with integrity, all this is commonplace and poses neither a burden nor a threat.

These general ethical norms apply to all businesses in all countries and across all borders; they do not depend on one's ethical theory. The norms are applicable whether one holds that consequences are most important in ethics or that moral rules are primary, whether one acts from Christian ethics or from Confucian ethics, whether one is from a developed country or from a less developed country.[23] Like all ethical norms, moral theories provide us with general rules about which actions are right and which are wrong. Any two or more of these rules may clash, in which case one or another must give way; and it is not always possible to tell in advance which ones should have priority. In general, life is more sacred than property, but even life may sometimes be sacrificed for other values.

The American system differs in some ways from the Japanese and German models of free enterprise, just as it differs from the former Soviet Union's system of socialism and from the mixed system of post-WWII Yugoslavia. That trade and commerce are possible and have been actual with all these countries shows that these systems share some common values. Some moral norms are so necessary for international business that their systematic violation undermines the business enterprise and renders it impossible. Any country or any firm that systematically violates these norms is clearly one with which business cannot be done.

These general norms and others like them apply to multinationals from the industrially developed countries that do business both in developed and in less developed countries. Doing business in less developed countries requires additional considerations and raises special ethical obligations for the multinationals because of the unequal status of the two parties, as we shall see in more detail later.

Integrity and International Business

Although it is not difficult to argue that multinational corporations should behave with integrity abroad as well as at home, what this requires of them abroad may be somewhat different from what it requires of them at home. A crucial difference on the international scene involves the absence of many legal and other restraints that constrain American businesses at home. A second difference is the varying outlooks, needs, and practices of foreign societies and of multinational corporations from those countries. A third is the presence of corruption at governmental and other levels within some societies that far exceeds the corruption found in the United States (which has its fair share). A fourth is the difference in economic power between the largest of the multinationals and the smallest and frailest of the less developed countries in which they sometimes operate.

Wherever a company seeks to act with integrity, it must possess a firm sense of its own values, moral imagination, and moral courage. No set of moral rules or norms can be exhaustive in their specificity, and no set of them can ever replace moral reasoning in given situations. Much of the time, individuals and firms can rely on their basic intuitions and on their sense of right and wrong. In difficult or unusual situations, however, ethical intuitions are not enough. We develop such intuitions to handle the ordinary, not the extraordinary. Thought and care are required to handle the new and different.

Moral imagination is necessary both at home and abroad, but it becomes especially significant in new situations. Non-Americans affected by a business's operations may view the world differently from the way most Americans see it. It is not easy to apprehend the issues from their perspective. Operating successfully in foreign environments while respecting the people and culture in those countries requires empathy and imagination.

Equally important is moral courage. Integrity requires not only that one determine what is consistent with one's values, but also that one act in accordance with them. The cost of acting on principle is sometimes high, even though we may nurture the hope that it will pay off in the long run. Even in the short run, acting on principle strengthens the company's self-image, promotes company morale, and helps enhance the company's reputation. Moral courage is vital to a company of integrity. This is especially true in the international context in which multinationals operate—a context that may appear to be drawn from several points of view, and that in some instances may appear to be an ethical jungle.

2

The International Ethical Context

An offshore oil-drilling rig is owned and operated by a multinational oil corporation. All the workers on the rig receive per diem and away-from-home wage supplements. But some of the workers come from the United States, some from the company's operations in Saudi Arabis, some from Venezuela, and so on. Since they are all working on the same rig, should the ones doing similar work get similar pay? Should they each get their regular salary and supplements, even though these vary considerably from country to country? Or should some other criterion be applied?

Ask what constitutes a fair wage, and you will get as many plausible answers as there are criteria of justice. Some will argue in favor of remuneration according to hours worked; others according to the quality of output during those hours; others according to need and the local cost of living; still others according to the importance of the contribution made; and many according to what the market bears or requires. Which is the right answer, if there is a right answer?

Americans look upon their society as being pluralistic—a society in which people have different backgrounds and hold a wide variety of beliefs, including beliefs about justice. But this diversity pales when compared with differences worldwide. The American experience shows that business can operate ethically within a pluralistic system, and that pluralism does not preclude acting with integrity. Yet a crucial difference exists between ethical pluralism in the United States and ethical pluralism on a global level. The American political system provides mechanisms for resolving disputes, including disputes about what is just and fair; and everyone is subject to the same rules. Globally, of course, this is not the case. Views of justice are often as diverse as national political systems, and no comprehensive global adjudication mechanism exists to resolve the disputes. Nor do different societies all share any uniform set of expectations about adjudication or about the expected results thereof.

Global Pluralism

Nonetheless, global ethical pluralism, like ethical pluralism in the United States, does support a good deal of basic agreement about which practices are ethical and which are not—even beyond the common basic moral norms. And this agreement forms the basis for international trade, commerce, and agreement. Joint ventures by companies from countries with different customs are becoming commonplace. No company would take part in such a venture if it thought the arrangement was unprofitable or unfair to itself.

Assertions about ethical pluralism often confuse and exaggerate differences. Ethical diversity is of several kinds, some of which are more significant than others.

The most drastic form of ethical diversity is radical ethical pluralism—a situation in which two parties (individuals or nations) differ so radically in their ethical views that they have no common ground for interaction. No individual society could long exist if it had such radical differences among its members, for it would have no cohesive basis. One nation will sometimes refuse to deal with another because of their radically different views about what constitutes acceptable action. Yet although some critics talk as if all instances of ethical pluralism present in the world are of this kind, it is in fact relatively rare. Since all countries inhabit a common globe, they are unlikely to differ so radically that they have no common basis for interaction with other countries. Even a shared desire for joint survival gives them something in common. Should a nation care only for its own survival, it might feel justified in doing whatever it wished to any other nation in order to guarantee this survival. If it also had the desire and ability to dominate others, it might get its way. Then, under conditions of radical pluralism, the only alternatives would be mutual isolation or war. Fortunately, today's world does not harbor such radical ethical pluralism to any significant degree.

A second kind of ethical pluralism consists of conflicting ethical judgments regarding the morality of specific practices. In Saudi Arabia, for instance, consuming alcoholic beverages is considered immoral; in the United States, it is not. This difference need not preclude trade. Morever, since it is not considered immoral in either country not to drink, Americans who refrain from consuming alcoholic beverages in Saudi Arabia in no way violate their integrity. Other issues are more complicated.

Within the United States abortion is a divisive issue. Some Americans believe abortion is ethically permissible; others believe it is ethically wrong. The issue divides the country, and attempts to resolve its legal aspects fall to the courts and to the political process. Differences of opinion on this issue are no less sharp if we consider abortion from a global perspective. In some countries there is little outcry against it. In the post-Stalin-era Soviet Union, for instance, abortion became the dominant form of artificial birth control,[1] and in China tremendous governmental and social pressures are brought to bear on pregnant women who already have one child to get an abortion. Other countries, such as Ireland, consider abortion unethical and ban it outright. Still others are as divided as is the United States. Each country can and does make its own rules concerning abortion, and the differences in rules each adopts do not preclude most trade and other interactions. But is it ethical for a company operating in a country where abortion is legal and is considered ethical to sell organs or tissues of aborted fetuses to hospitals or companies located in a country where abortion is illegal and is considered unethical? May someone or some firm in the second country ethically purchase such material? When differences in national viewpoints involve opposing notions of what trade practices are fair or just, no adjudicative body exists to resolve the differences. Some ethical differences between nations over practices become significant if those nations commercially interact.

A third kind of ethical pluralism consists of differences in ethical theory or in principles used to decide the morality of actions. Stealing is considered wrong in Islamic countries because it is prohibited by God through revelations to Muhammad recorded in the *Koran*. In the Judeo-Christian tradition stealing is considered wrong because it is prohibited by God in the Ten Commandments transmitted to Moses and reported in the Old Testament. In some tribal societies stealing is viewed as wrong because it is forbidden by tribal law. Different sets of moral principles may ethically condemn the same action. Arbitrarily killing members of one's society is wrong whether one evaluates the action from the point of view of Islam, from the point of view of Judeo-Christian morality, from the point of view of Confucianism, or from the point of view of one or another philosophical ethical position. The differences in basic principles sometimes—but by no means always—lead to different evaluations of practices. Islamic ethical views sometimes clash with Christian ethical views, leading to differing evaluations of specific practices; but on many issues they render the same judgments. When doing business in foreign lands, one should be aware of differences in principles; however, acting with integrity in international business is made possible by the significant areas of ethical agreement that exist in regard to many practices.

A fourth kind of ethical pluralism is the pluralism of lifestyles—the freedom an individual is allowed for self-development. The United States allows for a wide variety of lifestyles, and it is pluralistic in the diversity it tolerates and even encourages in this regard. Some countries are even more open to diversity, while others are less tolerant. In nineteenth-century Britain the characteristic ethically approved outlook consisted of knowing one's station in society and living by the rules that governed that station. For centuries Japan was (and to some extent it still is) a homogeneous society in which the permissible range of lifestyles is restricted. Tribal cultures often tolerate very little diversity of lifestyles, as do countries where religious fundamentalism is a dominant element in society. From a global perspective, one must accept the great diversity of styles and cultures. No culture is best, and no single culture is best for all people. Recognizing diversity of culture and the ethical legitimacy of the corresponding plurality of lifestyles is the starting point on the road toward international, multinational, and global business activity.

For the multinational that operates with integrity this means two things.

First, it should not impose its own views regarding lifestyles on its host countries. Second, it must accommodate itself to the local views on lifestyles, if it is to operate effectively in relation to the local population. Yet integrity may limit the amount of accommodation a firm can make.

Absence of Adequate Background Institutions

The major stumbling block to acting with integrity in international business is not ethical pluralism. Companies operate with integrity in the American context despite the pluralism present there. The significant difference is not the degree of pluralism involved but the context in which American and global pluralism exist.

The United States is often characterized as being a free-enterprise, democratic, and liberal society. It is all three only within limits, however, and it is correctly characterized as being all three primarily in contrast to other countries. American free enterprise is constrained in many ways by law. Its capitalism is tempered not only by industry-specific regulations but also by custom, by welfare and social programs, and by the business of government. It is democratic, but it is both a representative democracy and a democracy that limits what the majority may do or demand. Its liberalism is similarly restrained: it does not stand for unbridled freedom from government and social control.

Business in the United States operates in an environment that limits, restricts, and controls it in many ways. The plethora of laws, governmental regulations, customs, unions, consumer and environmental groups, and popular pressures, demands, and expectations make up what can be called the "background" or "background institutions" against and within which American business operates. Comprehending this background and these background institutions is vital to understanding American business. The limits they impose are significant. Built into many of the regulations, laws, rules, customs, and expectations are ethical criteria that the society (through the political process) has come to accept. In addition, included in the background are ethical expectations that have not yet been mandated by law. Law tends to lag behind ethics in the sense that legal regulations are often passed as a result of some unethical activity that becomes widespread or that seriously threatens the society's general interests. Thus, stronger laws against insider trading followed abuses by those inside a company who were perceived to be acting unfairly by those outside.[2]

Not only does the United States have a host of mechanisms that restrain businesses and help set national norms for what constitutes ethically acceptable behavior, but the society also contains the means for resolving conflicts in a peaceful way. Governmental administrative bodies and the courts provide various such mechanisms. Many intermediate private groups and organizations provide other sources. The mass media facilitate public debate on issues that can be aired, and these discussions sometimes suffice to generate a consensus. Within the United States, we do not live in an ethical jungle, much less in a state of nature. Nor do people inside other nations.

What is true of the United States is true of the other developed democratic countries of the world as well, even though their institutions may differ. Nondemocratic societies have their own means of dispute resolution, which may yield stability based on force and fear rather than on the impartial rule of law. In some less industrially developed countries the background institutions are equally little developed; and although these are sufficient for their internal needs, they are often inadequate to deal with the complexities introduced by multinational corporations.

The situation is very different beyond the national level. Dealings between two nations are often negotiated, but the context of the negotiation is not the same as negotiation within either nation. In international legal theory, each state is sovereign and equal, just as in the United States all citizens are equal before the law. But there is no effective international law comparable in scope or in existing enforcement mechanisms to the rule of law within the United States. Although states are equal in theory, they are very unequal in fact. Some are large, powerful, and strong; others are small, dependent, and weak. If they bargain, they do so from positions of inequality on many issues and on many levels.

As one passes from the bilateral to the multilateral to the global level, the differences between intranational and international relations become more pronounced. Not only do common norms become fewer, but constraints of every kind grow increasingly rare. Common expectations recede to a less and less manageable least common denominator. Effective implementation of laws, agreements, and decisions diminishes. The global pollution problem shows how little agreement there is on who should do what, and how difficult it is to enforce existing agreements.

This is the context for international business: law is often ineffective outside national borders; expectations vary from society to society or from region to region; and interests often clash in an environment where no clear method of resolving disputes exist.

In sum, a central difference between conducting business on a national level and conducting it on an international level is the absence in the latter setting of restrictive background institutions. In this situation a company without integrity—without a developed sense of what is ethically prohibited—seeks to promote its own interest in whatever way it can. Companies that feel constrained only by law and not by ethics in the United States feel few constraints in the international arena. They feel no obligation beyond obeying the local laws in each country in which they operate, and then only to the extent that the laws are effectively enforced. Only their own perceived interests guide them when they stand outside the jurisdiction of national laws. That some companies do operate in this way is a fact; that all do is not; and that any should be allowed to so act is a defect calling for a remedy.

The International Economy

Unrestrained free enterprise tends to result in the formation of monopolies, a policy of maximizing profits in any way possible, and a corporate attitude that discounts the general or common good in favor of the business's own vested interests. It also ignores those who cannot compete, is indifferent to vast inequalities in individual wealth and power, and declines to restrain the exercise of one's wealth and power in exploiting the weakness of others—be they workers, consumers, or competitors. Unrestrained free enterprise does not exist in the United States or in any other developed industrial country. In each country in which free enterprise flourishes, economic freedom is always constrained by its juxtaposition with existing political and social forces and structures. Free enterprise in the United States operates somewhat differently from the way it operates in Japan, Germany, or the United Kingdom. If free enterprise led to the starvation of significant numbers of people in those countries, or if those societies tolerated such starvation despite their prevailing affluence, free enterprise could not be ethically justified.

From an ethical point of view two major differences distinguish the American economic system from what might loosely be called the international economic system. The first is that the American system includes many restraints on monopoly formation, exploitation, deception, fraud, and various other harms to society, the environment, consumers, and workers that unrestrained capitalism tends to inflict. The government restrains competition and intervenes in the system in many ways and at many levels to prevent abuses and to confine the cycles of boom and bust within narrow limits. No such mechanism operates internationally. The second difference is that the American economic system functions within a specific political and social context such that those who cannot compete are not simply left to die. The United States operates an elaborate system of economic redistribution from the relatively rich to the relatively poor; an institutional means of providing education, roads, parks, and other public goods; and a welfare safety net designed to help those who are unable to compete or who fail disastrously. Internationally, countries or peoples who cannot compete are for the most part left to their own devices, since no international safety net or redistribution system exists.

Both the restraints and the redistributive mechanisms help make the American economic system ethically defensible.[3] But since both are missing from the global scene, is the international economic system ethically unjustifiable? Does their absence automatically taint all who operate within it, or can a firm of integrity operate within it and still maintain its integrity?

In regard to the presence of absence of constraints, the differences between the national and the international systems are significant.

To begin with, it is not clear how we should describe the international economy. Especially if we include China and other socialist and command-economy countries, we can hardly describe the global economic environment as constituting a single or unified system. We might therefore distinguish the economic world order or the mix of the many and diverse economies of the countries of the world, from the international market system that operates within it. Large portions of international business are conducted under conditions that share some features of a free-enterprise or market system: private ownership of goods and the means of production; available capital for investment and the purchase of goods; competition in prices, goods, and labor; and lack of any comprehensive government control over the setting of prices and the allocation of goods. In the context of the American political and social system these features are severely constrained. On the international level, restraints on competition and safeguards for workers and consumers are significantly absent. Of course, such restraints and safeguards are not entirely absent, since each country can control the amount of international commerce in which it engages, the extent to which it allows corporations from other nations to operate within its borders, and the conditions under which such companies can operate. Yet restraints on the natural tendency of competition to lead to exploitation vary from country to country and are often much less effective in less developed countries than in developed, industrialized countries. International free enterprise permits a great deal of unethical behavior that (especially) poorer, debtor, and dependent countries are unable to preclude.[4]

We have already noted that the most striking structural difference between the American system and the system of international business is the paucity of existing background institutions to control or guide business that crosses national borders. The situation is doubly bad with respect to developing countries, which tend to have inadequate internal background institutions as well. Such considerations have led many observers to conclude that ethics doesn't apply in international business, that American businesses cannot maintain a competitive edge internationally if they act ethically, and that—since corporations from other nations do not act ethically—American companies would be foolhardy to adopt ethical constraints unilaterally.

Although these claims fall short of the mark, it is certainly of central ethical significance that inadequate background institutions exist to constrain international business. Emphasizing this should lead not to the conclusion that anything goes but rather to the conclusion that it is morally imperative to establish equitable international background institutions. Their absence, instead of being interpreted as a license to act unethically, should be viewed as a continuing demand that these institutions be established. What this means in practice is open to discussion, since many different kinds of restraints (some of them mutually incompatible) may be justifiable and practicable. But until adequate institutions are operative, self-imposed ethics has greater rather than lesser importance for a company of integrity.

Although multinationals do not operate in a Hobbesian state of nature in which no external rules apply, the rules that do apply are frequently minimal.[5] Unlike in Hobbes's state of nature, the preconditions and mechanisms for establishing rules by mutual agreement already exist, and we have several models for developing the rules themselves. Some industry codes offer guidance, even though actual enforcement is left to the national governments. For instance, in 1981 the World Health Organization adopted an International

Code of Marketing Breast-milk Substitutes to govern the sale of infant for-mula.[6] Although some countries passed legislation to implement this code, its greatest impact has resulted from voluntary adoption of its provisions by multinational corporations.

Most international codes rely on voluntary compliance. The UN Eco-nomic and Social Council's Commission on Transnational Corporations has been working for many years on a set of guidelines for multinational opera-tions.[7] In 1976 the Organization for Economic Development and Cooperation drew up a set of recommendations it called Guidelines for Multinational Enterprises.[8] A number of church-sponsored groups have also drawn up model codes of international business conduct. In addition, some individual corporations have devised their own codes. Others, such as General Motors with its Sullivan Principles, have led the way in attempting to deal with the issue of apartheid and to stipulate conditions under which companies might ethically operate in South Africa.[9]

The overall international economic order contains many players besides nations and multinationals. Although nations are significant participants in international business, they do not operate always or exclusively as individual states. Many kinds of bilateral and multilateral government-to-government agreements affect, facilitate, or prohibit commercial interactions. In addition, affiliated groups of nations, such as the European Community adopt rules that govern aspects of their members' conduct. For many years the Eastern block of Warsaw Pact nations had special trading and other relations with the Soviet Union. To some extent these nations were not part of the overall international economic system, since their money was not convertible. Yet they clearly engaged in international trade with nations outside their bloc. Multinationals operate within the framework of these various groups, which often impose rules, guidelines, regulations, and pressures.

On the international level, a wide variety of organizations—both govern-mental and nongovernmental—mediate between nations, nation groups, na-tions, and enterprises of various types. Organizations such as the United Nations, the World Bank, and the International Monetary Fund help establish guidelines for international development and investment, and they facilitate industrial and economic growth in less developed countries. Equally impor-tant are international nongovernmental organizations (NGOs). Churches and church groups provide aid and charity, serve as conduits for private donations toward disaster or famine relief, and campaign for redistribution of the goods of the earth to help those in greatest need.

These institutions all serve as important mediating groups between indi-viduals and foreign nations and between nations.

The United Nations is not a worldwide government, nor was it ever in-tended to be. Its powers are severely limited. The UN cannot tax its members for redistribution of wealth, and all contributions to it are voluntary. The World Court depends on the voluntary submission to its judgments of the nations that come before it seeking to resolve legal disputes; it has no enforce-ment mechanism.

In this situation multinationals play an important role. They move into countries at the local level. They can perform extremely beneficial services: tie nations and peoples closer together; transfer knowledge and technology; and form the infrastructure for a truly global economy. Yet they can also do great harm: exploit the poor; disrupt cultures; and impose their will on those unable to defend themselves.

Central among the international issues facing business is the operation of multinational corporations. But equally important and inextricably tied to this issue are several other questions. One relates to the enormous debts that hamper the development of many less developed countries (LDCs), a large percentage of whose income goes to servicing the interest on these debts.[10] A second involves the complex of issues revolving around fair trade, protectionism, and dumping. A third inquires into the obligations (if any) of rich countries to poor countries, on the model of obligations of rich persons to poor persons within a single country. A fourth difficult question is whether to operate at all in a country whose structure is basically immoral—because of oppression of the poor by the rich, because of gross corruption of government, or because of immoral structures—and, if so, how to do so ethically. None of these are easy questions to answer. None exclusively involve ethical issues. But all have ethical dimensions that can, should, and must be faced if companies of integrity are to arrive at satisfactory answers.

The overall international picture of business has some structure, some interdependence, many possibilities, and a great need for developing more effective international background institutions of varying kinds and at various levels. Their absence does not preclude multinational corporations from engaging in international business ethically, but it does place an extra burden on those that wish to act with integrity.

The second major difference between the economic system that exists in the United States and the international economic order is that the former is embedded in a sociopolitical system that allows for transfer payments from rich to poor and provides a welfare safety net for its citizens. On the global level there is no systematic taxation of the rich to help the poor, no safety net for those unable to compete, no system of allocating or reallocating resources from those lucky enough to have them to those unlucky enough to lack them.

The international economic order is not found in any context of government and laws comparable to what exists in every national economic system. This glaring ethical defect becomes most evident when we consider what might be called global distributive justice.

International justice governs relations between states and/or firms. Global justice involves justice in the relations of individuals or groups of people to other people. The former, not the latter, pertains to multinationals. Yet deficiencies on the global level, like the absence of adequate background institutions, impose some special ethical demands on multinationals that wish to act with integrity.

In the United States and in most other developed nations needy individuals are cared for by the state. An internal system of entitlements and transfers of wealth makes this possible. In many developing countries, however, the extremely poor are not cared for at all. Redistribution clearly does not take place on a global level as it does on the level of nation-states.

The international order is notoriously bad at the task of internationally redistributing wealth and resources to those who are unable to take effective part in the international competitive process. The safety net of welfare that people take for granted in most developed countries is simply nonexistent in most LDCs. The mechanism of redistribution through taxation, which most national societies utilize, is not available on the international level. Rather than receiving the proceeds of some sort of redistributive scheme to the poor or to poor countries, LDCs, are saddled with burdens of debt and ingrained poverty, with no relief in sight.

Individuals who, despite their best efforts, are unable to provide adequately for their own subsistence traditionally make their first claim against those with whom they are most closely related—their family, then their community, then their state. If these prove unable to provide for their basic needs, the destitute people next have a legitimate claim against people of other states—first against the citizenry of states with which the individuals' state is most closely aligned, then against those more distantly removed. The basis for this claim is the traditional view (held cross-culturally in many theories of justice) than those with whom one has the closest relations are those with whom it is most appropriate to share benefits and burdens.[11] Given the political division of the world, the obligation to help the starving in Britain (if, despite its best efforts, Britain could not do so) would fall first to the United States rather than to China, while the obligation to help people starving in North Korea (under similar conditions) would fall first to China, rather to the United States, because of the respective ties of each of those countries to the others involved. In a truly worldwide community, one could invoke the principle of economic redistribution: from each according to his ability to contribute, to each according to his need for help in achieving subsistence at a decent level. But at present we are far from having such a community.

The demands of distributive justice on a global level, however, are much weaker than the demands of distributive justice within a given society. On the national level, distributive justice does not end with simply fulfilling minimal needs and providing equal access to goods. Social structures within a society make it possible to share both burdens and benefits through organized and accepted social institutions. The members of a particular society are related in many more ways than are the people of the world. Through the tax process, corporations and individuals are expected to pay a share of what is required to fulfill common and welfare needs. Multinationals operating across national boundaries can legitimately be expected to pay their fair share of taxes wherever they operate. What constitutes a fair share, as the notion of international justice suggests, may vary from country to country and may be subject to negotiation.

Global distributive justice requires some redistribution of wealth, resources, knowledge, and technology, at least to guarantee subsistence to all. Currently the difficulty in implementing global justice is not only the lack of theoretical agreement on the requirements of global justice, but also the lack of adequate transferal institutions on the global level. Global justice is difficult to implement, even at a minimal level where the will to do so is present, because of the lack of global background institutions. Less developed countries guard their national sovereignty just as jealously as do developed countries, and this is a central factor inhibiting the implementation of global justice. Those who object that nations and people have a legal and moral right to retain what they possess argue from a certain conception of justice. Their claims come up against claims based on a right to subsistence and on simple need, which are argued from different conceptions of justice. There is no easy way to mediate these conflicting views, since they are bound up with a range of other beliefs, values, and conceptions of self-interest.

Yet the best available vehicle for such a transfer of knowledge, technology, and wealth at the present time is the multinational corporations. By expanding operations in less developed nations, they can provide jobs, transfer skills and knowledge to local workers, and supply needed goods, while at the same time lowering their own costs and expanding their markets. The trick is to work out conditions that are advantageous and acceptable—and so fair and just—to all concerned. Negotiation in good faith, based on a commitment to integrity on both sides, would be the best road to a solution.

The obligation to develop equitable international and global background institutions is a pressing one. The lack of such institutions encourages the seeming ethical wilderness in which so much of world commerce still takes place. Rather than obviating the need for integrity in international economic transactions, their absence makes integrity all the more necessary.

Injustices in the international economic order are neither inherent in that order, such that they cannot be corrected, nor incompatible with reform (versus overthrow) of the existing order. Militating against wholesale replacement of the existing order by some other system are two points: first, it is not clear what other order is available; second, even if an alternative were available, it is not clear how it might be implemented. From a practical point of view, therefore, we should focus our attention on the order we have and on trying to make it better.

This is not necessarily bad. The existing conditions are open to corrections that result when competition produces greater efficiency and to negotiated changes that limit possible abuses. Such changes can even lead to a global redistribution of wealth from rich to poor countries, enabling the latter to develop their own capacities and to rise above the level of poverty. Although multinationals are central players in this scenario, the changes needed are primarily changes in political structure and are the province of governments, not of corporations.

Negotiating Justice

Basic to the ethics of international business is the task of determining what constitutes fair trade and fair practices. Rules, laws, agreements, and codes are needed, but what should these contain? In a global context that lacks adequate background institutions, what sense can be made of talk about justice? Just as one might ask "Whose ethics?" one might ask "Whose justice?" And although the answer "One's own" is a starting point, it cannot be the ending point: there are two sides to every transaction, and both should agree that the transaction is just.

Consider the denuding the Brazilian Amazon rain forest. That action affects not only Brazil but every other nation of the world, since all will be affected (and many adversely) by the resulting changes in climate. Should the decision to cut its forests be made only by the government of Brazil, only by the logging companies, only by the firms that purchase the lumber, only by the local farmers whose land can no longer support crops, or only by homesteaders who need wood for their houses? The decision is certainly a matter of interest to all of them. And unrestricted free enterprise imposes no limits on what companies might do in such a situation. Brazil—or at least some Brazilians— tends to see further deforestation as being in its economic interest, and it balks at being told that it cannot do with its own lands what the developed countries have already done with theirs. Yet other countries that are significantly affected clearly have a legitimate interest in this matter. Some have argued that, if other countries think that the forests are so important, they should buy them up and preserve them as parks, or they should otherwise provide Brazil with an attractive alternative to continued clear-cutting. If the free market cannot resolve the problem, negotiation is the only feasible approach—and one that may be aided by the action of intermediary organizations.

Neither the United States nor American multinational corporations are in a position to dictate what constitutes fairness in this and other international transactions. No country or group can or should dictate the rules of international commerce. Claims are often made about the dependence of the South on the North or of developing on developed countries. The demands raised a number of years ago for a New International Economic Order[12] were considered unrealistic by most Northern countries, and consequently these demands have been largely ignored.

Yet if justice and fairness are central to the ethics of international business, then one country cannot decide unilaterally what practices and background institutions are fair or just. All interested parties must be allowed to have a say. Justice and fairness in international business relations are not the result of imposing a preconceived set of structures or ideals on the world. Rather, they are arrived at by negotiation in such a way that all interested and affected parties are represented and have a voice in deciding the rules that will govern the international business game. The dominant position enjoyed by the developed countries financially, technologically, and historically does not give them the right to set the rules. But neither does the relatively undeveloped condition of poor countries give them the right to dictate the terms of trade or loans or aid. Mutual negotiations are necessary. International structures that all parties perceive as fair must be worked out; they cannot be imposed by philosophers or businesspeople or government bureaucrats. Nations, industries, and corporations should all have an opportunity for input and a voice in hammering out the new structures. It is as unfair to force policies on American multinational businesses as it is to force policies on poor countries or their local businesses. However, each must be willing to give up something. And in this regard U.S. businesses (and the U.S. government acting in business's behalf) have often been less flexible and more recalcitrant than is appropriate in a good-faith negotiation.

Ideally each transaction or case should be resolved in such a way that all affected groups and individuals believe that the resolution is just. Such a conclusion need not involve agreement by the participants on any particular notion of justice. Pluralism of principles, as we have seen, is compatible with agreement on practices, and it is the practices that produce the concrete results. Yet in order to resolve cases and to believe that justice has been done, each of the parties must have a conception of justice with which to assess the proposals under discussion. What is essential is to negotiate and compromise on issues of particular behavior in such a way that the results do not compromise one's principles or integrity.

In American society my beliefs about justice do not automatically justify my interfering with lawful practices that I happen to consider unjust. Many kinds of interaction are properly handled only through political institutions and procedures—that is, through a variety of background institutions. On the international or global level, issues of justice are even more complex. A first difficulty is that adequate background institutions, which normally provide touchstones for assessing what is fair or just in various negotiations or contracts, as well as the means for appeal in adjudicating disputes, are lacking. A second difficulty is that justice is always constituted within a system: it is a function of the accepted values and beliefs of the society in which it is found. In this sense, capitalist society has its own particular notion of justice, according to which (among other things) private property is justifiable. Justice within this system presupposes agreement on a background of accepted law, values, and beliefs. In a capitalist system disputes over property are adjudicated in an attempt to arrive at just results within the system. In a socialist society, the notion of justice rests on a different background of accepted law, values, and beliefs, yielding a socialist conception of justice. If this system establishes that private ownership of the means of production is unjust and illegal, the adjudication of competing claims about property in it will clearly differ from the adjudication of property claims in a capitalist society. Moreover, certain claims will be made in each of these systems that will not arise in the other. How to reconcile claims about property justly when the two systems interact—or when a country such as Poland switches from one system to the other—is a serious problem.

If we divide the world not according to their social structures but according to their level of development, we find certain aspects of justice common to industrially developed countries, and a different perspective on justice taken by developing countries.

From any given point of view, certain other systems and their practices might logically be condemned as unjust. If a socialist system of justice views private property as unjust, that claim does not carry much weight with people who live within the capitalist system—unless they can be persuaded that the socialist conception of justice is superior to the capitalist one. Because each theory of justice is substantively related to a set of practices, convincing others of the correctness of one's point of view most often involves prevailing on those persons to change some of their other beliefs and values. This is no easy task. Fortunately such conversions are not required for interactions between nations or between firms from different nations.

Protest and condemnation of what one believes to be another country's unjust internal policies are appropriate, and they may influence the views and beliefs of people living in that country. If a nation believes that the violation of justice is serious enough, it can move beyond issuing condemnations and forbear from dealing with the nation in question altogether. Thus, the United States, most European countries, and most African countries—which had long condemned South Africa for its apartheid policy—eventually imposed various economic sanctions on that country.[13] If enough nations act likewise, they can ostracize an offending nation from the community of nations. Yet the doctrine of national sovereignty, if respected, limits the extent to which any nation can intervene in the internal affairs of another nation.

The need to have a mechanism for resolving disputes arises once interaction occurs. Since international justice involves equitable transactions between different nations and national firms, it assumes some common basis for the interaction. Nations interact commercially for their mutual benefit; each expects to gain by the transaction.

Given this complex situation of differing conceptions and systems of justice, how may firms achieve justice in their interactions? A fair assessment of existing conditions must serve as the starting point. Although vested interests dictate initial positions in any interaction in the international arena, reciprocity is the procedural key to justice.

Justice as reciprocity means that each of those subject to the contract, practice, institution, or system agrees to the justice of the contract, practice, institution, or system. The agreement of the parties here is not about what in theory constitutes justice but about the justness by their own standards of the contract or practice or institution. From a practical point of view, a contract is just if everyone who is party to it, armed with all the relevant information, agrees that it is just. Similarly, an institution is just if all representatives of the various groups that have a stake in the matter accept it as just. On the international level, reciprocity requires that all nations affected by a practice or involved in a transaction agree to its justness, whatever conception of justice they hold. This suggests that a program that aims at developing just practices and just international and global social structures has the best chance of success if it can elicit reciprocal agreement in support of its endeavors.

Two background conditions for achieving justice on the international level can be identified: true participative reciprocity, and acknowledgment of the formal equality of states in the context of international relations and international law. The additional background already developed by tradition, custom, and law forms a limited basis for speaking of international justice and for determining just and unjust behavior with respect to states. To the extent that nations accept these background conditions, the conditions form a cross-cultural basis for developing additional just international structures. Many Latin American states claim that the international economic system is unjust because it favors developed nations and makes less developed nations dependent on them and subordinate to them.[14] Yet these less developed nations willingly acknowledge the justice of many individual transactions that they and their firms negotiate with other countries and their firms.

Exchange and trade are dominant forms of interaction among nations, and commutative justice governs such activities.[15] Whatever substantive differences may exist among the parties, based on their concepts of justice, commutative justice requires that equal be exchanged for equal and that those who enter into a transaction do so freely, with each seeking to secure its own good. If transactions are forced or take place at forced prices, they are unjust according to most theories of justice. Forced transactions are a form of exploitation, and if one state exploits another or if a multinational exploits a people or the resources of a state, claims for compensatory justice can be raised.

The component of reciprocity is essential in negotiating just commutative transactions. If two agents with different conceptions of justice wish to trade, and if their differing conceptions lead to different evaluations of the terms of the exchange, both must be willing to accept some accommodation of their positions, some agreement on terms, or some third position between the opposing positions. Otherwise, the transaction either will not take place or will be forced and so will be unjust.

Fortunately, moral pluralism seldom involves two countries' or traditions' holding opposite and nondiscretionary views of the morality of a particular action. Rarely does one side hold that an action is prohibited while the other holds that the very same action is obligatory. Most often what one side considers morally forbidden the other side considers morally permissible but not obligatory. In such cases, moral negotiation usually involves the latter country's accepting a restraint on its freedom to act in a way that it considers morally permissible. Thus, again, if an American firm wishes to operate in Saudi Arabia, it may have to enforce a ban on alcohol consumption by its employees. It (and they) may thus agree to a limitation of their freedom that their own morality does not require. Still, agreeing to abide by such a ban does not violate their principles. Similarly, suppose that an American company wishes to do business with a chemicals firm that tolerates a toxicity level at its plant that is harmful to the health of its employees. The American company may be willing to pay enough for the product so that the firm can bring its toxicity level down to an acceptably low level, and it may negotiate such conditions. Since it is extremely unlikely that the chemicals firm considers itself morally required to expose its workers to harmful conditions, such negotiations in no way violate the principles of the chemicals firm. On the contrary, they may enable the firm to do what it would have preferred but was financially unable to do.

Integrity requires fidelity to a personal sense of justice. This means that one cannot impose on others what one believes is unjust, even if they agree to the imposition, and that one cannot accept for oneself conditions that violate one's principles of justice. But neither of these criteria precludes accepting less than one thinks one deserves in absolute terms. Negotiation frequently consists precisely in each side's accepting less than each thinks it would receive in a perfect world, but not less than it thinks is fair under existing conditions. Just as this is true in national labor negotiations, so it is also true in international negotiations.

On the international level, their reasonably equal bargaining power prevents major states from forcing their terms on one another. This rough equality also provides the necessary background condition for arriving at a transaction that the parties agree is just, even if they make their judgments from different conceptions and theories of justice. The unanimous desire to avoid a nuclear war serves as a deterrent to any international act that would be perceived as so grossly unjust that it might provoke a nuclear confrontation. The mutual need for peace is the strongest incentive for cooperation in seeking what all sides consider a just solution to problems. Such state-to-state negotiations provide a framework within which individual commercial transactions can be worked out.

Cross-cultural divisions on the international scale include not only socialist versus capitalist, but rich versus poor, producer versus consumer, lender versus borrower, and more developed versus less developed. Countries lacking resources often make claims that are rejected by the developed countries, which feel that they have the right to their wealth, their resources, and the goods they produce. Chad had no greater claim to the oil produced in the Soviet Union than it had to the oil produced in the United States—even if Chad needed oil for its development. Any proprietary claim it might have made to American or Soviet resources would have met with the countervailing claims of these resource-rich countries that they had the right to use what they produced as they wished and to sell these products at prices they set. Similarly, less developed countries frequently claim that the conditions of trade worked out with more developed countries do not reflect true reciprocity.

What justice involves in trade, aid, defense, or other interactions between rich and poor countries is not a unilateral issue, even though unilateral judgments can be and are made. Differences in the judgments of parties cannot properly be resolved by expecting either side to adopt a different conception or theory of justice or by expecting the poor country to subordinate itself politically in service to one of the developed countries. Rather, a resolution should come about from negotiation on the terms of the transaction.

The pressure of argument, the appeal to moral values other than justice, the pressure of protest, the development of public and of world opinion, and the use of diplomatic, political, and economic pressure are all legitimate means of promoting negotiation between competing views. Negotiation over justice does not mean accommodation to injustice, as one sees injustice. It means widening one's perspective to recognize other claims to justice made from a conflicting perspective. On issues of internal national policy, no accommodation by other countries may be necessary, and an accepted modus vivendi may be mutually tolerated. Some issues, such as slavery, allow no accommodation by those who hold that slavery is unjust. On other issues, such as giving up some of the wealth that one claims to possess by right, or establishing institutions to foster global redistribution of wealth, accommodation does not involve acceding to injustice. The result of accommodation in appropriate cases comes close to an encompassing ideal of justice, mediated by actual conditions and less-than-ideal states of affairs.

International systems of justice can begin with negotiations between two states or among groups of states. Some of these, based on regional alliances, already exist. As these systems in turn interact, the net becomes broader. At its broadest the resulting single system would be truly global, comprising all states. But regardless of how many are involved, reciprocity requires that all affected states or parties agree to the justice of the terms.

This suggests that a just solution to the case of the Brazilian rainforest can only be achieved through negotiation and compromise by all parties whose interests are seriously affected. Those outside Brazil cannot expect Brazilians to forgo development and give up their right to manage their own resources. Brazilians cannot expect their actions—if they adversely affect others—to be simply ignored. A just solution will require imagination as well as negotiation. But only a settlement that all parties consider just will have any hope of permanently resolving the issue.

Integrity and Ethical Demands

A company that wishes to act with integrity faces many ethical issues as it engages in international business. First, integrity demands that it act in accord with its own self-imposed values—which cannot be less than the ethical minimum, but may well exceed this. A company may neither give nor accept bribes, but it has a good deal of leeway in what it will allow its employees to accept in the way of gifts, for instance. Some companies forbid their employees to accept even a cup of coffee or a cheap ballpoint pen. Others set limits at gifts worth $25 or $50 or more. There is no one ethically correct standard. Companies, like individuals, arguably have some obligations in the area of charity.[16] But how much and to what causes or organizations it should contribute are appropriately determined by the company in question.

Second, in addition to satisfying the basic moral norms applicable everywhere, any company of integrity will uphold other equally obvious moral rules. For instance, not only does one not kill a competitor, one also doesn't maim or otherwise harm that person. Such obvious rules do not require much thought or argument.

Third, built on these common rules are other obligations that one assumes by entering into contracts or giving one's word. Agreements in general are fair if both parties enter into them freely, both sides benefit from the arrangement, and both sides believe that the terms fair. Broader issues of justice may require compromise—not of one's principles, but of what one considers one's due in the face of opposing claims from others.

Fourth, the absence of adequate background institutions means that multinationals have special obligations in the international realm. Notable among these are special obligations involved in dealing with less developed countries—obligations that will be spelled out in more detail later in this book.

Fifth, firms have the general obligation to consider new practices, projects, and plans from an ethical point of view to determine whether they are ethically permissible. A company that acts with integrity considers the ethical dimensions of its actions, projects, and plans before acting, not afterward. What does this involve? In addition to the above considerations it means weighing the consequences of one's actions on all those affected, respecting the rights of all those affected, and acknowledging the just claims of all those affected.

The consideration of consequences is sometimes called a stakeholder analysis,[17] sometimes a utilitarian analysis,[18] and sometimes an ethical cost-benefit analysis.[19] Whatever its name, it involves trying to foresee, to the best of one's ability, the consequences of one's actins. It asks what are the good and the bad consequences of an action for all those affected. Clearly, unless a company expected to derive more good than bad from an action, it would not undertake it. But an ethical analysis requires that one consider not only the effects on oneself but also those on others. What are the effects on one's shareholders, one's employees, one's customers, one's suppliers, and the community in which one operates? What are the general effects on society? What would happen if others acted similarly, and if the actions one contemplated were publicly known? Weighing good and bad consequences is nothing new or arcane, but doing it objectively and trying honestly to foresee and weigh all the consequences to all affected parties is not always easy. In general only actions that produce more good than harm are ethically allowable, and one's own good and bad count for no more than the good or bad of others. Ideally one tries to act so as to produce a win-win outcome for all concerned. A business deal may well benefit one's own company, those that do business with it, and society as a whole. One company's gain may, however, be another company's loss—say, of market share—and so we have a zero-sum game. But that is known and expected. A company with integrity accepts this while trying to maximize the good results and refraining from actions that cause more harm than good overall.

Consequences are not the only consideration, however. Even good consequences cannot override the unalienable human rights of those affected.[20] We cannot justify paying workers less than subsistence wages or making them work in wretched conditions on the grounds that we may thereby produce and sell a product more cheaply and so benefit large numbers of customers. The benefit to the customers cannot justify overriding the rights of the employees. What rights do workers or consumers or members of society have? The Universal Declaration of Human Rights lists a large number (some of which are disputed, such as the right to employment, as well as some other economic rights).[21] Most of these rights are rights against governments. Yet some are rights that a firm that acts with integrity must respect. The right not to be discriminated against for non-job-related reasons, the right to a fair wage, the right to reasonable working conditions, and the right to organize are among the most widely recognized of these. A firm of integrity will recognize for its foreign workers the same human rights it recognizes for its American workers. Since human rights apply to all human beings, it would be inconsistent to do otherwise.

Finally, considerations of justice demand that each person be given his or her due. We have already seen that there may be differences of opinion about what people are due and what criterion of justice should be used in assessing this question. A firm of integrity acts on its best understanding of what is just, and it remains open to complaints from those affected that it is acting unjustly. It takes such complaints seriously and is willing to consider reasons it has previously ignored, points of view it failed to include, and claims whose potential validity it failed to recognize.

There is no simple algorithm or formula to follow in making ethical judgments. They are just that: judgments. Judging with integrity often requires using careful analysis and reasoning, as well as relying on one's basic intuitions. A company that acts with integrity takes into account consequences, rights, and justice, weighs them in cases of conflict; and ultimately acts in accord with its best lights. It is always willing to admit that it may be mistaken, and it is open to improvement.

The imperative to act with integrity cannot insist on moral perfection. It can and does demand taking ethical considerations seriously.

3

Multinationals and Less Developed Countries: Seven Guidelines

An American textile company in Mexico pays its workers the same wages as other local firms do. Critics in the United States charge the American company with exploiting the Mexican labor force. In response to the criticism, the company raises its wages. The local firms accuse it of enticing away the best workers, of attempting to foment labor unrest in the industry, and of forcing higher wages on the local companies to drive them out of business. What should the American firm do? Either way it acts, the American multinational faces charges of unethical conduct.

Another American multinational opens a plant in a Brazilian city that has a staggering unemployment rate. It provides employment and so a potentially better life for many who have no other hope. American critics explain that such a firm robs Americans of jobs and weakens America by exporting manufacturing. Although American multinationals enable the less developed countries to develop, critics accuse the firms of destroying the local culture.

Because different parties invoke varied conceptions of justice, American multinationals (and multinationals from other developed countries) repeatedly face dilemmas when they try to act ethically in less developed countries. No matter how they act, some group will accuse them of immoral or unethical behavior.

The many dilemmas that multinationals face arise from conflicting demands made from opposing, (and sometimes ideologically based) perspectives. Only some of these conflicts are ethical conflicts, even though critics on both sides tend to couch their demands and charges in ethical terms. Solving many of these dilemmas requires having the ability and the courage to sort out true ethical demands from self-interested, pseudo-ethical demands. To give an effective answer to poorly grounded charges of unethical behavior, a firm of integrity must be willing to speak in ethical terms and to engage in moral reasoning. Such reasoning helps the firm decide on the right thing to do, and then enables it to defend that position articulately in the public forum. Only in this way will it both act ethically and be perceived as so acting.

American business did not always operate as it does today. Our history records long periods of slavery, of sweatshops, of robber barons, of child labor, and of unsafe working conditions. If business no longer engages in these practices, it is not because businesspeople today are more moral than they were in the past—even though this may independently be true. Rather the explanation is that legislation has imposed certain restraints on employers, and unions have forced concessions for workers. In addition, new social structures protect workers, consumers, and the environment. Because of the presence of adequate background institutions, American businesspeople usually know what is entailed in ethical business action. They are aided in acting ethically if the firms for which they work are structured to reinforce and promote such action. The firms in turn operate in a society with background institutions that try to prevent business from harming or exploiting others, to provide safety nets for those unable to compete, and to protect the human rights of all involved parties. Although in some instances it may not be clear which action is ethically right, in most cases the problem is not a matter of knowing what is right, but of doing what is right.

The ethical dilemmas that multinationals face in dealing with LDCs arise from the fact that conditions are considerably different in those countries than in the United States, Canada, Western Europe, Australia, and Japan. The dilemmas come in part from the fact that the LDCs are industrially little developed and are typically poor: they do not trade or bargain from positions of strength or of equality with American multinationals. Even more important, until recently most LDCs had developed few of the legal, social, and employment restraints on corporate activity that the industrially advanced countries already possessed. In short, they lacked (and still lack) adequate background institutions.

The history of business in the United States and in other parts of the industrialized world offers a solution to the practices and charges of unethical conduct on the part of multinationals. It suggests that we should not confine ourselves to searching for ethical managers or for self-restraint on the part of multinationals; instead, we should expand our efforts to develop structural restraints that make profit possible while keeping competition fair and protecting the rights of all.

The required background institutions are needed on two levels: the international level and the national level in each country. We have already discussed the paucity of such institutions on the international level. On the national level, we can assume that each country knows best what is in its own interest. If the government of a country really represents the interests of the people as a whole and not just the interests of a privileged elite, it occupies the best position for determining how much and what kind of protection is required and what restraints should be imposed on operations from abroad. A growing number of LDCs have become increasingly sophisticated in dealing with foriegn multinationals.[1] One technique is to forbid entry to any firm that competes directly with the nation's own domestic industries. Another is to require home ownership of at least 50.1 percent of the stock of any foreign subsidiary—a practice that India has put into law. Still another is to allow tax breaks only for a limited number of years and only for industrial plants that require a large investment and are not easy to move once established. In this regard LDCs are learning from one another. But often the price of such measures is decreased outside investment, loss of potential new jobs, and a slower pace of transfer of new technology and skills.

The discipline that integrity imposes on a business is all the more necessary when operating without the external restraints of developed and enforced background institutions on the national and international levels. Central to that discipline is having a clear set of articulated principles that the firm can uphold, defend, and use to guide its activities. Is there any such set of defensible guidelines? Fortunately, the answer is yes.

We have already seen the general ethical requirements for a firm that wishes to act with integrity. Why do we need additional norms or guidelines for firms that operate in less developed countries, and why single out American multinationals?

The answer to the first question is that multinationals have come in for a great deal more criticism for unethical behavior in the less developed than in the more developed countries, for reasons we have already seen. We do not need more ethical norms per se, but clearly both critics and multinationals can benefit from a closer analysis of what the ordinary ethical norms require under the special conditions posed by operating in less developed countries. The need for guidelines is generally acknowledged both by multinationals and by the many groups that have been working to develop codes of multinationals. Most prominent among these have been the Organization for Economic Cooperation and Development (OECD), which has developed the voluntary Guidelines for Multinational Enterprises,[2] and the UN Commission on Translational Corporations,[3] which has been working on a code of conduct for multinational corporations. In addition, more specialized codes for multinationals have been developed by organizations such as the International Labor Organization[4] and the World Health Organization.[5] Many individuals and firms have also developed codes of conduct.

The codes vary in their specificity and scope, and some essentially express ideals toward which a firm aspires. None contain exclusively or specifically ethical guidelines, and in each case it is pertinent to ask a number of questions. Are the provisions of the code ethically mandatory or are they simply ideals? Are some of them self-serving and overly protective of vested interests? Can they be ethically evaluated? In evaluating them, what criteria can we use?

A company of integrity will ask these questions. By way of providing some response, I shall suggest and develop seven ethical norms or guidelines that are based on the general ethical norms we have already discussed. They are particularly appropriate for multinationals operating in less developed countries, and they implicitly ground many of the specific provisions of more elaborate codes.

In reply to the second question—why single out American multinationals operating in LDCs?—there are three reaons. The first is the lack of parity in such situations. Multinationals operating in developed countries usually operate under conditions of equality and reciprocity. American companies operating in Japan or Germany or France, for example, are constrained by the laws and other background institutions of those countries. On the whole these laws and background institutions suffice to regulate international business so that it takes place under conditions of reasonable equality and reciprocity. For instance, American businesses may complain of dumping or unfair practices by businesses from other countries, and vice versa. But the developed countries for the most part control such practices and handle perceived injustices among themselves through negotiation or the threat or enforcement of protective measures. LDCs do not have such parity vis-a-vis the advanced industrial countires. They lack both the power and influence of the developed countries. They do not have the necessary background institutions, which take years to develop—even though many of them are learning how to use multinationals to their own benefit and for their own purposes.

A second reason for dealing specifically with American multinationals operating in LDCs is precisely that they are American. Although the seven principles discussed here apply to all multinationals, the principles cohere with American values and so are especially appropriate to American firms that wish to act with integrity, even if their application in the way I note is not always clearly perceived.

Third, American multinationals have been a special and obvious target of criticism—only some of it justifiable. Not all the conflicting demands placed on them (such as those enumerated at the beginning of this chapter) are ethically mandatory. Sometimes demands couched in ethical language represent only the vested interests of particular groups. By clarifying the actual ethical responsiblity of multinationals in underdeveloped countries, we can establish a set of criteria for separating legitimate from ethically unfounded charges of unethical behavior. The norms can thenceforth be used by firms of integrity in determining their actions and by critics in evaluating them.

Ethical Norms for American Multinationals

Presupposing the general ethical rules for and approaches to deriving ethical norms that we have already encountered, what guidelines can we derive or develop for multinationals operating in less developed countries? I shall suggest seven, and offer justifications for each. The seven are interrelated, but they are not derived from any single high-level principle that might be supposed to be the only proper one. Most of them are overdetermined, in that one can derive or defend them from a variety of high-level principles. Nor is the number—seven—of particular significance. As we shall see, others can be developed as well. But these seven provide the basis for evaluating and responding to the charges of unethical behavior that critics have most frequently brought against American multinationals.[6]

G1.   *Multinationals should do no intentional direct harm.*

This is not a novel moral rule; nor is it applicable only to multinationals. But it is a general rule that can go a long way in guiding a multinational's actions in a less developed country. Doing intentional direct harm involves willfully harming another; this is generally immoral and is widely recognized as such unless it is done in self-defense or for some similar overriding reason. The norm of refraining from doing international direct harm can be derived from the norm of refraining from killing and the norm of treating other persons with respect—or for those who prefer a rights approach to ethical norms, from the right to life and the right to be treated with respect. An ethical approach based on consequences similarly can be used to show that adopting this rule yields more good than harm.[7]

This guideline requires a company's management to look beyond its own interests in its dealings with LDCs. The usual assumption that businesses make (legitimately) in dealings in the United States and in other developed countries is that each side can look to its own interests, since the background rules within which the interaction takes place tend to prevent direct harm from befalling innocent third parties. In dealings with poor countries, where negotiating power is not more or less balanced between the two sides, an American company has to consider potential harm to the other side. Dependency theory argues that developing countries are unjustly dependent on developed countries because of the actions of the latter.[8] Whether or not that claim is correct, the possibility of dependency and of producing harm must be considered. If the regime with which one deals is known to be corrupt, the difficult is exacerbated and the possibility of harming innocent third parties is increased. If one suspects that the government cares not for the interest of its own people but only for the aggrandizement of government officials or of a small elite, then in one's negotiations on behalf of a multinational corporation (MNC) that acts with integrity one must take on the delinquent government's role of considering the interests of its citizens who are affected by the MNC's action. This puts a burden on the MNC, but the burden is one it can neither relinquish nor ethically ignore. To ignore it is effectively to will the foreseeable harm that the MNC's actions will do.

In general this rule forces companies that operate on an international level consciously to consider factors other than direct business factors. Following this rule will not tell a business how to act correctly, but it will tell it how not to act, and thus will help it avoid acting unethically.

When applied to relations between U.S. companies and LDCs, the norm has a number of obvious implications. Dumping toxic products in LDCs, such as the children's asbestos pajamas that were prohibited from being offered for sale in the United States and Europe, is an example of doing harm knowingly and willingly and of benefiting from the lack of legal restraints to the detriment of the eventual consumer. Similarly, this rule prohibits selling pesticides and drugs that the seller knows will be misused or will cause harm even if properly used—an action of which some American multinationals have been guilty.[9] The rule forces companies to consider the degree to which their pollution of air, water, and ground harms the country, regardless of whether the host country's laws mandate such consideration. Obviously, if toxic wastes and chemicals cause harm, they must be controlled, even if such control is not mandated by law. Less obviously, if turning arable land into cash crops not only renders the local population unable to feed itself but also leads to malnutrition or starvation in the long term, the American agribusiness responsible for the scheme cannot claim in its defense either that what it did was legal or that it had no duty to consider the effects of its actions on the people of the host country.[10] In these circumstances the leaders of the country and the local entrepreneurs are not relieved of their responsibility, but their corruption or lack of moral integrity does not shield the American company from ethical culpability for the harm done.

The norm does not state that anything the FDA or some other U.S. agency prohibits from sale in the U.S. may not morally be sold abroad. The norm can be interpreted independently of U.S. regulations. Yet if there are U.S. prohibitions, the companies engaged in selling such products abroad should be able to show that they are not causing direct intentional harm and that valid reasons exist to explain why the U.S. standards—which are not in themselves moral standards—may ethically be ignored in the country of sale. The norm requires U.S. companies to examine the effects of their actions on the host country, and not to look only at the company's economic self-interest.

> G2. *Multinationals should produce more good than harm for the host country.*

This second norm builds on the first. Although the injunction to do no direct intentional harm applies to all companies in both developed and less developed countries, a multinational operating in an LDC should take into account the differences between its mother country and the host country. Given the great disparities, the multinational should go beyond doing no direct intentional harm; if its activity is to be morally justified, it must benefit the host country. This means that the multinational's activities must not only benefit it but also the host country. And in this regard, good to the multinational cannot be traded off against harm—even unintentional, indirect harm—to the host country.

While the first norm prohibits intentional harm, the second norm mandates actual benefit to the host country. This formulation is stronger than the one used in the first norm, and this norm does not apply across the board to a company's transactions within all other countries, especially within industrially developed countries. Why the difference? How can one justify this norm as a requirement for international businesses with regard to less developed countries?

This second norm presents a special instance of the application of a utilitarian[11] analysis: it does not allow the multinational to justify harm to the host country by appeal to the greater good produced for it or for the United States. To do so would increase the disparity between the status of the host country and that of the United States; it would benefit the well off at the expense of the poorly off; it would increase the dependence of the LDCs on the more developed countries; and it would eventually contribute to heightened world-wide tensions. This is enough to preclude the action on a straight utilitarian calculation, since overall the action would produce more harm and good. This norm is derived from that calculation.

The governing assumption in dealings with other industrially developed countries is that each has laws, treaties, and other background institutions that preclude gross exploitation by a foreign firm. Furthermore, since the countries carry on business from positions of roughly equal strenth, not every transaction need benefit the host country. On the whole and in the long run, both countries benefit, and neither country benefits at the expense of the other.

The same is not true with respect to American multinationals dealing with many LDCs. The allegation that MNCs exploit these countries cannot be sustained in every—or perhaps even in most—instances. Yet the charge carries some validity. Exploitation of the people and resources of developing nations has taken place in the past. And since exploitation involves the guest company's benefiting at the expense of the host country, the guest company must be aware of the potential for exploitation and must take steps to avoid it. Exploitation is possible because of the lack of equality in bargaining power and the lack of background institutions adequate to protect the workers and the resources of the LDC.

This norm places a burden on American companies. If an American chemical company builds a chemical plant in a less developed country, it must ensure that its plant brings more good than harm to the country. This means not only that it must make certain that the chemicals it produces and the jobs it supplies benefit the country, but also that its plant possesses and utilizes safety measures and devices necessary to preclude serious injury to its employees, excessive environmental pollution, and possible disaster to the population surrounding the plant. This heightened duty of the MNC does not relieve the host country of its responsibility to pass and monitor appropriate constraining regulations. But the American company shares responsibility for the ethical debacle if the project does produce more harm than good.[12]

The American company typically supplies work opportunities for the local population, and in return it receives a finished product that it can market locally or internationally. The trade-off is fair and represents the legitimate implementation of the principle of comparative advantage, provided that the good accrued to the country is greater than any harm done to it (through pollution, rapid depletion of its resources, deforestation that leads to natural disasters, the undermining of local industry, or the like).

A critic might claim that this norm is patronizing and assumes that LDCs are less able to protect their own interests than are developed countries. Yet such a reaction misses the point of the norm. If an LDC does adequately protect its own interests and does not allow foreign multinationals to operate within its borders unless the latter in fact produce more good than harm, the norm becomes at worst redundant; that is, what is required by the country in question is also required by the norm. But to recognize the difference in bargaining power between many LDCs and many giant MNCs is not patronizing. Recent history records many instances of exploitation that would have been avoided if companies had followed this norm. Under the guise of not being patronizing, one might conclude that anything one can get away with is legitimate.

A corollary to this norm of doing more good than harm to the host country is that *the good of the country is not the same as the good of corrupt leaders or the good of an oppressive elite of the country.* The good of the country must include the good of the ordinary people. This distinction is crucial. As a consequence of it, a multinational may be ethically precluded from operating in some countries or may have to operate differently in one country than it would in another. The situation in South Africa under apartheid illustrates this principle. Commentators who argued that American companies could not ethically operate in South Africa at all implicitly appealed to this corollary, claiming that the American companies might be inordinately benefiting the oppressive government or the elite, and therefore, in the long run, actually harming the ordinary people. The Sullivan Principles, which prohibited American companies from engaging in apartheid, represented an attempt to justify American operations in South Africa. According to these principles, if companies hired, trained, and promoted blacks, and if by their actions they helped break down apartheid, then they produced more good than harm for the people. The continuing dispute over the American presence in South Africa came to focus on whether, even if they followed the Sullivan Principles, the companies produced more good than harm for the ordinary people of the host country by doing business there.[13]

> G3. *Multinationals should contribute by their activity to the host country's development.*

The rationale for this rule is similar to that for the second rule—namely, the absence of reciprocity in power, the absence of adequate background institutions, the history of past exploitation, and the potential for present-day exploitation.[14] This norm, however, requires a different kind of consideration from that necessitated by the second one. Providing work for the local population and helping its members achieve or surpass a subsistence level of life might fulfill norm two. Norm three requires more: a contribution to the country's development.

Central to the interpretation and implementation of this norm is an understanding of the term *development. Development* in the context of international business usually means industrial development. An American multinational can contribute to a country's development by transferring knowledge, techniques, and knowhow to its local employees, or by sharing such knowledge with the host government, its advisors, or other appropriate representatives. The American company can help develop the missing infrastructure of roads, housing, transportation, and communication needed for the company to carry on its business and for the country to develop industrially. Such development is a feature of OECD and of many other international codes.[15]

Not all countries want industrial development, nor do they necessarily want machine-intensive (as opposed to labor-intensive) processes, since the latter supply work for more people. The multinational can serve itself and the host country by helping to educate the current labor force and the future labor force. Nonetheless, in helping a country develop, the multinational must be careful not to impose its notion of development on the host country. Once again, the OECD and other codes emphasize the need to consider the host country's aims, goals, and priorities.[16]

Financial institutions can play a significant role in the development of LDCs. But the past record shows that they can also be a destructive force if they leave a country with oppressive debts, the servicing of which precludes any further development.

Although this third guideline might seem paternalistic, it should not be so interpreted. It does not claim that American MNCs know what is right for the host country better than the host country itself does. Yet it recognizes that some actions of MNCs in the past have led to a deterioration of the host country's condition because of overwhelming debt, lack of investment capital, or failure to transfer appropriate technology.

In implementing this norm, MNCs should also consider the difference between the personal development of individuals' abilities and the industrial development of the country as a whole. Both can be proper aims. But industrial development should not be promoted in a way that leaves the people worse off than they were before, with fewer opportunities for individual development.[17]

A country and its people have the right to be independent and to become self-sufficient. This does not mean that each country must produce everything it needs. On the contrary, the doctrine of comparative advantage encourages different countries to support themselves in different ways and to get by trade what they do not produce. In light of this, *self-sufficiency* means utilizing the available resources and the talents and labor of a country's people to sustain the population at an adequate standard of living. Unless an American multinational can help the host country achieve such sustainable development, the company has not clearly justified its operation in that country.

> G4. *Multinationals should respect the human rights of their employees.*

Like the first norm, this one is not peculiar to American multinationals operating in the LDCs. All employers should respect the human rights of their employees. However, this rule takes on special importance in countries where the human rights of workers are not protected by domestic law.[18]

Multinationals tend to violate this norm primarily in the LDCs because of the great poverty and high unemployment rates found there and because these countries often lack adequate local legislation to protect their people's rights vis-a-vis employers. This norm precludes invoking the "when in Rome" doctrine to justify exploiting workers unconscionably. If the prevailing wage in a country is below the level of subsistence, an American company operating there cannot justify paying that wage on the ground that it is the prevailing wage. Respect for the rights of workers imposes on American companies obligations that may exceed what local laws require and what local industries practice. This does not mean that the "righteous American" demand for wages equivalent to those paid American workers must be met. It does mean that severe exploitation of workers is prohibited by ethics in places where such exploitation is not prohibited by law and where it may even be the prevailing practice. Just as an American company could not ethically engage in slavery or in apartheid simply because these institutions were lawful and customary, so it cannot engage in extreme exploitation.

Paying more than the going wage may cause problems for a multinational. As was suggested at the beginning of this chapter, it may result in the MNCs being accused of luring away the best workers or of forcing local industries to raise wages beyond what they can afford, and thus in effect of trying to drive them out of business. All of these considerations must be weighed. Yet none of them justifies failure to respect the human rights of workers. That local companies are guilty of this practice does not lead to the conclusion that we may ethically follow their lead. To the contrary, if others violate rights and we cannot compete effectively without also violating rights, either we must not compete or we must encourage the development of background institutions that protect the human rights of all.

According to norm four, American companies must pay at least subsistence wages and enough above that level to allow workers and their families to live decently. Companies must provide safe and healthful work environments. They must recognize their workers' right to form unions and to strike. Recognizing the human rights of workers does not solve the problem of determining what constitutes a just wage or safe working conditions. But failure to consider their rights usually leads to their exploitation in countries that do not protect workers' rights by legislation.

As stated, this guideline does not specify the precise content of "human rights," and to that extent it requires further clarification. There is considerable debate about exactly which rights are human rights, and against whom these rights are properly exercised. The UN Universal Declaration of Human Rights is a good starting point.[19] Widely accepted throughout the world, it serves as a working document from which an MNC should deviate only if it can fully justify the deviation. Many of the rights listed therein are rights of citizens against their own government, and these serve as guides to appropriate civil legislation. Even some commonly accepted rights—such as the right to free speech, or the right to freedom of conscience in the practice of one's religion—have very different applications within a firm and in civil society as a whole. A firm may not ethically discriminate on the basis of an employee's religion, gender, or race; and in general it should use only job-related criteria in evaluating employee performance. The right to free speech precludes an employer from firing employees for what they say off the job, provided that what they say is not job-related and does not, for instance, divulge trade secrets. But freedom of speech is not generally recognized as conferring on an employee the right to give speeches or to distribute non-work-related material on the job and during workings hours.

Exactly how the rights listed in the Universal Declaration of Human Rights are to be implemented also varies from country to country. The general injunction to respect the human rights of workers, therefore, is open to some interpretation and some variance in accord with local customs. But such leeway in interpretation can never ethically serve as an excuse for the violating a worker's human rights.

> G5. *To the extent that local culture does not violate ethical norms, multinationals should respect the local culture and work with and not against it.*

This norm reflects the charge made against American multinationals that they impose American values—and frequently bring with them the worst aspects of American culture—to the detriment of the native values and culture.

The norm requires multinationals to obey local laws, to respect local cultures, and to seek neither to undermine them nor to replace them. To do either would violate the first norm of doing no intentional harm, and this fifth norm is simply a particular application of the first one.[20] Moreover, as guests in a foreign land, multinationals generally have no right to interfere with the local government unless the latter is behaving unethically. They should not resist or lobby against reforms or laws that protect the country's workers or consumers, even if such laws make operating in these countries less profitable.

To do business successfully an American company operating abroad must recognize and conform to local customs. The present guideline is consistent with this observation, and it is also consistent with the third guideline of contributing to the host country's development. Respect for local culture, however, does not justify adopting or silently approving local practices that are unethical—such as apartheid. An ethical company must look at the impact of its activity on the culture of the country and must limit the adverse impact of such activity on that culture to the extent possible.

Instead of designing and building plants in LDCs exactly as they are built in the United States, for instance, a company must take into account the local architecture, the site plan, the customs of the people, and the impact that the plant and the product will have on the local culture. Not all the decisions about a plant, its operation, and its product should be made unilaterally by the American firm; consultation and sensitivity to the host country's culture are required. This is probably good business as well as the ethically correct action. The fact that good business and ethics can be mutually supportive is a prudential reason for acting as ethics demands, and it should not be ignored.

Implementing this norm is sometimes a delicate matter. Where women are kept in a subservient role, for example, it may take a good deal of thought and care to arrive at a practice that respects the rights of women and yet does not upset the local culture. Some ethicists may argue that, if women are not treated equally, the MNC has an obligation to change that custom. This norm does not go that far. Rather it says that the company may not treat women in a discriminatory way, even if other local firms and the general culture do. It places no burden on the MNC to take an active role outside its own walls in changing the local custom. The norm precludes the MNC from doing anything to prevent such change, but it does not preclude it from supporting any such change that is already taking place.

One underlying assumption of this rule is that the American MNC is not a citizen of the host country in the same way that it is a citizen in the American context. In the United States, lobbying by firms for legislation is an accepted part of the political landscape and is regulated to whatever extent the legislature at a given time thinks appropriate. Norm five precludes MNCs from engaging in such political lobbying abroad if their vast resources could easily skew the local political process (and hence the local culture) and in effect upset whatever natural balance exists within the country. Whether lobbying should be allowed by MNCs in developed countries is a matter for debate— one that properly should be decided by those countries. The difference in power and wealth justifies special consideration in this regard by MNCs in less developed countries.

American multinationals like to operate in countries that are politically stable because their assets are best protected in such societies. Because such stability is often achieved by repressive regimes, critics often charge that American MNCs favor conservative governments, even if they are military dictatorships. Norm five precludes American MNCs from collaborating with such regimes, even if the other four norms do not forbid their operating in such countries entirely.

G6. *Multinationals should pay their fair share of taxes.*

Since each country levies taxes and enforces payment, this norm, consideration of which takes up an entire section in the OECD Guidelines,[21] may seem superfluous. In fact, less developed countries frequently offer tax breaks as an incentive to American companies to establish operations within their borders. Then why is this norm necessary? In the past, some multinationals have avoided taxes through international price manipulation, transfer payments, and a variety of schemes that fall outside any country's control. Even the United States in 1990, Congress included in the deficit reduction bill a provision penalizing companies that underreport income from their foreign subsidies by more than $10 million; the purpose of this provision was to get companies to pay their fair share of taxes.[22] If the United States Internal Revenue Service has difficulty enforcing its tax laws on multinationals, it should not be surprising that many less developed countries cannot effectively enforce their tax laws.

To implement this norm, companies must be consistent in the values they place on products shipped from one country to another. All pricing of goods from a subsidiary should be done as if the transaction were an arm's-length transaction—that is, as if the goods were being bought or sold by a wholly unrelated firm.[23]

The absence of any international monitoring system allows multinationals to avoid oversight of their international operations at anything like the degree of scrutiny that they endure in their national operations. The fact that a company's national operations can nonetheless be profitable shows that price manipulation is not essential for economic viability. The absence of international control means that a company that wishes to act ethically must impose rules of fairness on itself that cannot currently be enforced internationally. Of course, a company that does so may feel that it is operating at a competitive disadvantage if its competitors do not live up to similar self-imposed standards. The solution here is not for all companies to sink to the lowest standards of practice, but for some companies to take the lead in working to establish international rules that will make competition fair while demanding in the interim that all companies adhere to basic standards of honesty.

> G7. *Multinationals should cooperate with the local government in developing and enforcing just background institutions.*

This norm calls for American MNCs to promote the development of just background institutions within the country, as well as on the international level. A narrow line separates the duty to work toward just background institutions internationally and in LDCs from the obligation not to interfere with the internal affairs of a country and to respect its culture and values. As guests in foreign lands, American multinationals are usually expected not to interfere in the operation of the host country's government or in its internal politics and affairs. However, this general expectation does not preclude the company's supporting (rather than undermining) attempts by the country's government to introduce and establish just background institutions, the purpose of which is to guarantee fair competition, the protection of human rights, and the conservation of the country's resources. It should be clear that supporting a government's efforts to establish just background institutions constitutes neither inappropriate interference nor the promotion of self-interest at the expense and good of the host country.

American multinationals have a good deal of power and can influence a poor country's decisions in various ways—subtle and not so subtle. In some countries managers of MNCs have opposed labor unions, the institution of minimum wage laws, and environmental protection measures. Norm seven precludes American firms that operate in LDCs from actively opposing the establishment of such measures, and it encourages them to support such measures and to help establish them to the extent appropriate. The justification for the norm derives from and constitutes an implementation of the preceding norms.[24]

Multinationals have an even greater obligation to promote adequate background institutions on the international level. Internationally MNCs are major players, and on that level they do not interfere with the internal politics of individual states. The existence of MNCs is a step forward in the unification of mankind and in the formation of a global community. They provide the economic base and substructure on which true international cooperation can be built. Because of their special position and the special opportunities they enjoy, they have a special responsibility to ensure that the international structures that they have so large a hand in forming are fair.

In the nations of the developed industrial world, the labor movement serves as a counter weight to the dominance of big business; consumerism serves as a watchdog on practices harmful to the consumer; and big government serves as a restraint on each of the vested interest groups. Similar international structures are necessary to provide proper background constraints on international corporations and competition.

Although this may have the appearance of asking the multinationals to act in opposition to their self-interest and to work for restraints that will hamper their activities, such an interpretation of background institutions is shortsighted. In the absence of adequate background institutions to promote fairness and efficiency, unscrupulous firms exploit peoples and nations, make gains by bribery and extortion, and succeed not on their efficiency or merits but on their ability and willingness to take advantage of the situations in which they operate. Equitable background institutions would preclude any company from gaining a competitive advantage by engaging in unethical practices. Firms interested in acting with integrity have a vested interest in playing on a level field, where they compete on their merits. Adequate national and international background institutions help ensure the creation and maintenance of such a level field. MNCs interested in acting with integrity have more to gain than to lose by helping formulate voluntary industry-wide codes (such as the code governing infant formula), UN codes, and comparable codes governing the conduct of all multinationals. Self-interest in this case is not at odds with ethical obligation but reinforces it for the ethically minded firm.

The foregoing set of seven norms is not a complete list of the ethical requirements that a multinational must meet to act ethically in an LDC. Yet the norms illustrate the ethical considerations that a firm must take into account if it is to act ethically and with integrity. In particular, they specify the kind of approach to operating in a less developed country that integrity requires. Observing these norms can also help American multinationals avoid some of the charges of unethical conduct to which they have been subjected in the past. Finally, the norms can help both American MNCs and their critics distinguish between justifiable and unjustifiable ethical criticism.

Ethical norms impose a level of consideration on a company that is not obviously and clearly business-related. As a result, many companies do not know how to integrate such considerations into their strategic planning, and they opt instead for the "when in Rome" solution. Too often the result has been exploitation, scandal, and corruption.

Many LDCs are becoming more sophisticated about controlling multinationals in ways that ensure that their presence benefits the nation. They have learned to bargain and to legislate. Some have learned faster than others. Yet the claim of dependence persists and poor countries often cannot police multinationals effectively.

Developing Ethical International Background Institutions

The solution to exploitation and oppression of LDCs by the industrialized nations involves not only having multinationals act ethically, but establishing structures of international trade and business that constrain their actions in a manner parallel to the way structures of the industrialized countries constrain the activities of businesses within their borders. The goals are to make and keep competition fair, to protect the rights of all, and to preclude the domination of the weak and poor by the rich and strong. Attaining these requires not only the development of just background institutions within countries, but also the establishment of such institutions on the international level. Ample precedent for such institutions exists, and imagination and good will can produce the structures required. Such institutions will clearly not be the result of the unilateral action of any country; nor should they be rules developed and imposed by any country or set of countries on others. If fair, they should ultimately help all countries and should be adopted by all because they promote the long-term interests of the entire community of nations.

United Nations commissions, church groups, the International Chamber of Commerce, the Organization for Economic Cooperation and Development, and other independent agencies have developed or proposed international codes of conduct for multinationals. Some codes have been developed by individual MNCs. There is no reason why multinationals themselves cannot take the lead in formulating and implementing industry-wide codes for governing their own actions.[25]

The hope for ethics in international business lies ultimately in the development of adequate international background institutions and in the willingness of multinationals to recognize their ethical obligations and act in accordance with them. Few companies take the lead in attempting to develop needed institutions, since such leadership involves taking various risks. Their motives are frequently questioned, and attacks come from companies less interested in moral actions.

General Motors played a major role in the development and implementation of the Sullivan Principles, written by Leon Sullivan, who was on GM's Board of Directors. That code precluded companies that adopted it from obeying the apartheid laws in South Africa. The success of the code among MNCs offers two lessons: concerted action can be developed in support of ethical principles, and ethically motivated members of large American multinationals can play an important role in developing just international structures.

The Interconnection of American and International Business

Consideration of norms for multinationals involves an additional dimension. Thus far we have treated the activities of American MNCs as if they were unrelated to the activities of the American business system at home. In fact, however, the two are inextricably intertwined: ethics in international business involves ethics in American business, and vice versa.

Consider, for instance, the export of industry and protectionism. The export of American manufacturing has been faulted from many points of view and is hotly debated. Can America maintain its preeminent world role without a strong and vital industrial base? Has the United States reached a post-industrial, service stage of development? And if it has, is this a positive or negative condition? Although some people complain when a company moves its factory from a northern state to the Sun Belt, where labor is cheaper, many argue this is morally and economically acceptable. But when the same company for the same reason—to take advantage of lower labor costs—moves from the United States to a foreign country, many of the same people condemn the action as immoral. They claim that, although the northern states may be adversely affected by the first move, the Sun Belt states benefit, and the overall benefit to the country remains constant. When industry is exported, however, Americans lose jobs and the country as a whole is hurt by the loss of industries and employment. This increases national unemployment, reduces the nation's tax base, and benefits the company at the expense of the country.

This argument, however, presents a one-sided view. It considers only the company and the United States. It fails to consider that exporting industry helps provide jobs for people in the host country, where typically the unemployment rate is staggering. Are jobs more important for Americans than for the unemployed of other countries? Arguments limited to the benefits for America and Americans are too narrow. The evaluation of good and bad in the ethical context demands the broadest possible perspective; that is, all parties affected by an action should be considered. From this perspective it is more difficult to determine the proper ethical evaluation of the problem. This does not mean that the export of industry is necessarily ethical or unethical. It does mean that, from an ethical point of view, the interests of others count for as much as the interests of Americans. If Americans prosper while others also prosper, so much the better. If in order for the disadvantaged in less developed countries to prosper at all, the standard of living of American workers must be somewhat reduced, then that is a cost that ethics may impose and that Americans (as well as others similarly affected) should be willing to pay.

Protectionism calls for similar analysis. The argument in favor of protectionist policies is that they protect our home industries from foreign competition. This helps preserve jobs for workers, but typically it also raises the cost of protected items for consumers. Moreover, protectionism denies less developed countries free access to our market. The harm done to them is sometimes greater than the benefit done to our own industry. Protectionism may be a justifiable tactice in response to protectionism practiced by other developed countries—if it aims for and actually results in the elimination of protectionism by all sides—but to the extent that it deprives LDCs of markets, it simply exacerbates their existing plight.

Ethics does not solve business problems. On the contrary, ethics imposes restraints on corporate activities. Ethics is a sieve through which proper corporate decisions must pass. The problems of international business and the conduct of multinationals are recognized as complex on the economic and business levels. They are equally complex on the ethical level. As with any other set of business considerations, determining the ethical quality of a firm's anticipated actions requires time, research, and analysis. Ethics interposes another layer of consideration on the part of corporate management, especially at the level of strategic planning. Some firms may have the expertise to deal with this layer. Others will have to develop it by forming ethics committees, by hiring people with skill at moral analysis, or by relying on outside help. Industry-wide panels may be set up to discuss some issues. But this added layer of consideration is required of any company that wishes to act with integrity. It is required of any company that wishes to be perceived as acting ethically. It is required of any company that wishes to preserve and develop a reputation for honesty and integrity—a reputation that in the long run can translate into profits and success. Moral action does not guarantee that a company will succeed. But no company can long succeed if it acts unethically or ignores moral considerations. In this sense competing ethically and successfully in international business is by no means a contradiction in terms. Ultimately the ethical level achieved in international business will reflect the integrity of those engaged in such business. Having ethical guidelines may help.

4

Applying the Guidelines:
MNCs and the Many Kinds of Harm

The members of one village in Ghana found that throwing pesticide into a lake made it easier for them to catch fish, a staple item of their diet.[1] Inhabitants of another gathered rain for drinking water in an empty steel drum that had been used to ship insecticide, assuming it was safe because they had rinsed it out with water.[2] In neither case did the producer of the product anticipate or intend the use to which their pesticide or drum was put. Does it have any responsibility for the local misuse of its products?

A U.S. agricultural company pays what it considers a fair price for some prime land in a Central American country—land that was formerly used to raise crops for the local population. The American company uses that land to grow fruit for export, and provides jobs for some of the local people. Food for the local population must now be imported, since the amount of food that can be grown on the remaining land is insufficient for the population's needs. The cost of food goes up, and many of those not employed by the U.S. company find themselves unable to buy enough food for adequate nutrition. The infant mortality rate rises, and the effects of malnutrition become obvious. Does the U.S. company have any responsibility for these results?

Imedla Marcos, Saddam Hussein, and many other former and current leaders of less developed countries, are alleged to have secret Swiss bank accounts. Colombian drug lords supposedly have such accounts as well. Do banks have any ethical responsibility if they act as havens for illegally obtained money?

The fairest way to make an ethical assessment in these and other cases is to examine them case by case. Broadside claims, such as the charge that all multinationals exploit underdeveloped countries or destroy their culture, are expressed too vaguely and at too broad a level of generality to permit one to determine their accuracy, even though many U.S. multinationals in the past have engaged—and some continue to engage—in unethical practices. Nonetheless, we can usefully discuss five types of business operations that raise very different sorts of ethical issues: drug and pesticide companies, agricultural enterprises, banks and financial institutions, extracting industries, and other manufacturing and service industries.

As we apply our seven general guidelines to each type of industry, we see some of the differences among them and many kinds of harm that MNCs should be aware of and should try to avoid.

Pharmaceutical and Pesticide Industries

Drug and pesticide companies encounter special problems abroad. Both have played a significant role in improving the quality of life in less developed countries. To the extent that they have done so, they satisfy the third norm (G3) of contributing by their activity to the host country's development. Yet both drugs and pesticides are potentially dangerous products whose marketing and use are tightly controlled in the United States. To act with integrity when they operate in countries without strict governmental controls, drug and pesticide companies must exercise a good deal of self-control and restraint. The special nature of their products empowers them to do great harm advertently or inadvertently unless they exercise the special care required by the circumstances in which they function abroad. The absence of adequate background institutions both on the national level in LDCs and on the international level is obvious and crucial in this situation.

That FDA standards are not ethically mandatory does not mean that drug companies are bound only by local laws. In some cases local laws may require less than morality does in the way of supplying adequate information and of not causing intentional, direct harm. The same is true of pesticide products. Although a pesticide producer operating in an LDC might not be required to adopt all the measures mandated by OSHA regulations, it cannot ethically leave its workers unprotected or expose them to preventable health risks. To do so fails to respect their human rights—a violation of the fourth norm (G4). Yet FDA, OSHA, and other American regulatory agencies are precisely that: American. Their function is to set regulations appropriate to American conditions, taking into account the American worker and consumer, the American standard of living, the degree of governmental paternalism sought by the American people through legislation, and the other background institutions already existing in the society. They do not presume to legislate for the whole world, nor do they claim that their regulations are ethically mandatory everywhere. At most they claim that the regulations are ethically justifiable, given the existing American context.

Yet the United Nations' Food and Agricultural Organization reports that 81 developing countries are not known to regulate pesticide use.[3] In these circumstances, pesticide companies that wish to act with integrity cannot rely only on local laws and regulations, or on local enforcement, to ensure the safety of their operations. Self-regulation is clearly necessary if harm is to be avoided.

Present-day drugs and pesticides are products of modern science. They have great potential for helping, improving, and prolonging life, but they are also capable of being misused and of causing great harm. In the hands of those who understand their proper function and use, they are a blessing; in the hands of those who do not adequately understand the results of misusing them, they are a constant danger. An important problem in less developed countries is the lack of adequate controls to prevent the actual potential use of such products in ways that cause more harm than good.

We shall consider two different issues. The first is the manufacture and sale in less developed countries of drugs and pesticides that are not allowed to be sold in the United States. The second is the promotion and sale of drugs and pesticides without due concern for the level of knowledge of the average user. Then we shall examine a specific (and well-known) case of alleged malfeasance by an MNC—Nestlé and its infant formula.

Products Prohibited in the United States

The claim that products prohibited from production or sale in the United States may not ethically be produced or sold in less developed countries is too strong. There may be reasons why a product not allowed in the United States should be allowed elsewhere. But the question of who should make that decision is difficult to answer. Placing the decision in the hands of the manufacturers may leave them without any practical restraints. A company with integrity will follow the ethical rule to do no harm and to benefit the host country and its people; one without integrity may not. LDCs need to establish the legal regulations that function in most developed countries, even though these may differ somewhat from one LDC to the next. The problem is that LDCs do not have the resources, for instance, to test all the products American governmental agencies can test and regulate. As a result, some simply adopt U.S. rules or outlaw any drug or pesticide banned in the United States. Lack of funds, however, frequently precludes an LDC from effectively enforcing laws it does adopt. Other LDCs, for whatever reason, have adopted no legislation governing the importation of pharmaceutical drugs.

Laws precluding the importation of drugs outlawed in the United States often provide insufficient protection, because unethical drug companies can get around them with relative ease. By adding an inert substance to a compound, a company technically makes a different product—one not banned in the United States—and can legally call it by a different name. A company could not get away with this in the United States, because the tests required before sales are permitted would immediately reveal that the product was functionally the same as the one banned. But a country that does not independently test pharmaceuticals might well allow such a product to be imported and sold. This deceptive subterfuge clearly violates the spirit (although not the letter) of the law, rendering it ethically unacceptable. Moreover, the product would produce the same effects or side effects on users in the LDC that caused it to be banned in the United States. Unless the product did not produce harm in the LDC, because of different circumstances, the company would violate the rule against doing direct intentional harm, even if the product also did some good.

Companies have a second way of introducing banned products into a country. Some LDC laws restrict the sale of any American-made product whose sale is restricted in the United States. Since the law is limited to products made in the United States, companies can legally introduce the product into the LDC if they make it elsewhere (sometimes also adding an inert substance and changing the product's name). It is then technically legal to import the drug, although it remains the same product that the legislation intended to exclude. LDCs have become more sophisticated in drawing up legislation to close such loopholes. But without the funds or laboratories to do their own screening, they rely on U.S. standards and risk circumvention of their laws by unethical companies.

From an ethical point of view, not all products banned in the United States need necessarily be banned everywhere. For instance, some pesticides are prohibited in America because they eventually contaminate the ground, the water supply, and the food chain, and because they increase the incidence of cancer. It is possible to imagine scenarios in which these banned chemicals may be the only ones powerful enough—as DDT once was—to rid a country of malaria-bearing mosquitoes or some other noxious insect that ruins crops or spreads disease. Using the pesticide for these purposes in an LDC may well produce more good than harm, and in such circumstances the country and its people may well opt to suffer the increased cancers in exchange for the elimination of the greater number of deaths from the other disease or blight. However, such choices should be made by the responsible governments or by the people who will suffer the harm—not by the pesticide companies.

The same sort of analysis pertains to the pharmaceutical drug industry. The side effects of a drug may make it undesirable in the United States. But in an LDC the side effects may be far preferable to the disease, and some factors such as difference in life expectancy might make the drug acceptable. What is not ethically justifiable is any instance of failing to disclose the real effects of a drug or of circumventing the laws through misrepresentation. As in the case of pesticides, the decision to accept whatever risk is involved is a choice to be made not by the drug companies but by those who suffer the risk: the patients or their legitimate representatives.

These scenarios provide grounds for not taking the U.S. standards as universally valid. But they do not justify deception or fraud. If a case can be made for their use in a given country, integrity requires that the case be made on its merits. The injunctions not to cause direct harm and to produce more good than harm to the host country remain the operative ethical norms, together with the general prohibition against deception and lying.

Abuse of Legitimate Products

A more difficult problem involves the misuse of drugs and pesticides in LDCs and the harm done by legitimate products. Both drugs and pesticides typically come with detailed instructions that describe the dangers of misusing them. A background of various assumptions controls the use of these products in the United States. Manufacturers assume that users are literate and that, in general, they know something about the potential dangers of the products they purchase and the importance of reading cautionary information printed on bottles or containers. Manufacturers know that commercial domestic use of the product must be made in accordance with OSHA or other regulations, and they take for granted that doctors or pharmacists will point out special dangers to avoid the misuse of prescription drugs. Manufacturers make many other acceptable and reasonable assumptions, as well.

Horror stories have emerged concerning the use of pesticides in some LDCs. The villagers who used a pesticide as an easy way to catch fish, which they then ate, and the workmen in the bush who used an empty pesticide drum to collect rain for their drinking water do not represent isolated examples. These and similar cases do not reflect any intent on the part of pesticide companies to cause harm; yet the misuse of the products can cause great harm.

The manufacturer's ethical obligation not to cause harm does not end with the selling of its product. A company is also responsible for predictable and preventable misuse of its product; and if some misuse is not predictable, the company is certainly responsible for preventing further misuse once an unforeseen problem is brought to its attention. A manufacturer with integrity must continually try to anticipate and to identify misuses, and it must do its utmost to prevent such abuses.

Critics rightly complain that some companies do not even exercise such elementary means of preventing abuse as painting a skull and crossbones on their insecticide drums. Pictures can convey appropriate cautionary messages to illiterate users. Clear and obvious symbols can effectively warn people; but some research may be necessary to determine what pictures, signs, or symbols are appropriate to different populations.

In the United States, strict liability laws make firms liable for harm done by their products not only when used according to directions but also when misused. The intent of these laws is to motivate companies to try to foresee and prevent misuses of their products by making them liable for damages that do not involve negligence on their part. They are in the best position to predict possible misuse and potential dangers and to learn quickly about other dangers from users. When manufacturers in developed countries are held strictly liable for harm, such that lack of knowledge or intent do not excuse them from liability, they often increase the cost of the product to cover their liability. In this way they indirectly insure their users in case the latter are harmed.

Many less developed countries do not have strict liability laws. Yet the ethical responsibility of drug and pesticide companies operating in these countries is just as real as it is in the United States. A company that acts with integrity will take this responsibility as seriously in one place as in the other, whatever the local laws or restrictions demand or allow. An ethical company must ask: "Who will use the product? Will protective clothing be necessary? How can I secure informed consent to the use of potentially dangerous products? How can I be sure that warnings are clear and understandable to those most likely to use the product? How can I prevent misuse of my product?" Integrity requires not only asking such questions but also answering them satisfactorily. The seventh norm (G7) requires that drug and pesticide companies cooperate in the development and enforcement of appropriate regulations and controls governing the sale, distribution, and use of potentially harmful products. Companies with integrity should have no reluctance to do so; and they would in fact gain if all companies in the drug and pesticide industries were adequately, fairly, and uniformly regulated so as to preclude any of them from causing direct or indirect harm.

The Nestlé Boycott

A study of the Nestlé infant formula case, the international boycott of the company's products, and the uneasy resolution of the problem is informative for the drug and pesticide industries. Women who are no longer able to or no longer wish to nurse their infants can substitute infant formula for breast milk. It is a good product when properly used, and it is very popular in developed countries. The formula is somewhat expensive and requires sanitary water in certain proportions if it is to serve as an adequate substitute for mother's milk. Use of the product is not unethical, nor is its sale in developed countries. Why then was selling it in less developed countries considered unethical?

Three basic charges were raised about Nestlé.[4] First, it was accused of misrepresentation and of attempting without justification to change indigenous behavior to the detriment of the health of the babies affected. Critics claimed that Nestlé ads showed white mothers feeding their babies infant formula, conveying the message that if native women wished to be modern and keep up with the times, they too would give up breast-feeding and use infant formula. This is a violation of norm five (G5), which is to respect the local culture.

Second, Nestlé was charged with giving away free samples of the infant formula while the mothers were in the hospital. The mother's milk would then dry up and she would be forced to use the powdered formula once she left the hospital. The samples were handed out to the mothers sometimes by doctors and sometimes by the company's representatives, who were often mistaken for nurses. This charge involves deception and alleges violations of the first three norms, which relate to avoiding intentional and net harm and promoting the good of the host country's people.

Third, the firm is accused of continuing these practices despite knowing that many of the mothers could not afford to buy the formula in the quantities required for proper nourishment and that, once they left the hospital, they stretched the formula by diluting it. As a result their babies received insufficient nourishment and eventually suffered from malnutrition. Moreover, hygienic conditions often did not exist, and unsanitized water or even contaminated water was frequently used to make the formula. Finally, during the first week or so of breast-feeding, mother's milk contains a rich supply of certain antibodies to common diseases, whereas the formula does not. The result of widespread use of infant formula in LDCs was a large increase in malnutrition, incidence of diseases, and death among infants in these countries. Critics charged that, despite being aware of what was occurring, Nestlé continued to advertise and to push its product aggressively. This again is a violation of the first three special ethical norms.

Critics organized a worldwide boycott of all Nestlé products. It lasted seven years, ending only when Nestlé changed its practices. Under public pressure, the United Nations drew up guidelines for the sale of infant formula. Nestlé and other infant formula manufacturers agreed to abide by the specified norms.[5]

The Nestlé case shows that the general public accepts the ethical rule against doing harm and holds the manufacturer accountable for the misuse of a beneficial product that results in avoidable harm. The case illustrates the responsibility of the manufacturer to prevent such misuse and harm, the power of public pressure and of moral censure to affect adversely a company's profits, the role an international organization can play even if it has no enforcement power, and the effectiveness of international industry-wide norms that keep competition fair.

In applying the seven norms for operating ethically in a less developed country, an MNC must consider the conditions under which its product will be used in the LDC, and it must take the proper precautions to avoid harm through misuse. This stricture affects the company's advertising, its marketing practices, and its responsibility for monitoring possible adverse effects from misuse after sale. A multinational cannot operate in an LDC as it does in a developed country, because the conditions, culture, literacy, and degree of familiarity with the products and their dangers are very different. The ethical norms demand more of MNCs that operate in LDCs, but no more than a company that wishes to act with integrity should be willing to acknowledge.

Agricultural Enterprises

Agricultural enterprises face other demands. The major complaint about agricultural multinationals in less developed countries is that they buy the nations' best lands and use them for export crops. Consequently, although prior to the conversion of this prime land to cash crops the local population could feed itself, after the conversion the local population has insufficient arable land to do so; and the MNCs are said to be the cause of malnutrition or even starvation. They violate the first principle (G1) because they cause harm; they violate G2 because they produce no net good for the country; and they violate G3 because they do not contribute to the country's development.

If the case were as simple as this, the critics would be correct to raise charges against the multinational agribusinesses. But cases are rarely this simple. Who previously owned the land, how was it used, and why did the owners sell? Usually a nation's best land is not simply there for the MNC's taking. It is owned by someone—either a large local landowner or local farmers. A large landowner may already have been growing a cash crop, in which case the MNC is not responsible for initiating the move to cash crops or for taking land out of cultivation that was previously used to grow local food. If on the other hand the MNC buys out small farmers who own the land, why do they sell? The scenarios one can devise are endless. If they were not swindled out of the land or forced off at minimal prices because of drought or other adverse conditions that a larger landowner could have lived through, they probably sold their land for what they thought was a fair (or even a handsome) price. If they were not forced to sell, the MNC can hardly be faulted for buying from a willing, even eager seller.

Unless the sale involved fraud or some other unethical behavior, it benefited the sellers, who probably either left the land to work in the city or stayed on to work for the new landowner. In either case, the money they received from the sale of the land compensated them and (in their eyes) made them better off. Unless critics are to ban such sales in the name of knowing better than the seller what is in the seller's best interest, such sales are ethically permissible.

The next step of the criticism involves denouncing the fact that the land is changed from local farming to a cash crop for export. There are two possible sources of criticism here. The first is that the land is taken out of local production. Yet that is not necessarily bad. The real issue is not whether the village or district or country grows enough food to feed itself, but whether the people have enough to eat. One way to have enough is to grown one's own. The other way is to buy what one needs, importing food if necessary. The MNC paid for the land, and it pays the workers who grow the crops. Both payments may give local residents more than enough purchasing power to make up for the smaller amount of food grown locally. The question is whether switching to the cash crop actually produces the harm claimed.

The second issue is that the cash crop is sold abroad. Hence land that was once used to feed the local population is now used to feed (or clothe) people in other countries. The other countries thus benefit at the expense of the home country. Moreover, if the MNC takes its profits out of the country and reinvests none of them, the MNC profits at the expense of the country and violates both the guideline to do no intentional harm and (probably) the guideline to benefit the host country.

If the MNC does in fact act contrary to those guidelines, it acts unethically—and some MNC agribusinesses have so acted in the past. Yet there are various ways to avoid the ill effects of the above scenario without forbidding all MNC agribusiness in less developed countries and without banning cash crops.[6] Both LDCs and MNCs have developed strategies that force or enable the latter to act so as to benefit the host country.[7]

One strategy is to allow only a certain percentage of arable land to be used for cash crops and to require that a certain percentage be reserved to produce food for local consumption. A second is to tax the cash crop at a high enough rate that the proceeds from the tax can be used to help redistribute money as needed to feed the population in other ways. A third is to restrict repatriation of all or some of the profits by requiring that they be invested locally and so benefit the country and its people (for example, by helping create more jobs for those who leave the land). Clearly this process depends on enlightened and progressive action by the host government. Unless it has the interest of its people at heart, it will not take the necessary action. If it receives payments from the agribusiness to ignore its people's interests, then it is doubly at fault—as is the agribusiness. The point here is not that agribusinesses and local elites and governments never act in ways that harm less developed countries. The point is that they need not so act, and that converting land from a local food crop to a cash crop for export need not in itself be unethical.

Second, agribusiness is charged with denuding forests. Again this is not necessarily bad in itself. For example, American settlers cleared the land for farming. Some of the denuding that occurs in less developed countries takes place because of the local people's desire for more farmland or for the wood that the forests provide.

Deforestation produces more harm than good when the resulting land cannot sustain farms for any extended period and is not usable for other purposes. The absence of trees allows rapid runoff of rainwater, causing flooding and loss of topsoil and even precluding reforestation. The result is often disastrous for the local people.

The cutting of the Brazilian and other rainforests has done extensive harm to the local people, to the country as a whole, and to the rest of the world, which may be adversely affected by the climatic changes such cutting introduces.

Once again the issue is far from simple. The land is sold voluntarily by its previous owners. Others who do not want the land to be deforested could buy it to preserve as virgin timerland.[8] But private individuals have no legal right to order those who own the land not to sell it, or to order those who buy it not to cut the trees. Our seven rules condemn some of the ways in which the forests are being cut, since these do more harm than good to the people and the country. Means of logging other than clear-cutting are available, including selective cutting of mature trees and immediate reforestation when trees are cut for wood.

Missing in the picture thus far is any action by officials of local governments, who see the actions resulting in deforestation as being in their national, bureaucratic, or personal self-interest; who are unable to pass and effectively enforce the legislation necessary to control waste and damage; or who do not care about these actions one way or the other.[9]

In terms of ethical responsibility, American multinationals are not major players in this case. Individuals, groups, or nations that are adversely affected may rightly protest, instruct people on the long-range effects of their actions, negotiate policies, or pay to have the policies or practices changed.

Protectionism gives rise to a third kind of criticism. The MNC is not directly blamed for protectionist policies. But the MNCs or the U.S. agribusinesses commonly back legislation in the United States that precludes entry of LDC products that would compete with American crops. Or American import taxes may make the imported crops more expensive than home-grown items. Critics claim that such policies with respect to coffee imports, for instance, have led some coffee growers to convert their fields to growing coca (the plant from whose leaves cocaine is derived).[10] Since the cases are complex and differ from one instance to another, no simple resolution is appropriate. But whatever the details of the case, the seven guidelines suggest the types of questions that should be asked of agribusinesses and the questions that a company of integrity will ask in developing its own policies. The guidelines do not mandate specific policies. They do prohibit certain actions and demand that a multinational carefully consider its actions from an ethical point of view as well as from a financial one.

Banks and Financial Institutions

When banks and other financial institutions open branches in less developed countries, they do not generally employ many people. Their service to a country does not involve providing employment but providing funds. Their putative primary function is to provide loans to finance various types of enterprises, and consequently they play a key role in the development of industries and private businesses in LDCs. Yet they clearly operate in such countries to make a profit.

With regard to the ethical obligations of doing no intentional harm to the host country and of helping it to develop, banks and other financial institutions have a mixed record. The major difficulties stem from three sources. First, financial investments, dealings, and transactions have most frequently gravitated toward government projects or toward development by the country's elite. Second, lax control of financing has often resulted in huge debts—often with little in the way of development to show for it. Third, banks have served as a conduit for flight capital.

The 1991 scandal involving the Bank of Credit and Commerce International (BCCI) epitomizes the harm a bank can do and the need for ethical and legal restraints.[11] BCCI was rightly condemned for practicing fraud and for stealing at least $5 billion from its depositors, both large and small. Its actions wreaked havoc with the economies of many small and developing nations, such as Cameroon, Nigeria, Sierra Leone, Botswana, and Zimbabwe. Beyond facilitating fraud and embezzlement, it provided a financial conduit for illegal drug and arms traffic, laundered illegally acquired moneys, supplied secret accounts for illegal flight capital, falsified its own records, carried bogus accounts, broke tax and other laws in many countries in which it operated, and avoided effective governmental oversight of its operations, in part by being chartered in two countries (Luxembourg and the Cayman Islands) that are noted for their lax banking regulations.

The BCCI experience shows the inadequacy of existing international banking regulations and reflects the paucity of meaningful background institutions at the international level. Banks are built on trust, and more than companies in other industries they must act with integrity. The less adequate the existing regulations are, the greater is the need for self-imposed standards of integrity.

Banking and Elites

American banks in South Africa did little—if anything—to hasten the end of apartheid. By lending money to the government and to white entrepreneurs, they actually strengthened the government's apartheid policy. An argument can be made that their willingness to overlook apartheid did South Africa more harm than good—an argument that a number of American banks considered valid.[12] These dissenting banks discontinued their South African operations, even before lending money to that government became financially risky.

Banks in less developed countries face a dilemma: the best prospects for large loans are the government and the country's elite. But the government and the elite do not always use their loans for the good of the country; indeed, they tend to use them for themselves and their own narrowly conceived interests. This should come as no surprise. Yet it places the banks in a difficult situation, if they can only justifiably operate in an LDC if their participation helps develop the country as a whole.

Large loans generate much more interest and income per dollar lent than do small ones. After the great jump in oil prices during the 1970s, Arab countries were awash in money, and the banks where they placed their money were anxious to lend it. Expanding industries and growing markets in less developed countries seemd to represent the wave of the future. It is not surprising that so many loans went to the better prospects in those countries.

Asking banks to promote the development of the LDCs in which they operate demands too much for some people and too little for others. It asks too much because it requires that a bank know more than it can possibly know. How is a bank to know what will in fact help a country and what will not? Hindsight shows that many bank loans were bad investments; but at the time they were made, few observers envisioned the burden of debt that would overwhelm those countries. To hold banks solely accountable for imposing that burden seems simplistic and historically dishonest. On the other hand, the norm asks too little because, since loans are typically earmarked for "development," every loan is justifiable if taken at face value.

The benefit of hindsight enables us to identify potentially useful guidelines for the future. First, banks should practice the same kind of restraint in lending to governments, institutions, and individuals in less developed countries that they do in the United States and other developed countries. This is not only ethically responsible but sound banking practice. Following this guideline is hardly a problem at present, since loans to LDCs have been drying up for several years. The basic banking policies of requiring collateral, sound business plans, and realistic schedules for repayment of principal and interest were often flouted in the rush to lend readily available money.[13] Nor did bankers typically consider the overall effect of the projects they were financing on the country receiving their loans.

Second, less developed countries require not only large development but also small entrepreneurial projects. Small projects often have a more positive effect on the quality of life of the common people than do large projects. But because small projects are more expensive per dollar to process and administer, they are less attractive to banks. They are often considered riskier— although recent experience with large developmental loans tends to suggest otherwise.[14] The norm that requires banks, like other businesses, to help develop the country may mean that some of a bank's business in an LDC should be reserved for this smaller type of development. Failure to grant such loans requires some explicit justification. The ethical norm legitimates the public's demand for such justification and places the burden of explanation on the banks. If all foreign banks in a country only supply loans for large enterprises, they must make the case jointly that they are truly promoting the development of the country despite jointly (albeit independently) avoiding the kinds of loans that might most promote grass-roots development.

Third, despite a bank's desire for profits, it must refrain from issuing loans that will be used to exploit the people of an LDC. When appropriate, banks can provide for the lessening of exploitation as a condition of loans. Since banks have a great deal of leverage, their positive influence can force a country to modify exploitative practices. Banks are similarly precluded from financing oppressive government policies, the purchase of arms or equipment that will be used to oppress the people, or unethical enterprises. Otherwise, the bank is an accomplice in these practices or endeavors. Ethically banks cannot knowingly fund or service drug traffickers, for instance, and they have a responsibility to determine who their large customers are.

Such criteria seems to impose an American view on less developed countries and to put American banks at a competitive disadvantage vis-a-vis banks from other countries, which may not be as particular about exploitation or about the sources of their depositors' wealth. Yet norm five (G5) precludes MNCs from violating human rights; and by providing funds to enable others to exploit their workers, banks knowingly contribute to that exploitation. To solve the problem of competitive disadvantage, banks should jointly develop guidelines that prevent any of them from lending money to enterprises that engage in exploitative or unethical practices. The Sullivan Principles are an indication that such joint action is not an impossible dream.

Debt

Financial institutions are an important source of aid for development, but the debts incurred by many less developed countries condemn them at best to their present level of development for the foreseeable future.[15] The World Bank Group, the International Monetary Fund, and the Agency for International Development are all key players in this situation. Yet the role of private financial institutions remains crucial and raises special and difficult ethical problems, if not dilemmas.

The debt problem resulted from a number of factors, including poor loans, lack of bank control over the use of money lent, variable interest rates, and unrealistic projections in connection with prospects for quick development.

Development of a country is not the same as development of the people within it. Yet developing the people and raising their standard of living depend on developing possibilities within the country overall. If a country uses all the dollars it generates from exports to service its debt, it cannot obtain further loans; consequently, it will never have the resources to emerge from its debtor status. At best this binds the people to their current standard of living, and more often it shackles thems to a declining standard of living.

The price of having massive external debts is paid not by those who reaped the benefits of loans but by those who inherited the obligation to repay. Justice requires that those who benefited pay, and that those who did not benefit should not pay. This means that the lending banks and the debtor elite ethically bear the burden of the bad loans and of the debt. Neither the ordinary citizen of the LDC nor the ordinary citizen of the United States should bear the burden, except to the extent that they benefited. This may be an elementary principle of justice, but it is extremely difficult to implement.

Starting in 1987, American banks began writing off some of the debt owed by LDCs as bad loans, and they have transferred some of their assets from elsewhere to cover the shortfall, conceding that the debts in fact will not be repaid.[16] They do not actually write them off and cancel the interest due on them, however, partly because they fear the precedent that this would set. Yet domestically, bad debts are written off all the time; bankruptcy is declared; restructuring takes place; and new loans are issued under controlled conditions. Doing something similar on the international level is neither unrealistic nor impossible. It also falls far short of the demand made by some bank critics that all the debts be canceled.[17] While the latter policy would leave the banks holding the bag for their part in generating bad loans, it would not place any burden on the governments and elites who borrowed and used the money for their own purposes. That problem must be solved by the nations in question, and requiring evidence that this is being done is a reasonable precondition for making any further loans to elites or governments of the countries in question.

Banks and Flight Capital

Banks do not only lend money; they also receive money. Offering customers secret unnumbered accounts and evincing a willingness to accept deposits without question make banks accomplices to exploitation, crime, and the flight of investment capital from less developed countries. It is ironic that the elite in many LDCs, who are in a position to get loans from American banks for developmental purposes, keep their private assets in American, Swiss, or Japanese banks. They do not trust the stability of their own economy and are unwilling to see the value of their money eroded by inflation. In this way they also keep their assets beyond the reach of present and future governments.

It is not only ironic but unconscionable that so much of the money lent to LDCs has found its way back to American banks; typically these amounts were skimmed or siphoned off the original loan and diverted into private accounts. Individuals in the borrowing country who did the skimming and siphoning acted unethically, but the banks were ready accomplices.

It is unrealistic to expect banks to investigate the legitimacy of all the money deposited in it. And it is not the bank's business to ascertain how one earns one's money. Yet between the extremes of probing into the origin of every deposit and of accepting without question any deposit of any amount into a secret account, there is a zone of banking behavior that balances the depositor's right to privacy against potential criminal abuses of the banking system.

The forms of illicit behavior are many, from laundering money obtained through drug trafficking and crime to facilitating the illegitimate flight of investment capital. Stocks, bonds, and real estate offer other avenues for protecting and investing illegally held money. National and international guidelines are needed to handle these problems. For example, the United States tries to trace illegal drug profits by requiring that any deposit over $10,000 in cash to be reported.[18] One can of course evade this requirement by making smaller deposits or (if the cumulative deposits are reported) by using many banks. Still, it does put some pressure on those who use the banks illegitimately, even though it also increases the cost of banking. The need for banking reforms was recogniized in 1990 by a study panel representing the Group of Seven industrial countries (the United Kingdom, the United States, Canada, France, Italy, Japan, and the Federal Republic of Germany) and was joined by representatives from eight other countries, including Switzerland, Austria, and Luxembourg. The panel recommended eliminating numbered and anonymous banks accounts.[19] As Swiss banks have become somewhat more cooperative in investigations of drug dealers and others accused of crimes, they in turn have sought to pressure banks in Liechtenstein to do the same.[20]

International agreements that open to inspection and freeze in place the accounts of depositors suspected or accused of major felonies are becoming more and more prevaalent. More agreements are needed. This approach makes the host government the investigator and places on the bank the burden of cooperating and (in some instances) of reporting special kinds of deposits. The latter responsibility helps in recovering flight capital hidden abroad by deposed corrupt leaders. It does not adequately handle the problem of flight capital generated by political and industrial elites, and it is unlikely that those elites in their own countries will establish rules banning or restricting the lucrative practices in which they engage. Nonetheless, public pressure can move banks and governments to develop guidelines that benefit the people of LDCs and help prevent their exploitation by their own elites through the medium of banks and other financial institutions.

A system in which those who reap the benefits of loans are not those who pay the penalties when the loans go bad is unfair. Loans should be so structured that those who benefit if they do well suffer if they do badly. This simply means that responsibility and control must go together. For instance, when a government guarantees loans but does not have control over them, it releases those who do have control from accountability and it allows them to use loans irresponsibly without incurring any penalty. Not only does this constitute poor business practice, it also invites rather than inhibits unethical practices.[21]

Dependence and Abandonment

The issue of the dependence of less developed countries on developed ones comes out most strongly in finance. Many critics claim that selfish interests brought the financial institutions into the less developed countries in the first place; banks sought to exploit the LDCs and their peoples financially; and in the process the economic nature of the LDCs changed from one of relative independence to dependence on outside support.

The claim here is not that the poverty of LDCs is entirely due to dominance by or colonial status vis-a-vis developed countries. The less developed nations were always poor. But the nature of their poverty changed as a result of the development introduced by (and usually for the benefit of) the developed countries. Since typically the financial institutions making the initial loans did not worry about satisfying the first three of our seven principles, structural changes were made in the LDCs' economies, and harm was done. Some development took place, but it occurred at the expense of former (often traditional) ways of living, lifestyles, and culture. The development led to urban emigration, extensive urban sprawl, and huge urban slums.

Dependence is partly a result of the change in lifestyle from an agrarian to a more urban society. This change in turn leads to rising social expectations, to the need for financing and technological know-how, and to the burden of debt. To continue in the direction of urbanization, an LDC becomes increasingly dependent on developed countries, which alone can provide the capital needed for development. If the LDC must send the vast majority of the hard currency it earns back to developed countries to pay off interest on its debt, it cannot save and so cannot accumulate the capital it needs for new projects. Meanwhile, inflation erodes whatever savings the people are able to maintain in their local currencies. At best the result is economic and developmental stagnation.

Arguably some LDCs are better off today overall than they would have been had the developed countries not intervened. Therefore, it is at least possible that the second and third of our norms are satisfied. But if LDCs had been left to their own devices, they could at least blame themselves for their resulting circumstances. As matters now stand, however, they cannot return to their old ways (which have been irretrievably displaced), and they cannot move forward on the path of development without external help.

The developed countries and their financial institutions have played a significant role in bringing LDCs to their present plight. If this is so, the least that can be expected as a matter of justice is that the financial institutions should not now abandon them. That they will abandon them is a growing fear of LDCs. They see American investors turning their speculative interest from possibilities in the less developed countries to more attractive prospects opening up in Eastern Europe.[22] The LDCs' fear is not unreasonable.

From a strictly financial point of view, abandoning countries that are already mired in debt makes some sense. Banks that have written off debts and forgiven portions of interest due can argue that they have learned their lesson and will not throw good money after bad. They may understandably feel that they have more to gain economically by looking to Eastern Europe.

Yet the ethical point of view reminds us that, since the developed world's financial institutions had a substantial hand in creating the conditions under which so much of the developing world now struggles, they should not simply abandon those countries. The financial institutions helped change conditions and practices in the LDCs, and they share responsibility for the LDCs' resulting dependence. They have an obligation not to abandon these nations, and they have a concomitant obligation not to worsen their plight. Instead, they must help LDCs move from a state of dependence to one of independence. The private financial institutions of the developed nations cannot do this alone. The project requires the prudent and decisive involvement of the governments of developed nations and of the various international governmental banks, funds, and agencies, as well as the discipline and hard work of the LDCs themselves. A financial institution with integrity will not abandon those it has helped to make dependent.

Extracting Industries

Extracting industries, such as mining and oil production, pose somewhat different problems. Critics accuse MNCs engaged in these industries of exploiting less developed countries by extracting their natural riches at very low cost and then shipping them abroad, where they are sold at handsome profits that bring little benefit to the original country.[23] Companies in the developed countries frequently use the raw materials to manufacture products that are subsequently shipped back to the LDC and sold at inflated prices. The LDC is thus doubly exploited: once when its natural wealth is taken without adequate compensation; and again when the finished products are shipped back to it for sale at prices higher than are asked in developed countries, where the competition is greater.

Although this accusation has some validity, MNCs need not act in the way described, and not all companies engaged in extracting industries do. Extracting industries are vulnerable to the charge of exploitation unless they can show two things: that they do more good than harm to the host country, and that the work they do benefits the people of the country. They cannot operate with integrity if their efforts benefit only themselves or themselves and a repressive elite in the host country.

Given the present economic and political division of the world, the natural resources of a country should benefit that country. They may do so in two ways. First, the country itself can extract its resources and use them to make needed goods for its people or exportable goods that can be used to generate capital to purchase what they need or want. Alternatively, the country can sell the resources to others who want or need them. In either case, the resources are only of value to the extent that they are used or consciously held as reserves for potential use. A country that has oil or coal or gold has valuable assets only if those items are useful and in demand. If they cease to be useful or in demand—that is, if they are no longer valued by someone—they no longer represent a valuable national asset.

No country should let others extract and export its resources without receiving adequate recompense when that resource is useful and in demand. An MNC that extracts and exports such resources without paying fairly for the opportunity to do so exploits that country. In many cases multinationals bought mineral-rich lands or the right to extract the minerals or oil underneath them at a time when those resources were readily available, the local economy was too weak or poor to exploit them itself, and the country was insufficiently developed to make good use of its resources. Even after conditions changed, the MNCs continued to benefit from having been on the scene early. Some countries nationalized their oil and mining industries, and so took back their resources, with or without compensation. Others did not.

What rights does a country have with respect to its natural resources, and when do the activities of multinationals constitute unethical exploitation of such resources? Clearly the answers to these questions turn on the meaning assigned to the terms *adequate compensation* and *exploitation*.

Adequate compensation means a payment equal to what the minerals in some sense are worth. In a competitive economy they are worth the price they will bring on the open market, as determined by supply and demand. Restricting the supply can to some extent influence that price, if one has a monopoly or if those involved in production agree on a fixed price, as in the case of a cartel. The OPEC countries dramatically increased the price of oil in this way, although they have not succeeded in keeping the price at the high level it once reached. Oil might be worth more if it were in short supply and if the cost of alternative fuels were higher, or if the price being paid for oil produced elsewhere (for example, in the developed industrial countries) were even higher than the price being charged by OPEC countries.

Oil and minerals are nonrenewable resources: once they are extracted, they cannot be replaced. Since any deposit of minerals is finite, it will eventually be exhausted. Thus countries with oil and minerals have valuable assets only while their oil fields or mines remain productive; once the resources are depleted, the countries' economic vitality must be based on other goods or services. It is at least plausible, given the division of the world into nations, to assert that each nation has a legitimate claim to the resources within its borders.[24] To protect their future, countries should use their resources in a way that benefits them now and in the future. Extraction of minerals, whether done by local companies or by multinationals from outside the country, need not harm a country. The ethical issue is not extraction per se but whether the extraction by the MNC yields more good than harm to the country. Of concern is also the third ethical norm (G3), which requires that the MNC contribute by its activity to the host country's development.

A government can help protect its nation's future interests by imposing a special tax on mineral and oil depletion. To some extent—depending on how the government handles the proceeds from it—this tax compensates for the country's loss of natural resources. Using the money wisely can help the country and its people develop in such a way that they cease to depend on the dwindling supply of minerals or oil. The norm of paying one's fair share of taxes extends to paying depletion taxes, if these are imposed. Observing this norm involves factoring the depletion tax into one's calculation of whether an MNC is producing more good than harm to the host country.

The OPEC countries claimed that they were being exploited when oil companies paid them only $2 a barrel for crude oil. By this they meant that the crude oil was worth considerably more than the artificially low price of $2 a barrel. The oil companies subsequently refined the oil and then sold various refined products for handsome products. The OPEC countries claimed that they were being exploited in two ways: they were subsidizing low gasoline prices for the industrially developed countries; and the foreign interests who were drilling the oil were making great profits while the producing countries were getting very little. The large oil companies in the industrially developed countries collectively determined and imposed on the producers the prices and the conditions of sale for crude oil, instead of negotiating the prices or letting free competition in an open market set the prices. The OPEC countries countered this situation by uniting; after trying to impose too high a price themselves, all parties eventually were forced to let the price of crude settle at a competitive world price that was considerably higher than it had been before the formation of OPEC but less than OPEC desired.[25]

The rise in the world price of oil adversely affected non-oil-producing LDCs even more seriously than it did the developed nations—and at a time when many LDCs were attempting to expand development rapidly. The abundance of petrodollars deposited in Western banks encouraged banks to make large loans to less developed countries, which eventually translated into mountains of debt. No matter how one assesses ethical responsibility and blame in this complicated scenario, some American multinationals must bear a substantial share. No company can foresee all the consequences of its actions; but a company with integrity does its best to foresee as many consequences as possible as far into the future as possible, and then takes steps to ensure that its actions benefit the host country more than they harm.

Although the seven norms offer no guidance on how MNCs should set prices, they do require that MNCs do the host country more good than harm and that their activity promote the country's development. The norms require that MNCs pay their fair share of taxes, which in this case includes their legitimate oil or mineral depletion taxes. But clearly no company voluntarily assesses taxes against itself and pays them to the local government. The taxes must be levied by the government. If the profits from extracting oil or minerals are great, some of these profits should go back into the local economy. One appropriate use of such profits would be to help develop the country's infrastructure, in the form of roads or schools.

Norm seven (G7) requires that multinationals cooperate with LDCs in establishing just background institutions locally and internationally. In the area of oil and mineral extraction some countries have acted to protect their interests faster than others, thanks to their relatively stronger bargaining positions. Justice requires MNCs that wish to act with integrity to consider this seventh ethical requirement seriously. They should welcome equitable international norms or rules and should willingly agree to prices that are fair to all.

The most difficult case arises when an autocratic government leader or a coterie of high officials sells a country's mineral rights to a multinational, sometimes at less than its real value, and sequesters all or a major share of the money in secret private accounts abroad. The government officials in effect divert the wealth of the country into their own long-distance pockets and use little or none of it for the benefit or development of the country. Typically such a government aggressively seeks buyers for its country's mineral rights or land from among foreign interests; if these are not purchased by one company, they will surely be purchased by another. Should a multinational refuse to buy mineral rights in such a situation?

If the land or rights are being offered for sale at less than their real value because the difference is to be paid in a bribe directly to the government officials, then the multinational is ethically obligated not to make the purchase. If this is not the case, the multinational may be unsure where the money it pays will go. If it is reasonably certain that that the money will in effect be stolen by government officials, it should not abet such activity. Most likely it will not know one way or the other, in which case the general norm applies that the multinational must do more good than harm to the country if its activity there is to be justified. It cannot change the government, and it has no right to try to do so. But it can avoid engaging in the gross exploitation that the situation appears to invite. Especially if it buys land or mineral rights for less than their fair market worth, it must return some of that windfall to the country—be it in the form of helping build roads, of supporting local schools, of transferring appropriate technology, or of engaging in other actions that might require imaginative and innovative approaches. It is also obligated to promote just background institutions in the country to the extent that it can do so, and this includes supporting governmental reform. The guidelines do not automatically preclude operating in countries where unjust or corrupt governments hold power. But they do require that in such countries the multinational take the extra steps necessary to ensure that it does not exploit the country or its people and that overall it benefits them.

Manufacturing

Manufacturing industries as a group have sustained charges of worker exploitation and of undermining the host country's culture.[26] The seven norms for MNCs operating in less developed countries provide guidelines for sifting the valid from the invalid charges.

The charge of exploitation of the workforce deserves special discussion. Norm four (G4) requires that the MNC respect the human rights of its workers: it must pay at least subsistence wages and as much above that as workers and their dependents need to live with reasonable dignity, given the general state of development of the society.

A company in the United States has no obligation to give all its workers who do the same kind of work the same pay, regardless of where they are located. The rule of equal pay for equal work means instead that no one should be paid less than someone else for the same work because of non-job-related criteria such as sex, race, or religion. But in the United States the cost of living varies considerably from one part of the country to another, from one city to another, and from the city to the country. Hence the going wage varies, even if the minimum wage is set nationally. For this reason firms frequently move from one part of the country to another where average wages are lower. The firm does not exploit the people in the new location simply because it pays them less than it paid its workers in the old location.

What is true on the national level is also true on the international level. The cost of labor has risen so high in the United States that many firms have moved their manufacturing plants to countries where the cost of labor is considerably lower. In some countries where high unemployment rates and subsistence wages prevail, an MNC can set up crowded and unhealthful sweatshops, demand long hours of work for little pay, and offer no fringe benefits. The MNC can then either sell its products in the United States for the same price as similar goods produced with higher-cost American labor or sell its goods for slightly less in order to gain a greater market share; either way, it still makes a large profit. Thus, the incentive for doing this is great. If the price of consumer goods manufactured under such conditions drops in developed countries, less developed countries are in fact subsidizing consumers in the developed countries; consequently, these consumers share ethical responsibility with the manufacturers for the exploitation of the workers in the LDCs.[27]

U.S. wages are, on average, the highest in the world. But they do not necessarily establish an ethical norm for the whole world or even for U.S. firms abroad. Internationally applicable, ethically mandatory standards that no corporation—U.S. or other—should violate and moral minima below which no firm can ethically go should not be confused either with standards specifically appropriate to the United States or with standards set by the U.S. government. Some of the putative ethical dilemmas faced by U.S. multinationals are actually false dilemmas created by critics on the basis of such false equations.

Exploitation of workers by local employers does not justify similar exploitation by MNCs. The seven ethical norms attempt to limit gross exploitation by establishing minimal conditions that MNCs must meet to justify operating in LDCs. But the norms do not claim, as do some critics, that American MNCs that wish to be ethical must pay the same wages abroad as they do at home. If there were such a rule, MNCs would have little incentive to move their manufacturing abroad; and if they did move abroad, they would disrupt the local labor market with artificially high wages that bore no relation to the local standard or cost of living.

Even if American companies operating in less developed countries produce their goods exclusively for export, they can help the host country. They do so by providing employment, transferring skills and knowledge, training managers, paying taxes, and helping develop the country's infrastructure.

Multinationals necessarily transfer some values, as well. The work may require punctuality, care, and cleanliness—characteristics that may or may not be valued locally. Thus, to some extent, MNCs affect the local customs and way of life. The norm of respecting local customs helps mitigate the harm that MNCs may do in this regard; and whatever harm they inflict on the host country must be offset by good of some kind, such as help in raising its standard of living. In the final analysis, however, the local country's determination of whether the effect is good or bad—not the MNCs—carries more weight. This means that the MNC must take into account the local country's evaluation of its activities; it cannot simply act on its own calculation without regard to the evaluation made by the host country.

Implementation of the seven norms varies somewhat from industry to industry and from country to country. The norms can help both critics and companies discriminate between justifiable and unjustifiable practices of multinationals in LDCs. But as norms they require objective and conscientious application, often on a case-by-case basis. Assessing whether a company does more good than harm to a host country requires detailed investigation, not an easy or intuitive assertion one way or the other. A company that wishes to act with integrity will apply the norms to its particular situation before it begins operating in a less developed country, and it will continue to monitor how well it is living up to them after it is established here. MNCs need not act unethically to prosper abroad, even though many have operated and do operate unethically. But operating with integrity in less developed countries is neither easy nor automatic. A company must rethink and (often) modify its home practices, and it must constantly monitor the results of its actions in the host country for compliance with the seven norms. Abiding by such a policy constitutes much of what it means to be a company of integrity.

5

Extending the Guidelines: Bhopal

On December 3, 1984, one of the worst industrial disasters in history occurred in Bhopal, India.[1] During the early hours of the morning a poisonous gas—methyl isocyanate (MIC)—used in producing the pesticide Sevin leaked from a Union Carbide pesticide plant. The gas hovered for a while over the desperately poor, very overcrowded shantytown that had grown up around the plant. By the time the gas dissipated it had killed at least 2,000 people (the final death toll was about 3,500) and injured over 200,000 others.[2] The incident shocked the world.

Under Indian law both a corporation and its officers can be held criminally liable for misconduct. The Indian government arrested the plant manager on charges of "culpable homicide through negligence." When Warren Anderson, then–Chairman of the Board of Union Carbide, Inc., who had flown to Bhopal immediately to survey the damage, arrived in India from the United States, he was charged with "negligence and criminal corporate liability" and "criminal conspiracy."[3] As late as May 1992, India tried to extradite Anderson to face homicide charges.[4]

The pesticide, Sevin, which Union Carbide made at Bhopal, was distributed in India. It is used on corn, soybeans, cotton, and alfalfa, and is especially effective on soybeans. The use of the pesticide in India increased crop yields by about 10 percent, providing food for about 70 million Indians who would otherwise have faced starvation or severe malnutrition.[5] Union Carbide could have supplied India with Sevin made in the United States more cheaply than it was able to produce it in India. Indeed, it would have preferred to do so, but it expanded its small existing Bhopal facility into a Sevin-producing plant at the request of the Indian government, which wanted to enlarge the plant to provide more jobs for Indians.[6]

In 1984 the Bhopal plant operated at a loss. It was underutilized, producing at only one-third of its capacity. Management was reducing costs through manpower reductions, and the parent Union Carbide Corporation was considering putting the facility up for sale.[7] At the insistence of the Indian government the plant was entirely run by Indian managers, who made all operating decisions and who ran the company as a separate entity—Union Carbide, India.[8]

The methyl isocyanate (MIC) from which Sevin was produced at Bhopal was kept in liquid form in large steel tanks. In May 1982, an inspection of the Bhopal plant by safety officers from the parent Union Carbide revealed ten major deficiencies in the MIC tanks.[9] By July 25, 1984, backup instrumentation to prevent the tanks from overflowing had been ordered, but it was not clear whether it had been installed before December 3, 1984. Local management determined the frequency of local safety audits. Although the parent Union Carbide had not inspected the plant during the two and one-half years since May 1982, Union Carbide, India, had sent it reports indicating that the safety defects either had been repaired or were being repaired.[10]

Five safety devices were in place to prevent what happened on December 3, 1984: a vent gas scrubber, a flare tower, a water curtain, a refrigeration system, and a spare tank. At the time of the accident all of these devices were under repair or failed to operate. The scrubber, filled with a caustic soda solution used to detoxify leaks, was under repair. The 30-ton refrigeration unit had been shut off for six months. The metal barrier (slip bind) that was normally situated in a pipe to keep water from leaking into the MIC liquid had been removed and had not been replaced the day before the disaster. Chloroform in a concentration thirty-two times higher than that needed was present in the solution; the concentration, which should have been monitored daily, had not been monitored for six weeks.[11]

At 11:00 P.M. on December 2, the MIC operator noticed that the pressure in the tank had risen to 55 pounds. The temperature of the liquid MIC rose to between 59 and 68 degrees Fahrenheit instead of remaining within its proper range of 32 to 41 degrees Fahrenheit. At 2:30 A.M. on December 3, the liquid MIC turned into gas. Two low-level employees failed to take countermeasures and fled.[12] A supervisor finally hosed the tank with cold water 45 minutes after the leak started, and thereby stopped it. According to one report, the supervisor finished his tea before taking action.[13]

Responsibility and Liability

Many people and nations lost no time in criticizing at the parent Union Carbide, a capitalist multinational, for exporting hazardous industries to underdeveloped countries, for using less safe equipment in India than was used in the United States, and for taking too few precautions with the lives of people in a less developed country.[14]

Clearly the Union Carbide plant caused the harm and therefore was causally responsible for the harm done. Did it bear other kinds of responsibility, too? If so, what did its responsibilities entail? To answer these questions, we have to look at all the information available, and at the four kinds of responsibility every company has—corporate, ethical, legal, and social.[15]

Consider first the purely corporate responsibility of the Bhopal plant. This responsibility stems from the ends for which the corporation is formed and from the interests of those who own or work for it. Making a profit is a corporate demand of shareholders and of the board of directors of any corporation. Management thus has the *corporate responsibility* to them to make a profit. Unless it does so, the board may replace the present managers with others who (it hopes) will do better. Yet the responsibility to make a profit is not a moral, social, or legal responsibility. If in a bad year Union Carbide fails to make a profit, its shareholders may be unhappy. But failure to make a profit is neither unethical nor illegal in itself. Since Union Carbide, India, was operating at a loss, those running the company understandably felt an obligation to cut their costs to the extent possible. Lower management decided to shut down the expensive refrigeration equipment cooling the MIC storage tanks so that the Freon could be used elsewhere in the plant. These managers laid off some workers, and they postponed maintenance and repairs. The fact that these actions were taken to reduce costs and operating losses does not justify them, but it does help explain them. In hindsight, the actions reflect poor judgment and lack of management skill, but they were taken in reaction to the corporate demand on any company to make as much money as it can or to lose as little money as it can.

The Indian managers running the company made these decisions, presumably in response to some implicit or explicit understanding of their responsibility to the corporation to do as well financially as possible. The available evidence indicates that the parent company in Danbury, Connecticut, did not know the actual condition of the plant, and there is no evidence that the parent company ordered these particular cost-saving measures. Whether it applied any pressure on Union Carbide, India, to cut costs has not been revealed.

In discussing the responsibility of Union Carbide, we can distinguish between the responsibility of Union Carbide, India, and that of Union Carbide, Inc., the American parent firm. In general corporate responsibility—especially the responsibility of managers to run a firm efficiently and as profitably as possible for the shareholders—never excuses a company for acting unethically. Any right that shareholders have to profits cannot be a right to profits made unethically. Although in this case the pressures to cut costs are understandable, the actions of the managers of Union Carbide, India, are nevertheless open to an ethical evaluation. Managers may act to fulfill their corporate responsibilities, but that does not automatically make such actions ethically justifiable.

Ethical responsibilities stem from moral imperatives and carry with them correlative ethical obligations. The seven norms we discussed in Chapters 3 and 4 are examples of ethical responsibilities. The ethical obligations they imply remain in force, whether or not they are enacted into law and whether or not they are socially mandated. Ethical obligations and the corresponding ethical responsibilities to fulfill them take precedence over corporate and other responsibilities. Shareholders have no right to demand that managers act unethically, and they have every right to expect that managers will act ethically. If acting ethically leads to a loss instead of a profit, shareholders have no right to claim that management should have acted unethically so as to satisfy their desire for a profit. The obligation to protect workers' safety and the safety of the public stems from the ethical rules to do no direct harm and to respect the human rights of employees. These norms take precedence over any obligation to make profits or to cut losses.

In the Union Carbide case, if safety measures were not taken that should ethically have been taken, then the desire to cut costs at the expense of safety cannot be justified. As a result of the incident many people in the United States pressed for legislation to control hazardous industries more tightly.[16] If such laws demand more than does ethics, they represent legal and social responsibilities—not ethical ones. Consequently, they need not be adopted as a matter of ethical duty by foreign companies operating in countries other than the United States. *Ethically mandatory* demands, on the other hand, apply across national borders.

We have seen that a multinational corporation is obliged to do no intentional direct harm (G1) and to produce more good than harm for the host country (G2). The intent of Union Carbide, Inc., was to do this, since it was willing to operate at a loss, and since Sevin was widely and beneficially used in India. There is no evidence that either Union Carbide, Inc., or Union Carbide, India, failed to respect the human rights of its employees prior to the disaster. The company attempted to respect those aspects of local culture that did not violate ethical norms, since they allowed local customs to prevail among their workers. Whether this tolerance of local customs was compatible with safeguarding the employees and the local population from potential harm is a disputed issue. The disaster suggests that Union Carbide, India, did not adequately safeguard either its employees or the local population, and that Union Carbide, Inc., did not adequately supervise its Indian plant.

If a legislature passes laws requiring companies to maintain certain standards of safety, those standards are spelled out as legal demands, and the corporation is *legally responsible* for meeting them. Through its police power the state forces corporations to comply with legislation. States also have the ethical and legal responsibility to pass and enforce regulations that protect the people they govern from danger, including danger posed by hazardous industries. A government that fails to pass such legislation bears some responsibility for harm caused in an avoidable disaster that breaks no laws. But the absence of adequate governmental regulations does not excuse a company from failing on its own to ensure that it causes no harm. Thus the general obligation not to harm people through pollution is ethical, whereas the specific obligation to avoid polluting by conducting one's business in the manner prescribed by law is legal.

Finally, *social responsibilities* are responsibilities imposed by a society or by a people through customs or demands that express social expectations. They often go beyond ethical demands. A society has the right to impose on corporations, as a condition for their doing business, particular requirements that promote the common good—whether or not they are ethically or legally demanded. These are sometimes expressed as the obligations of good citizenship. Such social requirements may appropriately vary from society to society. In some societies, for instance, corporations are expected to contribute to local charities or to provide company stores for their employees, although they are not required to do so by law. Each society may seek to achieve something different by permitting or encouraging the presence of corporations, and each operates under different specific conditions.

The existence of different conditions means that one need not expect the same safety practices, procedures, or laws to be implemented or followed in India as in the United States. But ethics demands an irreducible minimum level of safety in both countries, since no company may deliberately cause direct intentional harm. This means that a dangerous industry must take adequate precautions to prevent possible harm. Failure to do so violates the rule. But the United States may require safety mechanisms to be automatic and electronically controlled, while India may require safety measures to be more labor-intensive. The measures need not be the same in both places, even though the expected results of the safety practices should be comparable. Whether the differences between the plant in Bhopal and the similar Union Carbide plant in Institute, West Virginia, were justifiable on this point is still disputed. After the Bhopal tragedy a nonlethal leak occurred in the Institute plant, indicating that it too was not fail-safe.[17] There is reason to believe that, if the five safety devices had not all been in disrepair or disconnected, the controls at the Bhopal plant would have been adequate. Had the controls been automatic—rather than manual—and had they been similarly disconnected or allowed to deteriorate, the same catastrophe may well have occurred.

Society may impose on businesses certain legal demands that exceed what is ethically required. Ethics, for instance, requires that corporations be run honestly. But it does not require that the state or a local population of the state own a particular percentage of every firm that operates there. A corporation is not unethical if it completely owns its subsidiaries. India's 1973 Foreign Exchange Regulation Act specified that at least 60 percent of every "foreign" company must be owned by India or by Indian interests, and that at most 40 percent of such a company could be owned by foreign interests.[18] It also required that all plants operating in India be run by Indian personnel. Since Union Carbide's Bhopal plant was expanded by Union Carbide at India's request, India allowed Union Carbide, Inc., to mantain a 50.9 percent interest in the Indian company.[19] Nonetheless India enforced the legal requirement that the plant be manned entirely by Indians, including all levels of management.

Since India wanted Union Carbide to expand its plant in order to create more jobs for Indians, the government requested that the plant be more labor-intensive than the comparable United States plant in order to maximize the number of new jobs available. The plant did in fact provide work for a large number of Indians. As a result it drew a population of potential workers to it. Many of the people attracted to the area did not find work there, but they settled around the plant anyway, in what became the shantytown and slum over which the cloud of MIC drifted. Critics who condemned Union

Carbide for building its plant in the middle of a slum failed to recognize that the slum developed after the plant was built, and that the plant was built as it was in response to an Indian social demand. Nonetheless, neither Union Carbide, India, nor Union Carbide, Inc., prepared adequate emergency and evacuation plans for the slum dwellers once the shantytown did coalesce.

Up until December 3, 1984, did Union Carbide do more good than harm to India? The answer is arguably yes. Its product increased crop yields and helped feed additional millions of people. Its plant provided work for Indian citizens and was a source of income for the nation. It directly exploited neither its workers nor the country. It promoted the country's development. It paid its fair share of taxes, and it satisfied the other ethical norms we have discussed. Yet clearly, once the disaster took place, it was causally responsible for an enormous amount of harm. Is it ethically blameworthy for those deaths and injuries, as many nations and individuals claim? Whether it is or not, does the case suggest any additional ethical norms that might govern the transfer of dangerous industries to less developed countries?

Ethical Responsibility and Corporations

Warren Anderson, as Chairman of the Board of Directors of Union Carbide, Inc., stated that Union Carbide would not duck its "moral responsibility"[20] for the tragedy. What did he mean by this?

The moral status of the corporation is a disputed question. Milton Friedman, among others, sees the corporation as a legal entity only and denies that it has a moral dimension.[21] According to this view, the corporation can be held legally responsible for its actions, and perhaps its officers or workers can be held ethically responsible for their conduct, but the corporation itself can have no ethical responsibilities.

A second view holds that corporations are moral persons, comparable to human moral persons. Human beings are ethically responsible for actions they perform knowingly and willingly.[22] Insofar as corporations have an internal decision-making procedure, they act knowingly and willingly. Hence they are moral beings. This view would find Union Carbide ethically responsible for its actions, provided that they were done knowingly and willingly. The extent of a corporation's ethical responsibility is thus a function of its intent and freedom. Of course, it could also be legally liable.

A third view denies that corporations are moral persons but claims that they are moral actors.[23] They are not fully moral persons, since they have no moral worth in themselves. Because they are artificial entities established for limited purposes, they are not bound by the full range of moral norms that apply to moral persons. But since they act, they can be held ethically responsible for the harm they do. To the entent that they act, they are ethically obliged not to harm people. They can also be held legally liable for their actions.

In claiming that Union Carbide was "morally responsible" for the tragedy, Anderson clearly did not share Friedman's view of corporations and responsibility. Anderson's statement lends indirect support to the third view of a corporation's moral status and of its ethical responsibility. If Union Carbide, Inc., has ethical responsibilities—as Anderson and most others agree is the case—then those who say that corporations are not ethically responsible have to explain away the overwhelming sentiment against that view. The fact that people do not expect Union Carbide to act from ethical motives, even while expecting it to fulfill its ethical obligation to compensate those whom it has harmed, indicates that general opinion views corporations as having ethical responsibilities despite not being moral persons. Such sentiment does not solve the debate over the moral status of corporations, but it does lend the support of public opinion to the third view.

But exactly what Warren Anderson was claiming when he accepted moral responsibility on behalf of Union Carbide, Inc., and how much responsibility he was accepting were far from clear.

Union Carbide, Inc., initially referred to the disaster as an accident, as have a great many other commentators.[24] Ordinarily, one is not considered morally responsible for accidents. One is morally responsible for what one does knowingly and willingly—that is, intentionally. No one intends accidents, and an accident is by definition something unintended that happens. One can be ethically responsible for untoward or harmful results of an accident, however, if one was culpably negligent. The ethical culpability comes from failing to take the degree of care that an ordinary person in such a position knows should be taken. Although we can ask whether Union Carbide, Inc., or individuals within the corporation were ethically culpable in this sense, Anderson made no such statement. He did not say that Union Carbide, Inc., was ethically culpable through negligence; and he did not say that Union Carbide, Inc., was ethically obliged to offer compensation because it was the majority owner of Union Carbide, India, which was ethically culpable through negligence. But either Union Carbide, Inc., is ethically blameworthy because it was directly negligent with respect to the safety of people in the plant's environment—such as by not exercising oversight over safety controls at the Indian plant that it should have exercised—or it is blameworthy in a sense analogous on the corporate level to parents accepting responsibility for the damage done by their children.

In saying that Union Carbide, Inc., would accept moral responsibility for the damages caused by the disaster, Anderson meant at least that the American corporation would accept liability and pay compensation to those damaged. He did not attempt to restrict the prospective payment of damages to whatever amount the Indian company could afford; rather, he pledged to apply the resources of the American parent company. Nor did he indicate that he would refuse payment unless forced to pay as a result of a law suit. But he did not specify the amount that he felt the company had a moral responsibility to pay.

Anderson offered $1 million dollars immediately to relieve the greatest harm.[25] The Indian government refused the offer, although later it did accept $5 million in disaster aid from Union Carbide, without publicly acknowledging its source.[26] In addition, Union Carbide workers throughout the world established their own relief fund for the victims.[27] The government did not identify the source of this aid either. The Indian government's failure to acknowledge the source of such aid seems to have been politically motivated and can be seen as a form of misrepresentation by omission.

Union Carbide, Inc., is reported to have initially suggested a settlement of $50 million. The Indian government rejected the offer as ridiculously low, especially since Union Carbide was insured for damages of up to $200 million,[28] so that at least that amount could easily be paid. Paying some agreed-upon amount would have fulfilled the ethical responsibility of Union Carbide, Inc., to make good the harm done by its subsidiary, but this ethical responsibility is different from the corporation's legal responsibility.

The Indian plant caused the damage in Bhopal. The causal responsibility, therefore, lay with the Indian plant and its owners and staff. Since the plant and the damage were both located in India, any legal suit filed against the plant should logically and legally have been filed in India. After the disater, the plant was closed; and it has since been permanently closed at the insistence of the Indian government. That decision confirmed the decease of Union Carbide, India. Any civil suit directed exclusively against Union Carbide, India, if successful, would have enabled the plaintiffs to recover damages only to the extent that the company still had assets. Assuming that it could sell off any of its assets, the victims could expect to get only a small amount from Union Carbide, India.

To make matters worse for prospective plaintiffs, the lower Indian courts are severely overloaded with cases, and even relatively simple cases take years to adjudicate. These courts could not possibly handle individual suits from more than 200,000 plaintiffs. As a further complication, suits for damages are frequently not filed in Indian courts. For instance, no suits were filed after the crash of an Air India Boeing 747 in 1978 in which several hundred persons died or after 365 people died from drinking contaminated liquor in 1982.[29]

Because the majority (50.9 percent) owner of Union Carbide, India, was Union Carbide, Inc., the Indian government decided to sue Union Carbide, Inc., in U.S. courts on behalf of those injured. The U.S. courts did not have to accept jurisdiction for such suits, since the plant was located in India and since those injured were Indian; and ultimately they did refuse.[30] They also recommended negotiations to achieve an out-of-court settlement. The Indian government consolidated all the civil damage cases into one case, which was then presented to an Indian court.

A number of smaller industrial disasters have occurred in India, involving the deaths of up to several hundred people. In each case no damages were awarded to the relatives of those killed. Based on damages awarded in previous cases in the United States, the award to the relatives of those killed in Bhopal would have been about $500,000 per victim. The Indian government typically pays the equivalent of $794 to relatives of each person killed in disasters for which it is responsible, and it started making that very payment to survivors who applied for them in the Bhopal case.[31] Yet then–Prime Minister

Rajiv Gandhi asserted that India would demand the same compensation for Indians killed in Bhopal that would have been awarded if the victims had been Americans killed in the United States, on the principle that an Indian life is worth as much as an American one. He also pressed for punitive damages—which often exceed compensatory damages—even though Indian courts do not award punitive damages.

The statement by Gandhi that an Indian life is worth as much as an American life lacks substantive point. No price can be attached to any human life. To claim otherwise is to condone slavery and to treat human beings as objects only. Ordering payment of compensation for wrongful death should not be interpreted as putting a price on human life. The compensation is token and is intended primarily to ease the effects of the death on the remaining relatives, especially those dependent on the deceased. Any figure is arbitrary. One way to determine such compensation is to calculate the average earnings of an average person over his or her working life and then to take half or some other portion of that as the appropriate amount to award. The assumption here is that this amount will at least enable the recipient to make a transition from dependence on the former wage earner to relative independence some years after his or her death. Clearly the appropriate amount according to this scheme varies according to the cost of living, the standard of living, and the average wage of workers in a particular country. That far less compensation is paid to Indians in India than to Americans in America in no way implies that American lives are worth more than Indian lives. Since the Indian government typically pays only $794 for wrongful death, the logical inference to draw from Gandhi's reasoning would be that the Indian government values Indian life less than the American courts value American life—an absurd conclusion, given the relative wealth of the two countries.

Two commentators argued that, since the per capita gross national product of India is 1.7 percent of that of the United States, it would be appropriate to reduce the damages awarded by the court (if any) in a similar proportion.[32] The Indian relatives of those killed would then have received about $8,500; and injured Indians, an average of $1,100. Both figures would still have been much higher than is customary in India. If punitive damages had been awarded and similarly reduced, the total would have amounted to a judgment of $2 or $3 billion dollars, as opposed to $250 or $300 million if punitive damages were not awarded. Indian claims filed in court totaled over $15 billion;[33] the total assets of Union Carbide, Inc., were only $10 billion.[34]

Since punitive damages were not established in the United States to cover instances of damage done by a U.S. company operating abroad, imposing punitive damages on U.S. companies abroad would clearly put them at a competitive disadvantage with non-American firms that are not subject to such judgments.

Union Carbide and the Indian government for a long while could not agree on a settlement. The case went to an Indian court, and Union Carbide stated that it would fight any attempt by the Indian government to find it legally culpable. It claimed in its defense that the accident was the result of sabotage by a disgruntled worker and, therefore, not the result of any corporate action or negligence. The case was never argued in court.

On February 14, 1989, Union Carbide and the Indian government reached a civil settlement: Union Carbide agreed to pay $470 million in compensation to the victims. The court agreed to drop all pending civil charges and to absolve Union Carbide from any further claims.[35] The figure of $470 million was less than Gandhi had originally wished to receive and more than Anderson had initially been willing for the company to pay.

Gandhi's successor V. P. Singh, repudiated the court decision, saying that it was unacceptable. He declared that he would hold out for something closer to $3 billion, and he reinstated the criminal charges against Union Carbide officials. Many people seemed to agree with him that the settlement was too low. Yet it was not clear how they expected to reopen the possibility of extracting $3 billion, since the court had already settled the issue of damages.[36] To some extent his stand was purely political and gave him a platform from which to attack his predecessor. On October 4, 1991, India's Supreme Court upheld the amount of the original civil settlement, but allowed the government to pursue prosecution of criminal charges against company officials.[37] On May 1, as part of the continuing criminal proceedings, a magistrate in Bhopal ordered the seizure of the Indian assets of Union Carbide, Inc., even though the company had announced its plans to sell all its holdings in Union Carbide, India, and to build a hospital in Bhopal with the expected $17 million in proceeds.[38]

More than five years after the accident, relatives of 3,323 people who died had received only 10,000 rupees ($550), and some of those injured had received only 1,500 rupees ($83) from the Indian government, which does not consider these payments to be part of the settlement with Union Carbide, Inc. Starting in April 1990, the government announced that it would pay 200 rupees ($11) per month in relief payments for three years to each of 500,000 people who claim to have been in the vicinity of the disaster.[39] Finally, on June 21, 1992, India announced that it would pay from $3,840 to $11,530 to the next of kin of those killed, and from $1,920 to $3,840 to those injured.[40]

The blame for taking so long to reach a settlement must be shared by Union Carbide and the Indian government. But having received payment from Union Carbide, the Indian government now bears full responsibility for transmitting payments to those who suffered from the disaster. The longer it takes to make such payments, the more it is open to moral censure.

In this case moral pressure was a better route to follow than a legal suit. Moral pressure on both Union Carbide and the Indian government to reach a quick, equitable settlement could have produced the greatest amount of good for all concerned and could have achieved the best approximation of justice. Such pressure was applied both by the courts and by the general public. Warren Anderson had indicated that, if the suit went to trial, Union Carbide, Inc., would fight it. Even if it could not have proved sabotage, the corporation would have sought to place the legal blame on Union Carbide, India. It would have claimed that implementing safety procedures is a local responsibility, and that, if there was negligence, it was negligence on the part of the Indian managers and workers of the Bhopal plant. There was much evidence that safety measures were not enforced. Had Union Carbide won the case, the victims and their relatives would have received nothing. The pressure exerted by the threat of legal proceedings gave Union Carbide and India additional reasons to agree to a settlement. The length of time it took both sides to agree was unconscionable; yet it was significantly less than a final legal adjudication would have taken.

The Union Carbide Bhopal case shows the importance and effectiveness of ethical norms and pressures on multinational corporations. It also suggests the need for an ethical principle mandating that, when a multinational corporation does harm, it is ethically responsible for providing adequate compensation to the victims, even if the harm is not intentional. We can express this as a corollary to our first norm:

> G1a.   *Multinationals are responsible for making due compensation for any harm they do, directly or indirectly, intentionally or unintentionally.*

Parent and Subsidiary Companies

The Bhopal case raises the question of what the proper relation is between multinational parent organizations and their subsidiaries in less developed countries with respect to potentially dangerous industries. Is it ethically justifiable for developed countries to export hazardous industries to less developed countries? If so, under what conditions may they do so?

The guide to the first answer is the list of seven ethical norms. Multinationals may not transfer dangerous operations that are not allowed in the United States to less developed countries that lack regulations to prohibit such transfers. To do so would violate the first norm (G1), because of the harm the MNC would do or the threat of harm it would pose for the LDC. Even if an LDC permits dangerous plants to be built, the multinational must be able to show that such plants will produce no direct intentional harm, that they will help the host country and its development, and that they will be run in a way that respects the human rights of the workers and local population by adequately protecting them. For instance, some Americans were very concerned when asbestos factories moved from the United States to Mexico. They accused the asbestos companies not only of exporting their plants but also of transferring a high incidence of cancer from American to Mexican workers.

Application of the seven ethical rules shows that the transferring of plants is not in itself unethical. What is unethical is producing harm knowingly and directly, producing more harm than good for the host country, or endangering the lives of the workers. If the transfer of an industry does not violate the seven ethical norms, critics have the onus of showing that the transfer is unethical anyway.

The claim that any standards imposed by the United States should be met by American firms operating anywhere in the world is too strong and is a version of the "righteous American" position. Yet any multinational that follows lower standards abroad than at home should be prepared to show that those standards at least meet minimum ethical requirements.

Union Carbide initially satisfied all seven norms. It did not transfer dangerous technology that it did not use or was not allowed to use in the United States. It continued to run its Sevin-producing plants at home.

Yet the Union Carbide Bhopal case shows that, ethically, dangerous industries require special care and consideration. The case raises the issue of the relation between responsibility and control. If Union Carbide, Inc., had been only a 40 percent owner, rather than a majority owner, of Union Carbide, India, would it have had the same responsibility that it assumed and that was attributed to it? Is a multinational's best solution to the problem of potential liability to accept less than a majority holding? Would a company be acting ethically if it designed a plant, put in all the required safety features, turned the plant over to a local government or manager, and made no further attempt to ensure that the safety features continued to be implemented?

National pride sometimes motivates a country to demand control of dangerous operations, using a local population that has its own culture, different from that of the country that designed the plant's operation. Is it ethical of the host country to make such demands? Is it ethical of a multinational to accede to such demands? The Bhopal incident raises these issues in a dramatic way.

Ethics cannot determine the best business solution. It can, however, circumscribe the possibilities. Based on the Bhopal Union Carbide case, three additional ethical norms (G8 through G10) are justifiable.

> G8. *Majority control of a firm carries with it ethical responsibility for the actions and failures of the firm.*

This rule assigns responsibility for a company's behavior to those having financial control over it. There seems to be little rational reason for Union Carbide, Inc., to have insisted on a 50.9 percent share of Union Carbide, India, since it was unable to establish effective control over the Indian company. India's Foreign Exchange Regulation Act required all workers and managers to be Indian. Indians built the plant according to the parent company's design, which had been modified in accordance with Indian desires. Union Carbide, Inc., could and did inspect the facility periodically. Its inspections were less frequent than those of other major U.S. chemical companies operating subsidiaries abroad, but those other companies exercised a level of control that Union Carbide, Inc., may not have had. Evidently, reports from the Indian company to Union Carbide's Danbury headquarters were false, were exaggerated or were statements of intentions presented as fact. If Union

Carbide, Inc., had reinspected the Bhopal plant, it could not actually have performed the needed repairs or installed the needed equipment itself. This had to be done by Indians. It is not clear whether the parent company could have and should have inspected the plant and closed it until repairs were made. The plant's managers and workers and the Indian government might well have resisted such action.

Nonetheless, the rule that control implies responsibility remains valid. It applies in this case. Failure on the part of Union Carbide, Inc., to exercise effective control is no excuse. Hence, it was appropriate that Union Carbide, Inc., assume ultimate responsibility for the Bhopal disaster, even though the Indian managers and workers were immediately and primarily responsible. Union Carbide, Inc., as the majority shareholder, should have maintained greater control over safety than it did.

If majority control is indigenous, then primary responsibility is also indigenous. If a country insists on and obtains majority control, it becomes responsible for the actions of the firm. It cannot simultaneously have control and not have responsibility. If India had controlled 50.9 percent of Union Carbide, India, it would have had primary responsibility. If this had been the case, it is not clear that the plant would have been run differently or that the accident would not have happened. By norm eight, the primary obligation to provide compensation would have fallen to the Indian company and to the Indian government, rather than to Union Carbide, Inc.

Each country is responsible for the well-being of its citizens and for what foreign businesses it allows within its borders. If a country accepts dangerous industries, it cannot cede all responsibility for the safety of its citizens to the multinationals. The country must specify legal safety requirements. It should demand certain kinds of assurances, such as evacuation plans and emergency plans in case of malfunctions, and it should see that these requirements are enforced. Some LDCs that do not have the necessary technical expertise to draw up adequate requirements fall back on the expedient of using requirements drawn up in one or another of the industrially developed countries. Enforcement is difficult if the country has too few adequately trained inspectors to perform the inspections and to enforce the regulations it adopts. Enforcement is also difficult if firms bribe inspectors not to report violations—an unethical practice on both sides.

The continuing responsibility of MNCs in this area, even if they do not have majority control, suggests a second norm.

G9.   *If a multinational builds a hazardous plant, it has the obligation to make sure that it is safe and that it is run safely.*

This norm follows from the obligation to do no harm. It holds that one is morally precluded from providing a dangerous product (or plant) unless one can reasonably be sure that it will not cause harm—intentionally or unintentionally.

As Bhopal makes clear, a company cannot transfer production facilities without considering the people who will run them and the culture of the host country. Safety requirements must be negotiated with the host country, which will bear major responsibility if it is the majority shareholder or partial responsibility if it is not. The responsibility of the firm is to build a safe plant and to instruct workers in its proper use. Unless the parent firm can reasonably be sure that the plant will be safely operated, it has the ethical obligation to refuse to build it. Otherwise it knowingly and willingly acts in a way that brings direct harm to the country.

The implementation of this principle may in some instances be taken as an affront by the host country, since it may be interpreted by that country as insinuating that local technicians are less competent than their American counterparts. This consequence is unfortunate; but if the situation warrants it, the obligation not to build remains.

Nuclear power plants present a special case. The obligation to build a safe plant and to make sure that it will be run safely is especially important here. In the United States electrical power companies did not start building nuclear power plants until the U.S. government agreed to assume liability costs beyond a certain level in case of a nuclear disaster, such as the one at Chernobyl. It is unlikely that American MNCs will assume liability in other countries that they are unwilling to assume in the United States. Since primary liability will shift the host country, the builders of such facilities must obtain guarantees of the continued safety of the plant before building it, and they cannot ethically relinquish all responsibility for the plant once it is completed.

> G10. *In transferring hazardous technology to LDCs, multinationals are responsible for appropriately redesigning such technology so that it can be safely administered in the host country.*

This norm follows from the rule to do no harm and the rule to ensure safety.

Plants or processes may have to be completely redesigned in light of local customs, traditions, and capabilities. For example, it is now possible to produce Sevin by a process that stores very small amounts of MIC at any one time, precluding another Bhopal disaster. Transferring ownership of such a plant is different from transferring the plant that was established in Bhopal.

As this case shows, ethics for international business constitutes one more layer of analysis that multinational corporations must take into account in their business activities. The seven basic norms provide the initial ethical screen. Their implementation in particular circumstances and in particular industries may call for other norms or guidelines that can aid in ethically evaluating concrete cases.

By 1990 the chemical industry had sustained a good deal of criticism. In 1988 the Chemical Manufacturers Association of the United States adopted a "Responsible Care" program. On April 11, 1990, over 170 member companies of the Chemical Manufacturers Association (including Union Carbide, Inc.), in full-page announcements in the *New York Times* and the *Wall Street Journal,* announced their "Responsible Care" initiative, by which they committed themselves to the following set of Guiding Principles:

> To recognize and respond to community concerns about chemicals and our operations.
>
> To develop and produce chemicals that can be manufactured, transported, used and disposed of safely.
>
> To make health, safety and environmental considerations a priority in our planning for all existing and new products and processes.
>
> To report promptly to officials, employees, customers and the public, information on chemical-related health and environmental hazards and to recommend protective measures.
>
> To counsel customers on the safe use, transportation and disposal of chemical products.
>
> To operate our plants and facilities in a manner that protects the environment and the health and safety of our employees and the public.
>
> To extend knowledge by conducting or supporting research on health, safety and environmental effects of our products, processes and waste materials.
>
> To work with others to resolve problems created by past handling and disposal of hazardous substances.
>
> To participate with government and others in creating responsible laws, regulations and standards to safeguard the community, workplace and environment.
>
> To promote the principles and practices of Responsible Care by sharing experiences and offering assistance to others who produce, handle, use, transport or dispose of chemicals.

This initiative was an important step by the chemical manufacturers toward acknowledging their responsibilities. Whether following the initiative's principles would have precluded the disaster at Bhopal is a moot point. Since 1990 the chemical manufacturers of various countries have adopted codes of practice based on the Guiding Principles, have adopted specific targets to improve their safety preformance, and have set up norms against which they can be judged and can judge themselves. There are no official sanctions for failure to comply, but companies committed to the principles indicate that they will apply peer pressure to help ensure compliance. This instance worldwide of self-regulation by an industry serves as a model for other industries as well. This initiative followed the Bhopal disaster. Initiatives in other industries should not wait for comparable disasters before adopting similar self-regulatory measures. Companies of integrity in each industry can take the lead in articulating appropriate industry norms and in committing themselves to upholding them.

Case studies, such as the Union Carbide Bhopal case, are important not so much for the purpose of placing blame as for determining what practices, actions, policies, or norms might prevent similar disasters from taking place in the future. Bhopal and other smaller incidents have brought the issue of the ethical responsibilities of multinationals to the attention of both corporate leaders and the public. Corporations act with integrity when they accept and fulfill their ethical responsibilities. They thereby reaffirm the best of American values and of the American entrepreneurial heritage.

6

Ethical Dilemmas, Conflicting Norms, and Personal Integrity

Purchasing agents working for three different U.S. multinational clothing manufacturers in a Southeast Asian country all placed orders for 100,000 bolts of silk. Various factors led to a temporary shortage of silk, and all three orders were returned marked "Back ordered—estimate delivery 3–6 months." The day after receiving the returned order, Cathy Denton, the purchasing agent of one of the companies, received a call from someone who said that, for a separate cash payment to him of $1 per bolt, or $100,000, she could get her company's shipment within a week. She paid the money and received the shipment. Don Eden, the purchasing agent for one of the other two firms, called a local government official whom he knew and offered to pay him $100,000, no questions asked, if he could get his shipment within a week. The official agreed to do what he could, Don delivered the money, and the order arrived. Harry Goodman, the third company's purchasing agent considered it unethical either to offer or to pay bribes. He did neither and received his shipment in six months.

Ethical issues are always issues faced by an individual, either in his or her own right or as a representative of the corporation. Cathy, Don, and Harry confronted their situations on their own, and we don't know whether they acted in accord with company policy or in violation of it.

The ethical problems faced by people in corporations often arise from conflicts between personal and corporate values. Although some people consider any instance of an ethical conflict to be an ethical dilemma, a narrower definition of *ethical dilemmas* is situations in which neither of two available alternatives seems ethically acceptable.[1] People typically take such dilemmas at their face value and attempt to resolve them at the level at which they appear. However, some ethical dilemmas are in fact unresolvable when approached at face value. By staying at that level, a person may conclude that an ethical issue is unresolvable, except through some ethical sleight-of-hand reasoning. But our analysis of them should not end there.

Ethical Displacement

Ethical dilemmas can arise on any of the levels at which people and firms operate: the personal level, the level of the firm or corporation, the level of the industry or of other groups of firms, the national level, and the international level. Each level has its own problems. Yet ethical dilemmas at any level may yield to the technique of ethical displacement.

Ethical displacement consists of resolving a dilemma—or sometimes of solving an ethical problem—by seeking a solution on a level other than the one on which the dilemma or problem appears. Thus a dilemma encountered by an individual on a personal level may only find a solution on the corporate level; that is, the solution to a personal dilemma may require one or more changes in corporate structure. Corporate dilemmas, in turn, may require changes in industry structures to guarantee fair conditions of competition. Industry-wide dilemmas may require changes in national policies or legislation. National business dilemmas, such as pollution problems, may require changes in structures or agreements on an international level. And international dilemmas may sometimes only be resolved by moving simultaneously on that level and on the national level.

Many dilemmas faced by individuals in a firm cannot be resolved simply by the individual's acting ethically, and they are not amenable to intuitive solutions on the individual level. If the existing structures of a firm caused the dilemma, the only way to resolve it is to rise above the level of individual ethical analysis. Persons facing such dilemmas must still deal with the unresolved problem of how to act if they cannot effect change on the next level. But at least the person will have clarified the need for change at the next higher level if such dilemmas are to be resolved.

The technique of displacement analysis is initially a descriptive technique and then a diagnostic technique. Any solution that results from it will not be easy, since changing corporate structures and policies implies a host of considerations that must be worked through. The attitude that ethical issues are simple and are easy for ethical people to resolve intuitively must be overcome both at the personal level and at the corporate level. Acting with integrity does not mean acting only on the basis of one's moral intuitions. It also means being willing to make the effort and bear the cost of determining the right thing to do in a given situation. Clearly, conscientiously applying the seven ethical guidelines and considering which others might apply is not simply a matter of using one's ethical intuition.

Business executives would not consider approaching complex financial problems intuitively and without conducting an exhaustive study; neither can they hope to resolve complex ethical problems intuitively and without conducting an exhaustive study. Analyzing ethical issues in business within the framework of interactive levels is essential in approaching many problems, especially on the international level.

If a superior tells an employee to falsify a record, or if a worker knows that construction concrete is being diluted below specifications and may present dangers to the ultimate users, the employee or worker is placed in the position of either disobeying a superior and risking loss of job or acting in ways that are manifestly wrong. People in such situations need access to some other alternative, such as some means of making their situation known to top management (assuming that the improper orders do not come from there). This is important both for the individual and for the firm. Ethical hot lines and the position of ombudsman, instituted by a number of Fortune 500 companies, can help.[2] Employees can use ethical hot lines to report their ethical concerns or get their ethical questions resolved. Ombudsmen function as confidential intermediaries for workers; they try to resolve ethical conflicts while preserving the employee's anonymity.

Yet these approaches rarely lead to structural changes within a company or to genuine debates about the ethics of a company's practices. Such debates may take place in the board room or in the offices of the top management, but few companies consider it appropriate for lower-echelon employees to raise such issues. Ethical hot lines were not instituted to handle complaints that threaten the existing structure of the corporation but to answer or allay day-to-day concerns of employees, usually on fairly straightforward and obvious issues of right and wrong. A company that wishes to act with integrity should ask and answer such questions as these: Who attempts to resolve dilemmas involving ethical displacement? Where are the ethical gray areas in the company? Who internally challenges corporate procedures or structures from an ethical point of view? How might such questioning or attempts at resolution be institutionalized? Does the company need a devil's (or an angel's) advocate to do just that? Such questions are too seldom raised.

To be effective someone highly placed in a corporation (and who thus has other functions) should have the explicit task of anticipating complaints from workers, consumers, suppliers, and the general public, and of arguing from an ethical point of view for changes in corporate structures and policies. Only then will ethics be integrated into the company's operating procedures, as it must be in a company interested in acting with integrity. To be effective such a person should be rewarded for raising and pressing ethical concerns about corporate policies and structures and should be penalized for failing to do so (as evidenced by employee whistle-blowing or consumer suits). Multinationals have an even greater need than domestic firms for such positions, and the necessary structures become more complicated; yet the basic purpose is the same.

The widespread need for such persons emphasizes that many ethical problems faced by individuals in corporations are not simply a particular employee's problems. They cannot be resolved adequately by recommending that the individual act in accordance with his or her conscience or by seeking advice from someone in the company. The individual problem must be displaced to the institutional level, and a solution must be sought there—frequently through institutional change.

Individual dilemmas are replicated at the corporate level. Sometimes corporations in a given industry are driven to compete in ways set by the least ethical among them. In such cases the solution must be sought industry-wide. Ethical displacement thus operates at all levels and among all levels.

When dilemmas on a particular level can be resolved only by rising to a higher level, the solutions to them are seldom intuitive; and if properly approached, solutions that go beyond a corporation's immediate domain of action are often so costly, time-consuming, or unusual that people have an inherent reluctance to raise them. To the extent that they involve changes in existing structures or ways of doing business, they are seen as threatening and hostile; and so they may well be. If they were not, the moral dilemmas involving ethical displacement would not arise. Such moral dilemmas are symptomatic of the need for structural changes. Here ethical analysis yields both a threat and a possibility for creative corporate action.

Some ethical dilemmas at the industry or consortium level may only be resolvable by rising to the international level, as in the case of unfair international trade practices that no particular industry can change. Dilemmas at this level are even more difficult to resolve than are dilemmas at the industry level, but solutions are by no means impossible. They necessitate concerted international action, they may involve applying political pressure or negotiation, and they frequently require that someone or some nation be willing to take the lead. Other candidates for the technique of ethical displacement are global pollution issues, depletion of nonrenewable resources, and damage to the ozone layer of the atmosphere—problems to which a particular company may contribute, but that no individual company can solve.[3]

Bribery and the Foreign Corrupt Practices Act

Cathy paid a bribe in response to an offer. Don offered a bribe. Both got their orders filled quickly. Clearly there was some silk available. If we assume that there truly was a shortage overall, then they received their shipment while someone who would otherwise have received a shipment did not. Or perhaps the distributor sent all his customers the same notice, knowing that those who wanted earlier shipments would offer or pay a bribe to receive them. One might respond that such a system is the local custom: what is wrong with the custom, and what is wrong with paying or offering the bribe? Without the timely arrival of the silk, Cathy's and Don's plants might have been forced to close, putting their workers at least temporarily out of work and causing delays in filling orders for the completed garments, possibly until after the season for which they were intended.

Were the payments made by Don and Cathy actually bribes, or were they simply a way of doing business in a tight market?

To characterize the payments as bribes is to characterize them as unethical from the start, for bribery by definition involves unfairness. The case as described tends to justify that characterization.

Bribery is unethical for several reasons.[4] First, it undermines the fairness of the market, which presupposes a system of open competition. In a fair system, all compete on equal terms. In the given situation the fair thing for the supplier to do would have been either to deliver the silk that was available at its regular price on a first-come, first-served basis or to delay all orders, announce a $1.00 a bolt rise in price, and then sell at that rate on a first-come, first-served basis. Either method would have given all buyers an equal chance at getting their goods, since the increase in price reflects the shortage of supply as opposed to demand. The fact that some silk was deliverable to Don and Cathy raises the question of what the actual situation was and whether, if no special payments had been made, no one would have received silk shipments for six months.

In general, the presence of bribery on a large scale—especially if it involves highly placed government officials—is symptomatic of a contrived, manipulated, or otherwise inefficient market. If it possible for a firm to pay bribes over and above its normal costs for whatever it gets in return, the nominal price does not represent the actual market price. If the nominal price were the market price, no firm could afford to pay the bribe in addition to the standard price and still remain competitive. If a country sells its raw materials at below the world market price, its leaders or those who control the economy can ask for bribes and still hope to sell their resources. The reason is that the total price (fixed price + bribe) does not exceed the world market price. If it did exceed that price, companies would have no incentive to pay the bribe. Those in a position to set prices can set them so that they personally benefit from the difference between the real value of the goods sold or of the orders placed and the price asked. In countries where bribery is endemic, it is typically tolerated on the lower levels because those higher up also receive their cut or in other ways participate in the system of graft. Bribery thus not only undermines the fairness of the market but also indicates its inefficiency. The fact that Don worked through a government official is prima facie evidence of corruption within the system.

Second, the people who receive the bribes are not necessarily those who should have received any compensation at all in a fair market. As the situation is described, the money paid by Don went to a government official who was somehow able to influence the shipment of the goods—not to the manufacturer of the silk. The official in question was in a position to have the silk shipped, but the payment was neither the ordinary wage of that person nor the person's ordinary commission. The payment gained Don special treatment that he would not have received otherwise and to which he was not entitled in a fair allocation of goods. Cathy paid some unknown person— possibly a government official, possibly someone else. That person may have had legitimate access to the silk; but the request for $100,000 in cash makes that prospect seem unlikely.

Third, if there is a shortage, someone who would otherwise have received the goods under a fair allocation does not get them, and thus is unfairly injured through the payment of the bribe.

Fourth, since the payment is not stated as a legitimate increase in the cost of the goods received, it cannot be counted as such. If recorded, it must be recorded as a payment to an individual. If such payments are not allowed, they must either be covered up or be paid from unrecorded funds. Both approaches would violate U.S. and other tax laws and would not present an honest picture of costs and assets to the home office or to shareholders. Deception is involved in the payments; otherwise, they would not be bribes. Neither Cathy nor Don seem to be in a position to record their payments accurately and honestly.

If the $1 per bolt payment asked were truly and simply a temporary increase in the price, it would cause no problem. It could be paid, openly recorded, and managed as part of the normal way of doing business. But because it is not part of the normal way, because it is deceptive and unfair, it is unethical.

Cathy paid a bribe when it was requested. Don offered a bribe. Both paid the same amount of money and got the same delivery. Is there any difference in their actions? Cathy acceded to an unethical practice, initiated by an unknown individual. Don initiated an unethical action with a government official. In doing so, he not only acted unethically himself but also took the lead in possibly corrupting someone else. Perhaps that person was ready and anxious to be approached in this way by Don. Nevertheless, initiating a bribe is ethically worse than paying one, although both are unethical; and corrupting or abetting the corruption of government officials is worse than acceding to the blandishments of corrupt private individuals, since the former involves not only private but also public corruption.

Both Cathy and Don continued production, got their goods out on time, helped keep the workers in their firms employed, and fulfilled their customers' orders. Harry acted ethically, but his firm may have been forced to close down temporarily, leaving its workers without an income and its orders unfilled. The pressure on Don and Cathy to act as they did, rather than to suffer Harry's fate, is understandable. Arguably neither of them did what they did entirely for personal gain but did it to benefit the companies for which they work; and in the process they certainly helped their firm's workers and customers. Neither the actions of Cathy and Don nor the results for Harry, are completely satisfactory.

If we are to place blame, it should fall in large part on the system that allows the market to be skewed in this way through the payment of bribes. This analysis suggests a number of difficulties that require remedying on another level.

First, individual purchasing agents should not have to choose between obtaining material in a period of shortage through bribery or doing without. Even if it is widely practiced in a given society or country, bribery is unethical. The individual acting for a firm should decide, as Harry did, not to pay or to offer a bribe. But the result may damage his firm, and he may find his own job in jeopardy—especially if his competitors deliver the goods and he does not. It is unfair to place such a burden on the individual. The decision properly belongs at the level of the firm rather than at the level of the individual.

Making the choice at the level of the firm enables the firm and its employees thenceforth to follow an established policy. If the policy is to pay bribes or to offer bribes when necessary to get goods that are in short supply, the individuals who execute the policy may rightly feel uncomfortable (and they would be ethically justified in refusing to follow the policy), but at least the firm's expectations are clear and its decision has been made at the proper level. A firm that wishes to act with integrity will not adopt a policy of paying bribes, nor will it place its employees in the position of having to decide whether or not to pay bribes. The embarrassment most companies would feel at publishing a policy of paying bribes "as necessary" to accomplish economic objectives is an excellent indication that the policy is unethical. Moreover, such a policy, if explicitly acknowledged, would open a firm to suits and legal prosecution.

Having placed the decision at the level where it belongs, we must ask how a firm of integrity can compete ethically in this situation. The issue cannot be resolved simply by deciding not to pay bribes while ignoring the fact that other firms do. Although the company may stay ethically clean, it puts itself at a serious competitive disadvantage. Instead, it should seek to eliminate or circumvent the process of bribery by all means at its disposal. The most effective approach would be for all companies subject to the system to present a solid front and to refuse to pay bribes. By passing legislation that outlaws bribery or by enforcing existing legislation, a government can produce conditions of fair competition. Complaining about bribery, reporting it, and publicizing it are all legitimate reactions for an ethical business. Even if they ultimately prove to be ineffective, the present point is to see where responsibility lies and what level of response might provide a solution.

The U.S. Foreign Corrupt Practices Act

The U.S. Foreign Corrupt Practices Act was passed in 1977, partly as a reaction to a well-publicized incident in which Carl Kotchian, President of Lockheed, made $12.5 million in payments to Japanese agents and government officials to secure a large order from Nippon Air for Lockheed's TriStar airplanes.[5]

Japanese trade agents had approached Kotchian and told him that, if he wanted to make the sale, he would have to make certain payments. After making the initial payments, he was asked for additional ones. No one doubts that the TriStar was a good plane. But was it the best for the money that Nippon Air (the official Japanese airline) could get? If it was, Nippon Air should have bought it without requiring any secret payments; on the other hand, if the asking price was $12.5 million too high, Nippon Air should have negotiated the price down. As it was, Nippon Air paid the full asking price, but Lockheed netted $12.5 million less. The difference went into the individual pockets of intermediate agents and government officials who had the authority to order the planes. It is not clear whether Nippon Air would have agreed to buy the planes if Lockheed had refused the payments. The intermediate agents might have gone to producers of its second choice of plane and tried the same demands, and so on, until it found a company that would pay. The airline would then have purchased a poorer-quality airplane—the primary criterion being not the quality of the planes but the under-the-table payments to the agents.

If buyers require payments before they will even consider purchasing a company's products, they run the risk of ruling out the best product or the best value; consequently, they do a disservice to the country or to the people they represent. If buyers require payments only after an assessment of relative product quality has determined the initial choice, they again run the risk of not getting the best for their money. If the producer is willing to pay the bribes, it must still anticipate an acceptable profit; therefore, the buyers presumably could have negotiated the price down to the same level—to the benefit of the country's coffers instead of their own pockets. The paying of bribes must be covered up because it involves deception. It also invovles treating one or more third parties unfairly, so it is doubly unethical.

When the Lockheed payments were made public, Lockheed was charged with falsification of its records and tax violations, and its reputation was tarnished. Although such payments supposedly were an accepted way of doing business in Japan, news of the payments created a furor there. The government ministers in question were criminally charged, one committed suicide, the government fell in disgrace, the Japanese people were scandalized.[6] This is not the normal reaction to disclosure of an accepted practice. The claim that the practice was "accepted" really meant that it was widely practiced and that it was tolerated when kept secret. The Japanese public's reaction clearly indicated that the Japanese people did not subscribe to the view that the practice was acceptable or ethically justifiable. This incident illustrates the importance of publicity in judging and enforcing ethical rules.

The reaction of the U.S. government was to pass the Foreign Corrupt Practices Act. The drafters of this act recognized that the problem of bribery could not be solved satisfactorily at the level of the individual, of the individual firm, or even of a particular industry. Rather, the government had to face the problem at the highest level it could. In fact the problem is an international one and can be fully resolved only at the level of international agreement. The UN Commission on Transnationals recommends similar anti-bribery legislation for all countries, but many are reluctant to enact such laws.

The Foreign Corrupt Practices Act forbids the paying of bribes.[7] Later amendments to the act permit what are called "facilitating payments"[8]—a distinction we discussed in Chapter 1. Facilitating payments are not payments to pass goods that should not be passed, nor are they payments to obtain exclusive preferential treatment. They are payments to ensure receiving the standard treatment that one ought to get but otherwise may not. Although Americans would prefer a system in which no facilitating payments were necessary, U.S. law tolerates them in business abroad. Since such payments are legally acceptable, they can be reported openly.

The Foreign Corrupt Practices Act has been criticized for two main reasons.[9] First, some critics claim that it imposes U.S. ethical norms on conduct in other countries and is thus ethically imperialistic. Second, critics argue that it places American firms at a competitive disadvantage vis-a-vis firms from other nations that are not similarly disallowed to pay bribes by the laws of their home country.

The claim of ethical imperialism assumes that in some countries bribery is ethically permissible. Yet no country openly defends the demand for or the payment of bribes as ethically permissible. Bribery is a means of bypassing the normal way of doing business. If it were the accepted norm, it would simply become part of the price one paid to do business. It would be open, above-board, required, and legally sanctioned; it would cause no harm and require no deception. It would then not be bribery. Bribery is a way of getting preferential treatment. If it were part of the normal way of doing business, it would not be preferential. If it did not result in anyone's being treated unfairly as a result of the bribe, it would not have to be done surreptitiously, for no one would have any basis for complaint. Bribery is also a means by which an individual acquires wealth outside the usual ways of paying for goods and services. If it were simply a standard fee for legitimate services, it would not be a bribe.

In no country do high government officials openly practice and publicly justify the acceptance of large sums of money for preferential treatment. If the practice were ethically justifiable and acceptable to the public, the whole point of paying bribes would be lost. It would become a normal way of doing business, and no special advantages could be gained from it. This is not to deny that bribery is widely practiced in some places.

Since bribery cannot be ethically justified, at most one can claim that certain countries tolerate bribery or that many people justify their actions by asserting that such payments are necessary in a given country. These characterizations are compatible with the practice's being unethical in those countries. To call it unethical neither contradicts the ethical norms of other countries nor imposes one's own ethical views on them. American companies, when approached for a bribe, may reply that American laws prohibit such payments. This can hardly be equated with ethical imperialism, even if it may lessen the pervasiveness of bribery in some countries.

The second charge is that bribery puts American firms at a competitive disadvantage. The reply to this is threefold. First, if the action is wrong, the fact that other people do it does not justify American firms' acting in a similar way. To make the payment of bribes legal and reportable in the United States would be to put American firms in the position not only of paying bribes but of contributing to the continuation and promotion of bribery in other countries. This is a far more serious form of wrongdoing than ethical imperialism, because it amounts to promoting corruption.

Second, no hard evidence shows that American firms have operated at a competitive disadvantage because of the Foreign Corrupt Practices Act.[10] Part of the reason for this may be that data are simply not available. No published reports detail who pays which bribes to whom, and which deals American firms would have closed had they paid bribes to certain agents or firms. The evidence indicating that American firms now operate at a competitive disadvantage is at best anecdotal, and it is not very persuasive overall. A 1981 study by the U.S. General Accounting Office[11] indicated that less than 1 percent of the 250 American businesses surveyed claimed any loss of business due to the law. Since then, other studies have shown that U.S. exports have not declined as a result of the law, nor has the law made U.S. firms less competitive, even though some deals may have been lost.[12]

Third, if the American firms are at a competitive disadvantage because of the Foreign Corrupt Practices Act, their proper response should be to pressure the U.S. government to be more aggressive in protecting their interests by negotiating with other governments to pass similar laws in those countries. This would level the playing field for all. The technique of ethical displacement shows that the ultimate solution to the problem must be found at the international level. The UN Economic and Social Council has recommended a legally binding agreement on illicit payments similar to the provisions of the Foreign Corrupt Practices Act, as has the International Chamber of Commerce in its International Code of Marketing Practice.[13] Binding agreements are possible, although they are not yet in place.

Conflicting Cultural Norms and Values

Various kinds of ethical conflicts must be resolved on a higher level. Three kinds of conflicts are commonplace: pressures on individuals to violate personal norms; inconsistent cultural norms; and host-vs.-home-country interests and values.

Pressures on Individuals to Violate Personal Norms

Individuals working abroad in multinational firms experience more than the usual degree of pressure to violate their personal norms. First, they are away from their ordinary milieu and supporting culture, and they are psychologically and geographically distant from the parent company. Second, a multinational operating away from home functions in a mix of cultures and values that tends to undermine the authority of both the home set of norms and the norms established in the host country.

The psychological and geographical distance involved means that the home office has less control over daily operations and less detailed knowledge of actual conditions in the subsidiary abroad. One of the easiest ways for managers to pressure their employees to act unethically is to give them such unrealistic goals or assignments that they can only fulfill these by cutting corners or acting unethically. The manager who says, "Get this done by such and such a date. I don't care how you do it, but get it done or I'll find someone who can," is inviting unethical behavior. Home offices may make unrealistic demands on a distant subsidiary because they lack day-to-day knowledge of the subsidiary's operations. Because of the great distance, the home office is also less able to see how its orders are implemented down the line on a day-to-day basis, and it may fail to exercise adequate control. Often, those who implement the orders do not feel responsible for what they do, since they are simply following orders. Not only does each office tend to take less ethical responsibility for its actions than it should, but each may act progressively more unethically. Such a situation calls for more conscious responsibility and for altered procedures that compensate for the distance. The changes should reinforce ethical behavior, rather than making unethical behavior more probable.

Subsidiaries in less developed countries need ombudsmen and ethical hot lines like those that have been instituted in many firms in the United States. These should be linked to the home office so that ethical difficulties encountered in the MNC abroad can get a hearing at home as well.

The mix of employees and managers from two countries—the United States and the host country—increases the likelihood that individuals will feel pressured to do things they feel they should not do. Whose ethics should the MNC follow? We have already seen that a company with integrity will not change its ethics as it changes locales. Hence the ethical norms of the American parent firm should be inculcated and followed by the firm wherever it operates. But non-American workers in the multinational abroad will certainly want to follow their own sense of what is right and wrong, as they should. Their consciences are no less to be respected than are American workers' consciences. The potential for what appear to be ethical conflicts in this setting increases the need for ethical mediators. The ombudsman or the person on the answering end of the ethical hot line should know the customs and values of both countries and should have the confidence of workers and managers from both countries. Companies need to think about ethical structures and to develop a corporate culture that reinforces the importance of personal integrity and upholds corporate integrity while at the same time respecting the legitimate values and customs of the host country.

Conflicting Cultural Norms

The problem of conflicting cultural norms is experienced on a day-to-day basis by individuals, but it is actually a structural-level problem. Norm five (G5) requires multinationals to respect the customs of the host country to the extent that the local culture does not violate ethical norms. But the mere introduction of a new industry or of new technology usually disrupts some aspect of the culture of less developed and only slightly industrialized nations. It is not so much that one country considers ethically right what the other considers wrong as that one way of doing things may be incompatible with another.

The requirement to respect local customs does not mean giving up one's integrity, nor does it mean giving up one's way of doing things. But it does mean that American workers abroad should accommodate themselves to the local ways to the extent compatible with ethics.

Certain industries demand punctuality: what one person does depends on what others have just done. Such industries may demand punctuality from workers whose notion of time is very different from the standard American view and who in other facets of their lives are not constrained by the clock. Extreme heat may demand that work stop during midday and continue farther into the evening than in a typical American factory. Although this is not an ethical issue, respecting customs and accommodating corporate practice to them are. Everyday practical issues that individuals face should be addressed in company policy—a policy that must take into account the local culture and that should not be set unilaterally by the home office.

Host-vs.-Home-Country Interests and Values

A multinational company chooses to operate in a less developed country for specific reasons; the country allows the MNC to operate within its borders for different reasons. Each has its own interests at heart, and these interests differ even though they both lead to the MNC's operating in the country. The MNC may want to employ less expensive labor than is available in the United States; the host country may want to provide more jobs for its people, given a prevailing situation of high unemployment. The MNC's desire for markets may match the host country's desire for the products the MNC makes. The MNC's desire to locate where taxes are lower than in the United States may be matched by the host country's desire to increase its tax base. But the two sets of interests do not always match.

The MNC may wish to keep wages as low as possible, while the country may wish them to be as high as possible. The same is true of the price of goods. Since the MNC wants to obtain the greatest profit possible, it wants to charge the highest prices it can competitively get; conversely, the host country wants the lowest prices. The MNC wishes to pay taxes that are as low as possible, while the host country wants to receive as much tax revenue as possible without driving away foreign firms and investment.

Neither side's legitimate desires are unethical, even when the interests involved are at odds. Self-restraint and a balance of power tend to keep each from acting unethically. But unless there is such a balance, the MNC may be tempted to seek its own interests at the expense of the host country, in violation of the second and third norms. If the host country pursues its interests too zealously at the expense of the MNC, the latter is likely to close down or sell off its operation and leave.

Moral Imagination

Clearly, in dealing with cases of ethical displacement, analysis is often not enough. Solutions and guidelines must be implemented, and they can be implemented only by individuals. Personal ethical commitments are not irrelevant to corporate, industrial, national, or international guidelines and policies. They are the starting point for discussions that lead to broader guidelines and structural changes on various levels. These corporate guidelines must cohere with the personal values and ethical beliefs of individuals if they are to be effective and if they are to be followed. In crisis situations, personal moral courage and integrity are necessary to ensure ethical economic survival, as well as to implement the required changes. Corporations with integrity are ultimately a function of individuals with integrity.

Many people of integrity ignore or underplay the importance of moral imagination. Yet no fixed code or set of rules can suffice. There is a difference between learning the rules of drawing—such as the laws of perspective—and creating a work of art. The latter requires imagination as well as craft, innovation as well as mastery of the rules. Ethics is similar. We start by learning the moral rules—the Ten Commandments, or the ordinary rules of decent moral behavior. Living by these rules has become second nature to most people and requires no great effort. We all know that, in general, lying is wrong and that it is ethically impermissible to murder our competitors, no matter how tempted we may be to do so on some days.

Moral imagination enters the scene in at least four ways. The first involves attempting to walk in someone else's shoes. *Stakeholder analysis* is a popular term in business ethics. It means that, in trying to assess the ethics of a particular course of action, we should consider all those who have a stake in the firm.[14] Shareholders are only one set of stakeholders. Others include the employees of the firm (managerial, secretarial, and blue collar); its customers; its suppliers; its creditors; its neighbors; the government; and the general public, insofar as it is affected by the firm's action. A stakeholder analysis considers each of these interests, imagines standing in each place, and looks at the action from each perspective. It is no easy task; and if it is to be done objectively and fairly, it requires not only practice but imagination. How does it feel to be laid off in an economic downturn? How does a neighborhood view a plant's closing? The neighborhood may consist of small shopkeepers—a baker, a shoe repair man, a corner grocer, a dry cleaner; they may have located near the plant to provide services to those who work there. The city or town may have invested in roads, sewers, and streetlights; it may have borrowed to build them; and it may have counted on taxes from the plant to pay for them. A supplier may have been led to believe that it could count on future sales to the firm. What are the consequences for each of them if the plant is suddenly closed?

The point is not that sentimentality should decide what is ethical or what a business should do. But analyzing the impact of a plant-closing, for instance, involves more than just abstractly considering the money a firm can save by having fewer workers and paying less in overhead and taxes. A very different view of fairness emerges if you put yourself in the shoes of each affected stakeholder, rather than merely considering the closing from the point of view of the shareholders or of management. Using moral imagination means thinking concretely instead of abstractly about the effects of one's actions. Using one's moral imagination to represent the interests of a firm's various international stakeholders requires knowledge of such stakeholders and is clearly more difficult and complex than considering only American stakeholders.

A second aspect of moral imagination involves considering how someone whom one admires as honest and upright might act in a given situation. Ethics is often taught not only by rules and precepts, but also by stories. Religious traditions include stories of holy people or saints, which present them as models for conduct. Their stories stick in one's memory and help stimulate one's moral imagination. Where are the ethical saints and heroes in business, and even more in international business?[15] Surely such saints and heroes will not be exclusively American. Who are the paragons of virtue that MBA students and managers working abroad should be taught to emulate? Business has undoubtedly produced many such models. But neither business nor anyone else has yet produced the litany of business saints necessary and sufficient to illuminate the moral imagination of the business student or practitioner. The recently established Business Enterprise Trust hopes to identify such models. It gives national awards annually to persons and firms that have shown the "courage, integrity and social vision" that "exemplify the highest standards of business responsibility."[16] Anyone deserving such an award will certainly have exercised moral imagination, and may in turn serve as a model for others. The need for similar models on the international level is clear.

A third way moral imagination provides insight into the effects of a proposed action and perspective on the ethical propriety of that action is by envisioning how it would be described the next day in a local newspaper if it were known. Since appearances can make or break reputations, actions in business should not only be ethical but also appear to be ethical. A cynic might say that they need only appear to be ethical, but that view is short-sighted. Publicity is an excellent guide to what is ethical. If Carl Kotchian had imagined the headlines that revealed Lockheed's $12.5 million payoff in connection with the sale of TriStar planes to Nippon Air, he might have resisted making those payments. If the Japanese officials who profited from the TriStar payoffs had imagined the headlines that ultimately appeared in Japan, they would surely have acted differently. A person who would be ashamed to have an accurate account of the deal currently being negotiated appear in the paper the next day should reconsider its ethical propriety. The simple act of imagining one's spouse, mother, children, or best friend reading the account in the paper can throw a bright light on the ethics of the act. The trick is to imagine the news item not as we would like to see it portrayed but as a reasonably objective investigative reporter would describe it. Ethical rules demand the moral minimum. But a firm that wishes to act with integrity will imagine, consider, ponder, and attempt to achieve the ideals it holds and the possibility of going the extra mile beyond the moral minimum, even though such actions rarely make the headlines.

The fourth aspect of moral imagination invovles continuing to look for alternative solutions to a moral dilemma when none may at first appear to exist. In a moral dilemma, neither identified option seems ethically acceptable. For example, either one must lie or one must reveal a trade secret. Neither is the right thing to do. If in fact those are the only possibilities, then one must choose the lesser of the two evils. But rarely are one's options so narrowly circumscribed. Frequently other alternatives are available, if only one uses one's moral imagination. Alternatives include evading the question, changing the topic of conversation, walking away without answering, and spilling a drink to create the needed diversion. Mahatma Gandhi exemplified moral imagination on a grand scale when he devised the technique of passive resistance. On a less dramatic level, an employee who is told to do something he or she feels is unethical (and who feels trapped between a sense of obedience as a subordinate and an unwillingness to act as commanded) should look for other alternatives. Surprisingly, an often ignored alternative is to discuss an inappropriate command with the person who issued it, stating one's objection to the action, and suggesting some alternative that can get the job done to everyone's satisfaction. The latter may involve applying imagination that the boss should have had. But moral imagination should be treasured wherever it is found.

Leon Sullivan exemplified moral imagination when, as a member of the board of directors of General Motors, he came up with the Sullivan Principles for American firms operating in South Africa.[17] Previously it had seemed that American firms must either engage in apartheid or leave South Africa. But Sullivan's principles provided a strategy whereby U.S. companies could refrain from engaging in apartheid while continuing to operate in South Africa. It was a noble experiment, even though after ten years Sullivan himself finally judged it to have failed as a means of undermining apartheid in South Africa.

Moral imagination is a key ingredient in the technique of ethical displacement.

Moral Courage

Firms that act with integrity must possess corporate courage, both on the level of the firm and on the level of the individual within the firm, if their ethical concerns are to be taken seriously. Often the most difficult task is to acknowledge that being ethical is not always profitable and may even be costly—at least in the short run. People who claim that ethics is good business are only partly right, and any company that acts ethically only to increase profits runs the risk of resorting to unethical behavior whenever an ethically right action and economic self-interest fail to coincide. In such a situation, moral courage and a commitment to ethics above profits are essential.

Employees need moral courage to say no when corporate superiors instruct them to falsify documents, backdate reports or orders, or produce goods that fall below contracted specifications. Although these are mundane examples, such refusals nonetheless constitute instances of moral courage. More dramatic instances are the famous (or notorious) whistle-blower cases.[18] The film *Silkwood* dramatized one such incident—a case in which a worker's moral courage led to her death: dramatic indeed. Newspapers and the literature on business ethics are peppered with others: the three engineers at

BART who warned of a defect that could lead to a train wreck;[19] Dan Gellert, who blew the whistle on Lockheed for a defect in the 1011 aircraft design;[20] Frank Camps, who went public with his concerns about the safety of the Ford Pinto.[21] To draw attention to what they considered dangers to the public, these individuals risked their jobs. Whistle-blowers tend to be depicted in the business ethics literature as heroes, but one aim of business ethics is to preclude the need for whistle-blowing. If firms were sensitized to respond substantively to the complaints of their employees about such things as product safety, the employees would not have to go public. Responding appropriately also takes courage.

Although we usually refer to moral courage as the courage of individuals, we can also speak of a morally courageous firm. Blowing the whistle on unethical industry practices may make a firm unpopular in the industry—or it may make the firm a leader, as moral courage frequently does among individuals. In some instances moral courage means simply refusing to do what is unethical, as does IBM, which is known for its policy of not paying bribes, even in countries where bribery is considered endemic and "necessary" for doing business. Clearly if a company is good enough, bribery is not necessary.

Moral courage may seem to come more easily to the big, successful, industry leader than to the struggling, marginal firm. Yet the best of the leaders started out small and showed their moral courage early on. In part they became successful because of that courage.

Johnson & Johnson demonstrated its courage in the face of the Tylenol tragedy,[22] when—as we noted earlier—three of its executives looked a $100 million cost in the face and ordered the removal of Tylenol from all store shelves nationwide. The action required courage, which the individuals responsible for the decision had—courage that they claim was fortified by the knowledge that the company would support their decision and by the company's Credo, which they all respected.

Operating in a corrupt environment raises the need for moral courage of another kind. In the 1980s, Colombian drug lords made death threats against the lives and families of Colombian judges and politicians.[23] The courage required of those people parallels the courage required of firms that refuse to do business with drug traffickers in such environments. The local drug pusher is easier to refuse than the national drug lord; but both refusals require moral courage, and that courage does not come overnight. It must be developed the way character is developed, by many small acts of courage over time. A corporate culture can carry the seeds of moral courage and provide an environment where it can eventually blossom under stress.

Like personal courage, corporate courage is not a trait that is in constant view. Courage is manifested and is most needed in trying conditions, but it is not the same as foolhardiness. The truly brave do not claim to be brave; they simply act appropriately when the need arises. No enforceable rule can tell an individual or corporation to be brave, and no code can make people or companies courageous. Yet moral courage is central to acting ethically in difficult situations.

The Cost of Being Ethical

Moral courage means doing the right thing, and that sometimes leads to failure. Of course, we hear less about the failures than about the successes. The courage to do the right thing does not mean the courage to keep one's business afloat no matter what the cost and no matter what action that requires. The courage to do the right thing means the courage to do what ethics requires, even if the result is bankruptcy or failure.

It would be convenient if ethics always led to profits and if being ethical always resulted in business success and increased profits. Unfortunately, that is not always the case. In general honesty *is* the best policy. But crooks sometimes succeed in the short run, and now and then they succeed in the longer run as well.

At times, acting ethically takes some toll on a company, and it may even threaten its existence. Although we hold human life sacred, it is sometimes right to lay down one's life for a friend, for one's family, for one's country, or for a cause. Similarly, might not a CEO justifiably lay down the life of the corporation for a cause or principle? Should the CEO at any cost refuse to yield to corruption or extortion, or refuse to engage in unethical practices? The simple answer is yes. But that is the extreme answer, just as sacrificing one's life is the extreme answer. Ordinary life situations rarely require such sacrifice, either of individuals or of companies.

If a firm cannot operate ethically in a corrupt environment, it must either withdraw from that environment or work to change it. American firms are not forced to continue operating in Colombia, should they find that they cannot operate there ethically. If they do operate in a corrupt environment, they must use a good deal of moral imagination to avoid engaging in corrupt activities. At the same time they should do what they can to change the environment, as American firms in South Africa did. The particular circumstances determine the specific requirements. But past experience teaches us that in such a situation neither isolated individuals nor single companies can do much by themselves. Both must rise to a higher level of action. The situation requires a concerted effort by large groups of people or by groups of firms powerful enough to offset the entrenched practices they are opposing. The example of the citizens of Eastern European countries who demonstrated against their nations' corrupt communist governments shows the importance and effectiveness of moral courage. These events also teach us that courageous ethical action can have costs. A company with integrity must be willing to act courageously when necessary and must be willing to pay the cost that integrity sometimes exacts.

7

Strategies for Competing
with Corruption

A company intending to begin operations in South Africa in the 1960s or 1970s faced the problem of how to deal with the then-existing apartheid laws. Could it ethically start operations in a country governed by such laws? A company considering opening a plant in Colombia in the 1980s had to decide how to relate to the country's guerrillas and drug lords. Could it operate ethically in such an environment? A company thinking of starting a subsidiary in an LDC where bribery at the highest levels is endemic must decide how it will respond to the pressures it will encounter at all levels to pay bribes to carry on its legitimate activities.

The task of competing in a more-or-less ethically structured environment that includes adequate background institutions is relatively unproblematic, even if doing the right thing is not always easy. But competing in less developed countries that lack adequate background institutions is more difficult and poses special ethical problems. And competing in a country whose business environment is thoroughly corrupt poses the greatest ethical difficulties. The rules of the game are fairly clear when all the players operate ethically and legally. Do the same rules apply when some of the players do not operate ethically or legally, when extortion and intimidation are rampant, and when the government either is ineffective in combating the problem or itself participates in the corruption?

There is no obvious, easy, or intuitive solution to the problem of corruption, because our general ethical intuitions develop in a context where corruption tends to be the exception rather than the rule. Multinational corporations can decide not to operate in such an environment and can decline to enter such areas. But this is not a solution for established and indigenous firms that operate there. The ultimate solution is to eliminate corruption, but the interim solution consists of adopting effective ethical strategies for operating in such situations and for moving toward the elimination of corruption.

Ten Strategies for Dealing with Corruption

The ethical problems and dilemmas that arise from operating in a corrupt environment or from facing unethical competitors have no uniform or easy solution. Yet it is possible to cope with such situations, and the previous chapters suggest a set of ten strategies that will often help in facing such situations.

> 1. *In responding to unethical activity do not violate the very norms and values that you seek to preserve and by which you judge your adversary's actions to be unethical.*

One is never ethically permitted to do what is unethical. In confronting immoral opponents one may be tempted to retaliate in kind, or even to go them one better. The temptation is natural and is a manifestation of righteous anger. But to give in to the temptation is to stoop to the adversary's level, to give up one's own integrity, and to give up morality in the process.

A company must counter a competitor's lies with the truth, not with lies of its own.

A cynic might reply that following this strategy puts a person of integrity at a disadvantage versus an unethical adversary. The unethical adversary is not inhibited by moral rules and so has the competitive edge, while the person of integrity is constrained by morality. People who are not worried about the morality of their actions are free to do whatever they want and whatever they need to do to win. If winning is one's goal, then restrictive rules and moral qualms simply get in the way of achieving one's end.

There is some truth to the cynic's analysis. But for a company of integrity, success or victory won at the cost of one's own principles is hollow. Principles cannot be turned on and off at will. If they do not guide one's response to wrongful activity, there is no assurance they will guide one's response at all. Morality may demand the difficult. It cannot allow the contradictory without our having to give it up as an intelligible (much less as a defensible) enterprise.

Some firms that operate in corrupt environments claim implicitly or explicitly that they are ethically justified in doing whatever they must to stay in business. Their usual assumption is that a corportion has not only the right but the obligation to continue to exist. Unless the corporation continues to exist, they reason, it cannot do all the good it might be capable of doing. But from an ethical perspective such a claim is much too broad to be defensible. If valid, this argument would justify the company's doing anything (including engaging in catastrophically immoral acts) that would ensure its continuation—even when the costs incurred by others could never be repaid by "all the good" the corporation might later do.

Ethics does not require that a business capitulate to corruption. Although turning the other cheek and accepting martyrdom may be personal ideals, they are not usually corporate ideals or corporate ethical requirements. But even in the usual case when economic survival and self-defense are morally justifiable aims, these must be pursued ethically.

---

2. *Since there are no specific rules for responding to an unethical opponent, in responding ethically use your moral imagination.*

An ethical response to unethical activity must be at least as imaginative as the unethical activity.

The injunction to think and act imaginatively is designed both to offset the tendency to consider morality only in terms of cut-and-dried rules and to encourage people of integrity to reconceive the situation in which they find themselves. More alternatives are usually available than the unappealing dyad of suffering at the hands of an unscrupulous opponent or adopting that opponent's tactics. Either/or situations occur less frequently than one might think. Moral imagination pushes ethical individuals to seek advantages that they do not ordinarily consider, to look for weaknesses in their adversaries, and to search for analogies with the responses of those whom they admire. Literature, stories, and the lives of heroes and saints can be more helpful as sources for imaginative ethical responses than any set of rules.

In responding to bribery, as well as to other kinds of corruption, imagination is extremely helpful. When a customs official assessed one firm a higher-than-normal fee, company officials sent 500 letters to various government offices asking for an explanation. Customs officials finally found that it was preferable to pass that firm's goods through at the standard fee rather than attempt to extract a higher fee and be besieged in such a way. Why bother with that company when so many others that would make no protest were available?[1]

---

3. *When your response to immorality involves justifiable retaliation or force, apply the principle of restraint and rely on those to whom the use of force is legitimately allocated.*

This principle states that force must be used only in reaction to unethical acts or practices, that it must be justified as the ultimate solution, and that it must consist of the minimum force necessary. The reason is obvious: force always involves harm, and the basic moral minimum is the injunction not to do direct intentional harm.

A corporation operating in an area where it might be attacked by guerrillas and where its personnel might be kidnaped is ethically permitted to use sufficient force to prevent those activities. In general businesses rely on local police forces; and in times of grave crisis, on the host country's army. Security patrols and personnel are legitimate safeguards, if allowed by the host country. Self-defense is a right exercised by each person and by corporations in defense of their employees and representatives. But the waging of personal wars is clearly not ethically justified, even against guerrilla forces, drug lords, or other such groups.

The principle of restraint requires that the powerful, regardless of the immorality of an adversary's actions, use no more force and cause no more harm than are necessary to accomplish justifiable aims. The more powerful one is, the greater is the restraint one must exercise. Adults dealing with children must apply more restraint than adults dealing with other adults. Police are empowered to exercise civil force, but they are expected to use it with restraint even against suspected criminals. Armies are given a monopoly over the major implements of force, and they are accordingly expected to be restrained in its use.

More is appropriately required of the strong than of the weak, because they can inflict so much more damage. This ethical need for restraint leads to the next principle, with which it is closely linked.

---

4. *In measuring your response to an unethical opponent apply the principle of proportionality.*

This principle requires that any force used must be commensurate with the offense and harm suffered and with the good to be achieved. It also requires that those who use the force must have some hope that it will be effective in achieving the end for which it is being used. The principle of proportionality is widely used in military ethics but surprisingly little invoked in business ethics, where it is also applicable. The principle applies to economic and political force, as well as (ultimately) to military force.

A company that suffers from a competitor's spying can seek legal redress and can loudly complain to the competing company. The principle of proportionality requires the company to keep the harm done to it in perspective, however, and to keep its planned retaliation (if any) legitimate by ensuring that this be proportionate to the offense.

---

5. *In responding to unethical forces apply the technique of ethical displacement.*

We have seen that, in a situation where bribery is the prevailing practice, a company that acts with integrity may have no option but to opt out of it and so lose business. This is blatantly unfair, yet a company with integrity can neither demand nor accede to bribery. At the level of the individual company injustice seems to triumph. Only by rising to a higher level can the disadvantage be overcome. Legally outlawing bribery makes the field of competition fair on the national level. The same is true on the international level.

The U.S. Foreign Corrupt Practices Act, which precludes American firms from soliciting or paying bribes, equalizes the playing field for all American companies. Ethical U. S. individuals and firms do not have to shoulder the complete burden of their integrity. The next step is for all other countries to enact similar legislation. The European Community is currently under pressure to adopt similar rules for European firms.[2] The American and European groups must then get Asian nations to outlaw the practice. The complete solution will only be achieved slowly, but in the long run it is the only adequate response. Simply saying that all individuals and all firms throughout the world should act with integrity and should not solicit or pay bribes is not enough.

Nor should one draw the conclusion that law is the only solution. Americans and American companies operating in South Africa faced the local government's demand that they practice discrimination as specified in the South African apartheid laws. Any individual or firm that violated those laws would be prosecuted or be forced to leave. The successful strategy for disobedience in this case consisted in having a large number of American firms agree that they would all publicly violate the apartheid laws by following the Sullivan Principles that precluded discrimination. Together they were so powerful that the South African government had to ignore their violations of its laws. Individual integrity was not enough, even though it took individuals and firms with integrity to pursue the course that they adopted.

The moral to be drawn is that, at the individual level or at the level of the firm, unfair or corrupt competition can sometimes be met only by rising to a higher level—to a level of cooperation among firms or countries that is adequate to deal with the injustice that prevails at the lower level. Integrity is required to muster the forces necessary to achieve the end at the higher level; but individual action is not enough.

> 6. *In responding to an unethical adversary, system, or practice use publicity to underscore the immoral actions.*

Corruption operates most effectively in the dark. It is never publicized as justifiable or defended for what it actually is. In this setting publicity serves three functions. First, it opens up the practice to public scrutiny. The public can then evaluate it for what it is. There is a difference between public awareness that corruption exists and the public knowledge of specific instances of corruption. Public revelation of particular corruption focuses attention on the corruption and forces an open ethical evaluation. Corruption thrives on people's unwillingness to confront it, either by hiding from it or by hiding it from themselves.

Second, publicity enables one to mobilize public pressure against corrupt practices and their perpetrators. What is tacitly known and quietly accepted becomes intolerable when fully illuminated. Publicity demands a public reaction, and it makes possible a joint response that individual persons may be too intimidated or frightened to make. For instance, since extortion always hurts someone, it cannot stand the light of publicity. No one openly admits engaging in extortion; much less does anyone engaged in it attempt publicly to defend it in any particular instance. Where adequate background institutions do not yet exist, publicity is frequently the necessary first step in fighting a corrupt practice. If the society is such that it does not object to the practices, publicity can bring outside pressures to bear in defense of those subject to the harm that corruption imposes.

Third, publicity forces a government to come to terms with corruption within its borders and, at the least, to be consistent in what it can demand of law-abiding citizens, given that it is unable to protect them and unable to enforce its laws.

Of course, if the government itself is corrupt and controls all avenues of publicity, this strategy is precluded within the country. Publicity may also bring retaliation of various kinds on those using it. This consideration leads to the seventh strategy.

> 7. *In responding to an immoral opponent seek joint action with others and work for the creation of new social, legal, or popular institutions and structures.*

Individual or personal integrity is not enough when the structures within which one operates hinder rather than foster moral action and so lead to moral dilemmas.

Joint action by companies is often much more effective than individual action, and joint action by nations is similarly more effective in international business than unilateral action by any single nation. The stumbling block in working through UN commissions is the difficulty of getting unanimous agreement. But such total agreement is not always necessary on the international level, and the agreement of groups and corporations is often preferable to individual action.

> 8. *In responding to unethical activity be ready to act with moral courage.*

Competing with integrity in a corrupt environment requires moral courage, both personal and corporate. A corporation cannot act courageously unless those within it (especially its leaders) act courageously. Personal moral courage is necessary when one's actions may produce serious personal harm— dismissal, destruction of one's property, business failure, or bodily harm to oneself or one's family. Such actions are not to be undertaken lightly.

Moral courage requires one not only to determine what is consistent with one's values but also to act in accordance with them. Frequently it may be easier to ignore the unethical activities of others—even of one's opponents— than to take any action against them; and sometimes it is both proper and wise to do so. But in other cases and at some stage, it is necessary to face the perpetrator of injustice or terror. Knowing where to draw the line and when to respond rather than to forbear requires prudence and judgment. But such lines can be drawn, and being willing to draw them requires the courage of one's convictions and the willingness to stand up to immorality and to take the risk that this involves. This is especially important when ignoring injustice will encourage the perpetrator to continue to commit similar actions or to escalate the degree of terror or injustice.

Responding with courage means being willing to stand up to immorality on one's own, if necessary. But often more important is the realization that in unity there is strength, and that a collective response to injustice is usually stronger and more effective than an individual response. Thus moral courage in conjunction with the previous guidelines, involves being willing to take the initiative in mobilizing others or to join the initiative of others who take a stand. The point of the assertion that integrity is not enough is to emphasize that any individual or company is limited and to acknowledge that immoral forces generally can be overcome only by mobilizing forces at least equal in power to those on the other side.

Companies should be willing to join other companies to fight immorality and should join forces with legitimate governments and organizations as well. This general principle is often ignored by some American companies operating in Colombia, for instance, which prefer to negotiate with drug traffickers rather than join others in opposing them.

> 9. *In responding ethically to an unethical opponent be prepared to pay a price—sometimes a high price.*

Unethical activity may initially be cheap for the perpetrator. It is always costly to the victim. Ethical responses may be more costly still. Just as moral courage is required, so is a willingness to bear the costs.

A company with integrity should realize that operating ethically in a corrupt environment carries with it a cost. Some firms that operate in corrupt environments claim implicitly or explicitly that it is ethically justifiable for them to do whatever they must to stay in business. But their claim is too broad to be defensible. Ethics does not permit a company to capitulate to corruption.

The cost of an aggressive war on those attacked, as well as on those who attempt to repulse or counterattack the aggressor, is obvious. The same is true for businesses. A company of integrity hopes that its ethically justified responses to immorality, despite the cost, will be cost-effective in the long run. In the short run such responses may enhance the company's or nation's self-image, promote morale, and help enhance the company's or nation's reputation. Facing immorality or an immoral opponent early rather than late may lessen one's eventual total cost. History teaches us that those who profit from immorality tend to continue more aggressively in their ways rather than resting content with one round of ill-gotten gains. One aim of the rule of law is to make sure that immorality does not pay. But in the process innocent people must pay the costs others impose on them by their actions.

> 10. *In responding to unethical activity, apply the principle of accountability.*

This principle demands that those who impose costs, do damage, and inflict harm on others be held accountable for their actions. Consequently, those who engage in immoral practices should know that they will be held accountable for what they do. The intent of accountability is to preclude anyone (to the extent possible) from benefiting from immoral activity, and so to help remove any incentive for so acting. A rule of law imposes accountability and holds people responsible for their actions.

In a business situation accountability is often enforced through the courts and through civil suits in which those adversely affected seek redress from the guilty party. Criminal charges also come into play. In the insider trading scandals and the S&L debacle we saw and will continue to see both sorts of penalties imposed, as guilty parties are held accountable for their actions. In Colombia, the Colombian government is attempting to hold drug lords accountable for their actions, and the fear of the extraditables is that they will be held accountable under the American legal system, which they are less able to manipulate and coerce than the Colombian one.[3]

Imposing accountability on multinational corporations is difficult, since they operate in more than one country and since insufficient international rules and enforcement mechanisms exist as yet. This both points up the need for such mechanisms and underlines the importance of accountability.

Despite the difficulties involved in enforcing accountability, the principle is essential in dealing with unethical forces. They must be held accountable by general public opinion, which is mobilized by publicity; by legal bodies, where these have jurisdiction; and by the community of nations, when the offenses are between nations. Imposing accountability and fairly enforcing it set important precedents that can help dissuade others from acting similarly in the future. The moral courage to impose accountability is just as essential as is developing adequate mechanisms to assess the proper reparations.

Holding corporations, nations, and their leaders accountable for their actions and for the damage they do to others is necessary if we are to achieve a truly civilized world. International mechanisms must be developed and supported that help prevent future harm. Those involved in the process of assessment must be people of integrity if the process is to enjoy the moral support of others and to avoid falling into the trap of vendettas, individual justice, and an eye-for-an-eye mentality, in which integrity quickly goes by the board.

The ten preceding strategies go together. They outline a pattern of appropriate responses to unethical behavior on the part of one's competitors or to unethical elements in any society. Although the list is not exhaustive, it is systematic in the sense that the strategies are interrelated. They are rules of thumb in that they are not exact formulations of duties or obligations but rather describe and prescribe approaches to immoral forces. They organize a number of disparate reactions and preclude inappropriate and immoral ones.

They suggest ways of dealing with unethical competitors and of operating in conditions of corruption.

Competing in Corrupt Environments

Companies may compete in at least four different types of corrupt environments, although these types are often found intermingled. The first environment is that of a society with an unethical social system. The second arises when the government and leaders of the country are corrupt, although the social system itself is not. In the third environment, the system is not corrupt, but influential private elements engage in illegal and unethical practices and pose frequent threats to individuals and ethical businesses. In the fourth, the government of a country is not corrupt, but it is ineffective in enforcing its own laws. By looking at each of these environments in turn we can see whether and how our ten strategies can suggest ways of competing with integrity amidst corruption.

Competing in a Corrupt Social System

The white population and government of South Africa, under that country's apartheid laws, radically and unjustly discriminated against the nation's black majority. Starting in 1948, the laws mandated segregation in restrooms, dining halls, and living areas; they prohibited blacks from being employed in managerial positions that would place them in charge of whites; they reserved certain occupations exclusively for whites; they permitted lower pay for blacks who did the same work as whites; they limited black ownership of land to native reserves that made up only 13 percent of the nation's land surface, although nonwhites accounted for 83 percent of the population (17.7 million, as compared with 3.8 million whites); they prohibited blacks from voting outside the native "homelands" and from having an effective voice in the South African government; they required blacks to obtain special permission to enter urban areas.[4] Even though a majority of white South Africans for many years supported the apartheid laws as ethically justifiable, given the special circumstances of South Africa, the laws were widely condemned internationally as unjust. Numerous countries applied economic sanctions and political pressure on South Africa to change the laws. Many white South Africans acknowledged that the laws were unjust, as well. The problem was how to dismantle the laws with a minimum of risk to their safety and property when the black majority acquired the right to vote.

South Africa under apartheid laws constituted an unethical social, economic, and political system. It was inherently unethical because its faults could not be changed or corrected by anything short of an outright overthrow of the system of apartheid. Just as one cannot ethically permit a little slavery, so one cannot countenance a little apartheid. Given this state of affairs, could a firm ethically conduct business in South Africa? If so, how?

The general ethical rule is that one is not allowed to engage in an unethical practice; therefore, no individual in a firm and no firm in its policy may engage in such a practice. This means that neither a firm nor an individual in a firm may ethically practice apartheid or obey the apartheid laws. The same sort of judgment was made in modern times with respect to plantations or businesses that practiced slavery in the American South and in other parts of the world. One might argue that, given South Africa's apartheid laws, it would be better for a company to run a business that treated blacks reasonably well, even while obeying the apartheid laws, than to close down and leave the field entirely to those who would treat blacks worse; however, any such defense ultimately fails to justify participation in the system. A kind slave owner is better than a mean slave owner, but neither is ethical.

A white South African manager who abided by the apartheid laws acted unethically, and yet such a person may have seen neither migration nor unemployment as an attractive alternative. In this situation some people rationalized that the system was not really unjust. Others rationalized that, although unjust, it was the lesser of two evils—better than the chaos and violence that the end of white rule would bring. Still others claimed that, since they had no viable alternative, they could work from within to help change the system. These arguments may have been honest justifications or convenient rationalizations, but they cannot excuse the apartheid policy of firms, of highly placed officers, and of others who did have real alternatives. No matter how one evaluates the moral reasoning of white South Africans who engaged in apartheid practices, foreign investors and multinationals could not validly use such reasoning to justify their obedience to the apartheid laws, because they did have an alternative—namely, to leave South Africa.

Could American multinationals ethically remain in South Africa if they did not obey the apartheid laws? If one grants that there is no ethical way to obey the apartheid laws, can one ethically operate in that unethical or corrupt society?

The suggestion of Leon Sullivan, a Baptist minister and a member of the board of directors of General Motors, was that it might be ethically justifiable to operate in that environment if two conditions were fulfilled. The first was that the companies should not obey the apartheid laws. This was a form of passive disobedience. Disobedying unethical laws is ethically justifiable; otherwise, one is forced to conclude that one has an ethical obligation to act unethically because it is commanded by law. The second condition was that the American firms should actively promote, in whatever ways they could, the abolition of the apartheid laws. This was a necessary condition if the firms were to produce more good than bad for the South African people overall, since by their presence and their tax payments the American firms helped support the white apartheid government. Sullivan used great moral imagination in proposing this plan, since it was not an obvious strategy. Proposing it and following it required moral courage. General Motors took the lead in adopting the principles, and other firms followed. Faced with large-scale civil disobedience by MNCs, the South African government chose to ignore their activities, thus silently capitulating to their violation of the law.

The solution was an instance of moral displacement and could not have been exercised effectively by a given individual in a firm. Any American who worked for an American multinational operating in South Africa could not individually have chosen to disobey the apartheid laws. The only recourse would have been to refuse to work in South Africa. Nor is it likely that the South African government would have allowed any individual firm to break the apartheid laws with impunity. But when faced with a strong coalition of large and important American firms, the government decided it had less to lose by allowing them to act on the Sullivan Principles than by closing them down or trying to force them to obey the law.

Did the Sullivan Principles succeed in undermining the apartheid laws and help bring about their repeal? Critics have argued that the South African government allowed American companies to follow the Sullivan Principles because it reaped more benefit than harm from the continued presence of the American firms involved; hence the government must have seen tolerating the Sullivan Principles as, on balance, a reasonable price to pay for keeping the MNCs in South Africa and (indirectly) strengthening the government.

In 1987, Leon Sullivan decided that ten years of applying the principles had failed to undermine apartheid and that observance of the principles no longer sufficed to justify the continued presence of American firms in South Africa. Shortly thereafter, many American companies sold their plants or left in one way or another.[5]

We can draw several lessons from this study about how to operate in a structurally corrupt environment. The first is that firms may not engage in unethical practices even if those practices are legal. MNCs have alternatives: they can disinvest, leaving the country if they are already there, or they can opt not to go there in the first place.

The second lesson is that disobeying unjust laws is more likely to go unpunished if companies act in concert. Operating together, the American firms were powerful enough to refuse to follow unethical practices. This is a classic example of an ethical problem that resisted solution at the levels of the individual and of the individual firm, but that could be solved by joint action at a higher level. It is also an instance in which publicity in the United States pressured American firms into following the Sullivan Principles.

Nor was that the only instance in which the technique of ethical displacement was implemented. Nations around the world exerted a great deal of pressure on the South African government to change its apartheid policies. Even if the economic sanctions that many countries imposed did not take a severe toll, they played a role in bringing about change, as did the moral pressure and condemnation and the political and social ostracism that were imposed on South Africa by African states, the United States, the European Community, and others.

The third lesson is that publicity was important in effecting change. Publicity threw light on actual conditions in South Africa and on the country's apartheid policies, and it focused attention on companies that operated in South Africa. This forced American companies to think through their policies, to adhere to the Sullivan Principles, and in many instances to divest their holdings in South Africa.

The fourth lesson is that refraining from engaging in unethical practices oneself is not enough. Individuals who operate in an unethical system can only justify their continued presence by establishing as a reasonable expectation the prospect that their activities are undermining or will undermine the system. This means that their actions must do more good than harm to the people of the country, as required by rule two (G2) of the initial seven. Sullivan had the courage to say that a ten-year trial was adequate. He did not try to justify an open-ended time frame that offered no clear means of determining the effectiveness of the firms' tactics in undermining apartheid. The latter approach would have presented too weak a criterion to justify the continued presence of American firms; it would have licensed them to stay in South Africa indefinitely, even if their presence had been counterproductive to achieving their claimed ethical goal. A firm that is unwilling to end its no-longer-justifiable operations at some cost to itself lacks ethical integrity.

The fifth lesson is that some industries, such as banking, cannot ethically justify their operating in a corrupt system. Our initial guidelines continue to be applicable, even when the situation involves operating in a corrupt social system. Banking and other financial industries do not employ many people, and they typically benefit mostly the entrenched powers—in the case of South Africa, either the state or the local enterprises that enforced the apartheid laws. To the extent that such industries have this effect, they violate the second ethical guideline (G2). Nor can industries that directly help the government to enforce its unethical policy be ethically justified. Hence any arms or equipment that might be used by the government or by the police in surveillance or law enforcement cannot ethically be sold to the government because of the known improper uses to which they will be put. Anything that helps support a corrupt system is not ethically justifiable.

Competing in Environments with Corrupt Governments and Leaders

When the source of corruption is not the system but the government or the country's leaders, the problems are different. Doing business in such a situation does not involve committing direct unethical acts, and no laws require that one discriminate or treat any individuals or groups unfairly. Theoretically one could operate in such a situation without acting unethically.

Yet two types of ethical problems arise. The first involves the extent of a business's collusion with corruption, if the government or leaders of the country are corrupt: the leaders are unjust to their people; they are tyrannical, repressive, or exploitative; they use public money for their own benefit; they amass great wealth at public expense; they divert aid or loans from legitimate projects to their own pockets. The second type of problem stems from government officials or police who exercise their authority capriciously, who do not enforce the law, who seek bribes and payoffs, or who demand payments to keep them (or others) from damaging a firm or its property. In such a situation the government is not the source of remedy for one's ills. The government is the illness, or at a least part of it.

The easiest course of action for a multinational is not to enter such an environment in the first place. But what if a firm is already operating in the country when the corruption begins? The general rule that one may not engage in unethical practices still holds, as does the rule that one cannot help those who do engage in such practices.

Countries with strong leaders are sometimes attractive to multinationals, even if the leaders are repressive or tyrannical toward their own people. The companies feel that such societies are relatively stable and that business property in them is safe from nationalization. The second of our initial seven guidelines (G2) requires that the multinational produce more good than harm to the host country. The corollary to that rule specifies that the good of a country cannot be understood as the good of an elite or of certain corrupt leaders of a country. We can now add that, not only is the good of corrupt leaders to be discounted in determining whether the second rule is fulfilled, but supporting such a government or social elite is not ethically permissible.

The argument that this policy imposes American rules of ethical justifiability on foreign governments and their elites cannot be taken seriously. Anything that helps governments and elites exploit their people or siphon off funds for their own purposes is not ethically justifiable. If by operating in such a country a firm helps the corrupt government, its operation is not ethically permissible. The proper question is whether one can both operate in such an environment without helping the corrupt government or elite and bring more good than harm to the people of the country. The odds against this are sometimes high. But because the system itself is not corrupt, some ethical way of operating there may be possible, given integrity, ingenuity, and moral imagination on the part of the firm.

The second type of problem raises the question of what constitutes a proper response to governmental extortion, to unjust laws, or to selective, punitive, or arbitrary enforcement of laws against those who do not pay bribes to prevent officials from enforcing the law. Two principles apply here. The first is that an unjust law is not ethically binding. The second is that people have the right to protect themselves and their property, and that each firm has the right to protect itself and its employees to the extent possible under the circumstances.

The claim that corrupt laws are not ethically binding means that, if the laws are corrupt in what they command (as are the apartheid laws), they cannot ethically be obeyed. If the laws are corrupt because they are selectively enforced against certain people (such as those who do not pay off the officials whose job it is to enforce them), the laws may be resisted by any means possible, and they may validly be protested.

Individual protests against unjust laws or their enforcement, against extortion, or against governmental bribery do little good if the government itself is the problem. Joint protests by major firms and by one's home government may or may not be effective, but they are appropriate nonetheless.

Paying extortion is less bad than demanding it; but like paying bribes, it is unethical. Paying extortion reinforces the practice; it acquiesces in evil rather than resisting it. At best it may be the lesser of two evils. Although difficult to avoid on the individual level, it can sometimes be fought effectively by uniting with others similarly extorted, by mutually helping one another, and by taking a stand together. The broader the group—and the higher the level at which support can be mobilized—the better the chance of resisting extortion. The obligation to resist corruption thus becomes an obligation to unite to fight it. Since large companies are better situated to lead the fight than are small companies, they have a greater obligation to do so.

Civil disobedience that consists in nonviolently breaking one law to publicly protest other unjust laws or government practices is an ethically permissible tactic for firms as well as for individuals. To be effective, it must arouse other people to protest and to action; hence, publicity is a key ingredient. There is no obligation to engage in civil disobedience if it will be ineffective. A person or a firm is ethically required—as opposed to being ethically permitted—to engage in this or other kinds of protest against unjust government laws and policies only when the disobedience is likely to achieve its intended goal, and when it is the only alternative to acting unethically. The latter condition is seldom fulfilled, as long as withdrawal remains a possibility.

Are multinationals allowed to take part in, help foment, or give monetary support to the overthrow of a corrupt government? The general rule that multinationals should not enter into the politics of the host country presumes the legitimacy of the government of the host country. But by what right may they decide on the legitimacy of a government and interfere in its operation? Surely, if they are suspected of planning to take part in the government's overthrow, they will not be allowed to operate in the country. Indeed, a frequent complaint against multinationals is that, as long as their own interests are protected, they care little about the corruption to which the people of the country are subjected.

Our seven guidelines require MNCs to walk a narrow line. They may not take part in corruption; they should not succumb to corrupt demands; and they should not support a corrupt government, even if the government does not extort or impose corrupt demands on them. When a government is corrupt, the people ultimately must take over and depose those in power. The people's revolts against corrupt regimes in Eastern and Central Europe is a lesson in the effectiveness of mass movements and protests. The fact that the people in these countries did not act in concerted fashion to overthrow the Communist regimes for forty years shows that state power can keep a people cowed for a long time. Yet even that does not justify any MNC's leading a revolution or directly fomenting or supporting one, even against a corrupt government. Such intervention is overwhelmingly likely to produce more harm than good.

Once a company understands what it cannot morally do, it can turn to the strategies for operating in a corrupt environment. The need for moral imagination here becomes paramount. Uniting with other firms of like mind in pursuing whatever strategy is effective is more likely to produce positive results than trying to operate independently. Citing the Foreign Corrupt Practices Act as a legitimate reason not to pay bribes has proved effective in many instances. Publicity is a tool that one can sometimes use—if not in the first instance, then as a later defense against continued extortion or unfair treatment. Probably the most important strategy is to promote just background institutions. Operating under a corrupt government does not preclude respecting the human rights of one's workers or ensuring protection of the environment to the extent one can. As we have seen, the cost of operating with integrity in such an environment may be high. If it becomes too high, the obvious solution is not to capitulate to corruption but to leave.

Competing in Corrupt Private Environments: Drugs and Syndicates

The third type of problem in dealing with corruption arises when neither the system nor the government is corrupt, but when corrupt private elements dominate or set the environment in which business is done. Examples include parts of the United States during prohibition, where rival groups of gangsters controlled certain industries; parts of Sicily and mainland Italy where the Mafia is powerful and influential;[6] and parts of Colombia, where the drug lords are the major economic powers and the richest and most influential people—but hardly the country's elite. Other countries have similar situations.[7] In Bolivia, 25 percent of the country's gross national product comes from coca for cocaine production; and coca is the biggest foreign currency earner in both Bolivia and Peru.[8]

The Mafia can be traced back to the thirteenth century in Sicily, where it operated a system of private justice during periods when official despotic rulers oppressed the poor. The Mafia not only dispensed its own version of justice but sometimes shared with the common people the wealth it stole from the rich. To some extent the Mafia developed its own "ethics" or rules of behavior, built on notions of revenge, disdain for the official authorities, silence, and loyalty to one's extended family or group.[9]

The drug lords of South America have learned from the Mafia. They have gained the support of the farmers who grow the coca leaves by building schools and by taking care of the farmers in ways the government does not.

Collaboration with corruption—be it the activities of the Mafia or of South American traders in illegal drugs—is unethical, and all who engage in it are tainted. The Colombian situation is dramatic, and the Colombian government has rightly practiced the technique of ethical displacement in seeking solutions to its problem, arguing that a permanent solution to the dependence of peasant farmers on coca production cannot be found on the level of the individual farmer. It is easy for outsiders to say that, even if threatened with harm, the farmers should not grow coca. It is easy to say that they should grow other crops even if they cannot sell them for as much money or that it is better to starve than to act unethically. But this puts a far greater burden on the farmers than is justified. If they are to stop growing coca, then someone— their own government, multinationals, other governments—must not only protect them from the threats made against them, but also help them change from coca to other crops. They need money and seed to get started; they need markets for their products. They need help to solve their ethical dilemma of either producing coca and keeping their families alive or not producing coca and seeing them die. They cannot solve their problem on the level of the individual or even on the level of individuals acting together.[10]

The Colombian situation is dramatic because the government declared war on the drug lords, and the drug lords retaliated with a series of bombings to instill fear in the people and to turn them against the government and its attempts to control the drug industry.[11]

In such a situation legitimate multinationals have little incentive to carry on operations. The cost of protecting their key people and their property is high. The instability of the political situation is not good for any kind of legitimate business, even though it is not unethical in general to do business in such a situation. But it is unethical to do anything that helps those involved in the drug industry. And this raises questions about what it means to do business with those in the drug industry and what is and is not ethically forbidden.

Since no one is ethically permitted to do what is unethical, no firm may ethically sell goods that it knows will be used in the drug trade or will be helpful to the drug trade. Clearly, the sale of arms to any buyer who is likely to employ them or resell them for any illegitimate purpose is unethical. Drug lords use armaments of all kinds against the government, against other factions that threaten their business, and against various third parties.[12] Similarly, the sale of chemicals that are used in Colombia to derive cocaine from coca leaves, such as ether and methyl ethyl ketone, is unethical. Surprisingly, the United States, which is interested in stopping the flow of cocaine from Colombia, did not prohibit the sale of such chemicals by U.S. firms, and had to be asked to do so by Colombia.[13] Yet even before the sale was declared illegal, it was unethical.

By similar reasoning other manufacturing, service, or banking companies have the obligation not to take part in cocaine production and not to support and abet those who do. This poses special problems for companies that choose to operate in Colombia. Trucks, computers, and various other products play a key role in drug traffic. How far must a company go in determining who its customers are and how its products will be used? Although there is no general rule or hard-and-fast line separating acceptable from unacceptable practice, the requirement not to take part knowingly and willingly in helping drug traffickers means that a company with integrity will try to determine who its customers are and whether their purposes are or are not legitimate.

One might argue that, if one supplier does not sell drug traffickers the goods they want, another will. As in other cases, the reply is that one unethical act does not justify another unethical act. One useful strategy is for all ethical merchants and firms to band together in opposition to the drug traders. In some cases refusal to sell goods leads to threats and (subsequently) to harm, which necessitates joint action between the government and the populace to offset the power of the drug traders.

The claim by merchants that they do not know who is involved in the drug trade is often untrue. Reports indicate that the exclusive social clubs in Colombia, for instance, do not admit drug lords, despite their wealth.[14] They are denied prestige and social acceptability, but they are sold goods and services. If they are known for one purpose of exclusion, they are sufficiently known for the other. Those who cooperate cannot claim to be acting with integrity. And whatever excusing conditions might apply to local firms, these cannot serve to excuse MNCs, which always have the option of withdrawal.

The argument goes even farther. American, Swiss, and other banks cannot ethically accept drug-generated money, much less launder it. Real estate owner should not sell drug lords land, and stock exchanges should not offer them investment opportunities. Where does one draw the line in accepting drug money? Even though we can draw no precise line, the general rule that it is unethical to take part knowingly in drug trafficking or to support those who do requires that one exercise due care in determining who one's customers are and whether the money one accepts is legitimate.

Some may claim that this requirement is too strong, that it violates the rights (for example) of the drug traffickers or of their families. Yet they have no right to any goods if the money being used to pay for them was illicitly obtained. There are some people with whom one cannot ethically do business. The existence of unethical bankers, black-market munitions suppliers, and unscrupulous merchants is no justification for others to act in the same way.

The efforts of individuals and firms needs to be reinforced by law. The link between arms and corruption makes it difficult—sometimes even impossible—to fight corruption effectively without also controlling access to arms. A society serious about fighting violent corruption must be serious about controlling firearms. Likewise, laws should prohibit the sale of materials used in the drug trade, the sale of trucks and other legitimate items to drug traders, and the handling of drug money in Colombia, in the United States, and in other countries. Action on the government level and on the international level between governments can reinforce the inclination of individuals and groups at the lower levels to act as they should.

The Colombian government has moved along these lines and used moral imagination in freezing all the known assets of the drug lords until they come forward and justify their holdings.[15] That action is appropriate, even if in one or another instance a person's legitimate holdings might be inappropriately frozen until the person does indeed justify them. The harm such a person suffers is not sufficient to render the practice unjust.

These actions are not a solution to the drug problem, which would certainly involve cutting demand as well as restricting supply. But they do suggest a first answer to the question of how business can ethically operate in a corrupt environment: it can only do so if its activities do not help those who act corruptly, if it does not itself engage either directly or indirectly in any activity that is unethical, and if it cooperates with those who are fighting the corruption.

The claim of the Colombian government to have declared war on the drug lords and on those who produce and traffic in illegal drugs is noteworthy, since it is a declaration of war on Colombia's own people. The United States government has used the rhetoric of the "war on drugs" domestically, too, but it has not taken the rhetoric seriously. Colombia has. War is legitimate only as a response to an unjust attack; it is a country's means of self-defense. Even then the means used must protect the innocent and the amount of violence used must be proportionate to the threat.

In Colombia the very existence and normal functioning of civil society have been threatened. The analogy with war is not altogether misplaced, even though the rules of war cannot be totally invoked or enforced, for the state must continue to guarantee the civil rights of its citizens. Yet the Colombian declaration of war is more than merely symbolic and rhetorical. The war involves the use of police and of the armed forces to pursue drug lords and to engage in search-and-destroy maneuvers against coca crops and cocaine laboratories.

Especially significant at all levels is the mobilization and reinforcement of moral courage of the type demonstrated in war. A stigma attaches to those who give aid or comfort to the enemy, by supplying them with goods or aiding them in other ways. By officially declaring war, the Colombian government has in effect branded the drug traders as enemies of the people and of the state and has put pressure on the general population to ostracize them.

The technique of displacement looms large throughout this analysis. Given the physical threats and the economic forces at work, American companies that choose to locate in Colombia can legitimately take any precautions and use any force necessary to defend themselves, their property, and their personnel. But they cannot claim neutrality in the drug war or argue that they have no connection with it. Once a company chooses to operate in such an environment, it takes on responsibilities, including the duty to protect its employees—both American and Colombian—to the extent possible. Such a company cannot cooperate with guerrilla and drug lords on the one hand and seek the protection of the government on the other. Integrity requires that it be clear in its refusal to deal with those outside the law. Self-interest and prudence impel it to cooperate with other companies in joint plans of action and to cooperate with the government in its battle against corrupt forces. True courage will often be necessary to cooperate, despite threats, with lawful authorities. The alternative is not to stand alone but to leave.

What of the other side—the ethics of the drug lords or of the guerrillas? Rather than siding with the government, wouldn't it be more reasonable to negotiate differences with both sides? The simple answer is no. Attempting to render drug traffic morally justifiable stretches the notion of morality too far. Not everything is justifiable, even if some people engage in the practice and somehow justify it to themselves. Integrity requires that one sometimes draw the line.[16]

Competing in an Environment of Corruption and Ineffective Government

Equally difficult problems arise when a government is not corrupt but is ineffective in enforcing certain laws and in controlling some of the corrupt elements within its borders. On one level the paradigm of this situation involves the reluctance of many Italians to pay taxes and the response of the government to build in a presumption that the figures on tax forms are underreported. On another level it is the inability of many governments to curtail the power of crime syndicates and their tolerance of petty bribery and of illegal payments to officials, despite constant complaints about such payments.

What are individuals and companies ethically required to do when the vast majority of other people and firms do not obey the official rules?

The answer arguably is that one is ethically required to play by the rules that are actually followed, provided that in doing so one does not harm others. We can usefully distinguish between ethics and law for this purpose. Since one may never ethically do what is unethical, and since harming others for no good reason is unethical, one may never legitimately harm others without having some justifying reason. Moreover, in general one has an ethical obligation to obey the just laws of a legitimate state. But an unenforced law has dubious standing as a law, and such a law is in general not binding.

The Italian tax procedure[17] acknowledges that a good deal of the Italian economy is an underground economy, in which goods are traded for other goods or services, and in which not all exchanges are reported.[18] In part the underground economy developed because of the inefficiency of the government and its bureaucracy. When rules become too difficult to follow, or when people cannot ascertain the actual rules (that is, rules that are really enforced), they tend to circumvent the nominal laws to the extent possible. This results in loss of control by the government and inefficiency. Yet analysts credit the underground economy with making the Italian system work. It works not because of government but in spite of it. To call such economic transactions unethical judges them by a totally inadequate criterion. The proper question is whether the transactions are in general fair. If they are, the second question to ask when doing business in such a society is, what are the common practices? That the practices diverge from the letter of the law does not make them unethical within the system. This reasoning does not justify unethical practices or unfairness. It simply does not decide what is unethical or unfair on the basis of the letter of the law.

The distinction between ethics and law is also important in considering unenforced laws. An unenforced law loses its effectiveness and penalizes those who follow it to the letter while allowing those who ignore it to profit from noncompliance. If the law prohibits an unethical practice, the practice remains ethically impermissible whether there is a law or not and whether the law is enforced or not. But the purpose of some laws is to make competition fair. And if they are not enforced, they fail in their purpose and hence are of dubious validity. As an example, consider an air pollution case.

A statute is passed requiring pollution control and specifying maximum levels of sulfur emission. The law is a good one. Pollution is harmful, and setting limits imposes the same standards on all. Controlling pollution is costly, but the law places the cost on those who produce the pollution instead of on those who suffer its noxious effects. Violating such a law is in general not only illegal, but also unethical, since the firm that ignores the law does not bear its fair share of the burden of pollution control. But what if none of the firm's competitors abide by the law? They take the attitude that they will put in pollution control devices only when—if ever—they are monitored and are forced to do so by direct, specific order. In the meantime, despite the law's having been passed, no one monitors and no one forces compliance. Does the simple fact that the law has been passed mean that an ethical firm must put itself at a competitive disadvantage by spending a considerable sum on installing pollution control equipment while other firms do nothing?

From an abstract ethical point of view the answer would seem to be yes. But practically speaking, one firm's installing the mandated equipment will not materially reduce the total amount of pollution, if the pollution is caused by effluents from a large number of firms. The harm done is not caused by any one plant acting alone but by all the plants together. Hence each one individually can claim that alone it would not ethically be bound to control its emissions, since the emissions from one plant alone would not be dangerous. If this is true, then it is only together that the plants are harmful; and only if all of them (or at least the vast majority of them) control their emissions will the level of pollution be reduced sufficiently to be safe for all. The point of passing the law is to require from each firm the same conditions of pollution control and to make the air safe for all. But if the law is not enforced, it fails in its aim and the resulting situation is not fair. Clearly a law that singled out one or two firms for expensive pollution control and that ignored all the others would be unjust. Lack of enforcement amounts to the same thing. Hence this law is not binding unless enforced.

This does not mean that, if a firm knows it is doing harm by polluting, it is ethically allowed to continue doing so until forced to stop by law. A plant that dumps toxic waste into a river acts unethically and should refrain from so acting whether forced to by law or not. Unlike the situation in the air pollution example, the firm's actions are harmful even if no other plant dumps any waste. But laws that aim to create conditions of fair competition must be enforced to be effective. Unless they are effective they give those who choose to ignore them a competitive advantage. The law imposes a restraint and a cost only on those who obey it. In such a situation a firm that acts with integrity will not act unethically. But it does have several options. It may not only obey the law but also demand that the law be fairly enforced, requiring others to comply as well. It may comply whether or not others do. Or it may do its best to identify what ethics requires of it in terms of reducing its pollution, and then act accordingly, rather than expecting the law to determine its fair share of the burden. If the law allocates responsibility for pollution control fairly, it sets norms that coincide with what is ethically required.

The principles that a dubious law does not bind and that an unenforced law is a dubious law do not justify disobedience to laws just because others break them. Despite the law, ethical rules always apply; and if the law prohibits what ethics prohibits, those actions remain ethically impermissible whether the law is enforced or not. Nor does the fact that some laws are frequently broken allow others to break them, provided that the government makes reasonable attempts to enforce them. The American prohibition laws were laws that everyone was ethically required to follow, even though they were so widely broken that they were eventually repealed.

What about laws that are enforced to some extent? For example, suppose that a firm is inspected for compliance, but it pays the enforcing inspector not to report violations. Or suppose that an inspector comes around every year and takes emission readings; if the readings are over the specified amount, the plant is fined a certain sum each day until it comes into compliance. To be effective, the fine must be so high that it is cheaper for the plant's owner to install the pollution control equipment than to continue paying the fine indefinitely. But suppose that the firm pays the inspector the equivalent of one week's pay not to file charges, and that this payment is much cheaper than installing the equipment.

No firm with integrity will make such payments. But is compliance in such a situation very different from the case in which a firm complies with unenforced laws? What is the purpose of laws in such a situation, and how do the inspectors get away with such procedures on a large scale? That is a point of entry for an ethical analysis.

A complying firm may protest the system and the corruption to whatever authorities will listen (and who are not in turn receiving some of the payment to ignore violations). An individual firm may have little impact and may receive little attention. But a group of complying firms will get more attention.[19] And as a group they may seek media coverage to bring the situation to public light and to garner public support. One or all of the firms interested in compliance may refuse to comply with the law in order to get cited and thus bring the case to court for judicial action. Other techniques, requiring imagination and courage, are possible.

If in the end local apathy, public indifference, or official ineffectiveness do not change the unfair situation, is the law unjust? The answer is yes. To the extent that it is unjust, as in the case of nonenforcement of air pollution standards, the affected firms are not ethically bound to comply. But unlike in the prior case, they will be fined for noncompliance unless they pay the inspector. Paying the inspector not to report violations is not a facilitating payment—that is, a payment made to get an official to do his or her job. In this case paying the inspector not to do his or her job is unethical and, usually, illegal.

There is no easy or happy solution to this situation on the level of the firm.

Although ethics does not strictly bind the firm to obey the ineffective law, ethics does preclude the firm from paying off the inspector. The only way to achieve a true solution is to rise to a higher level, which involves trying to change the system. In most societies publicity is the key. In almost any society, if the corruption is gross enough and at a high enough level, people may be moved to apply real pressures or to take significant action. But with low-level petty corruption, marshaling public opinion may be difficult if such corruption is rampant. It is not that people think the corruption is ethically justifiable; if it were ethically justifiable, it would not be called corruption. Rather the corruption is so pervasive that people feel it would take too much energy to fight it in one place, knowing all the while that it is also present and every bit as bad in several dozen other places as well. Why get aroused about this particular instance simply because one company or group of companies complains?

Multinationals have several options. Presumably they locate where they do because it is profitable to do so. If abiding by the laws—even though these are only selectively enforced due to illegal payments—makes it unprofitable for them to operate in a given area or country, they can leave. Making public their reasons for leaving would be a service to the country. And if the companies are big enough to provide many jobs and significant tax revenues, they may be important enough to make a difference. A company's size and its importance to a community or region are factors that may enable it to act ethically and profitably. Willingness to act with integrity means willingness to close down if it becomes impossible to operate both ethically and profitably.

Small firms do not have as much leeway as large firms. If a multinational closes down a firm in one location, it still has other locations and the possibility of opening up new facilities elsewhere. A small firm that has few other locations and no relocation possibilities may face a choice of being ethical and going bankrupt or making unethical payments and staying afloat. Sometimes one cannot compete ethically and survive in a corrupt environment. But even a small firm can use imagination; attempt various means of getting public attention and publicity; name and embarrass those engaged in the unethical practices; protest to high-placed elected officials, to the courts, and to the media; and do whatever else is possible. This effort consumes time, is costly, and puts one more strain on a firm that may be only marginally profitable.

The burden of fighting petty bribery is sometimes made greater by the threat of violence or by the strict enforcement of other laws that are on the books but are not generally enforced. Any troublemaker—that is, anyone who complains too loudly or who threatens to upset the vested interests of the officials involved—is open to legal harassment at best and to physical threat to himself or his property at worst. The cost of being an individual reformer of the system is high, so it is not surprising that few choose to be reformers. For this reason a system tends to remain as it is. On the individual level, the cost of being ethical may well take the form of an inability to compete effectively. An adequate solution can be found only when businesses interested in being ethical join forces against the corrupt practice. As a unit they can fight for their standards, get more effective enforcement through changes within the government, marshal public opinion, or join with firms that are large enough to exercise leadership. In these ways they can initiate or support significant change.

Competing with Multiple Corruption

The question of how to compete ethically with corruption is still partly unanswered. Add political corruption to the corruption of crime syndicates, and consider operating ethically in such a situation.

A large multinational may have the resources to operate ethically even in this situation. It may be able to protect itself against criminal violence when the police or local authorities are unable to do so, and it may be so important to the economy of the country that its protests about bribery are effective in changing how it is treated. In the first case, self-defense is an established right; if a government cannot provide adequate protection, multinationals can frequently hire the protection they need for their key personnel and their facilities. This is a cost of doing business in some areas. If the cost is too high, the firm closes down or moves.

In a society like the United States the institution of investigative reporting is an effective means of uncovering corruption by public officials. Although publicity is a powerful tool against corruption, a difficulty of operating in some countries that have corrupt governments is that the governments control the media. Hence the internal use of such organs to throw light on corrupt practices is precluded. The use of media outside the country may be possible, and it may or may not be effective. Almost certainly a repressive government will do what it can to disallow such outside reports, and to forbid a company from issuing any such reports as a condition of its continuing to do business there.

Sometimes, those interested in acting ethically can organize and present a common front against those who threaten them or who compete unethically. If the legal system is effective, such organizations can keep competition fair, making it possible for individual firms to compete ethically and successfully.

No special rules permit a marginal company to act in a way that would be unethical if it were a profitable company. No company has a right to continued existence analogous to a person's right to life. A starving man may be justified in taking a loaf of bread from an affluent neighbor if that is the only way he can keep himself alive, arguing that the right to property is a lesser right than the right to life. A sinking company, however, has no right to take property from an individual or from any other company, for it enjoys no comparable right to life.

Suppose that firms in a given city cannot get their truck deliveries unless they give the drivers additional payments. Traffic is always so congested that any driver can plausibly claim that it is impossible to get access to the delivery area. But if all those from whom such payments are demanded banded together and refused to make such payments, the drivers' employers would soon ensure deliveries or the trucking companies would go out of business. But the problem does not threaten the existence of any firm, and the remedy costs more than any firm feels impelled to spend. Often firms complain but they continue making their payments to get what they should get without such payments.

The truck drivers act unethically in demanding extra payments. Is it unethical to make such payments? If they are made secretly (and hence in a way not reportable for tax and other purposes), the answer would have to be yes, because of the duplicity, lying, and manipulation of funds that go along with it. But suppose that the payments are made openly and are reported as a legitimate expense of doing business?

Consider a rule that says that any such payment necessary for doing business is permissible provided that it is made publicly, at least in the sense that it is claimed as a legitimate cost of doing business. *Publicly* means that, at a minimum, it is entered on one's books as a business expense and is reported to the tax or other authorities.

It is hard to imagine any company publicly announcing that it is paying extortion and then defending its payments to its shareholders and to the public by citing this rule. But if it is both necessary and ethically permissible, why not? When nations engage in what they consider just wars, they publicly justify the killing, bombing, maiming, and destruction of the lives and property of the enemy. A reasonable way to test the morality of paying extortion in a corrupt environment is to see whether it is reported openly and whether it is justified as necessary because of the circumstances in which one operates. Publicity as a contributory justifying condition helps open the practice to public opinion and to possible governmental and intergovernmental action. Those who demand extortion or facilitating payments usually do not accept checks or anything else that can be traced, and they do not give receipts. Even if the extortionists explicitly impose the condition that the payment not be reported, a company of integrity (according to this rule) may only make payments if it can publicly report them.

Publicity is one of the most important tools in dealing with corruption of any sort, because it can arouse popular resistance and possibly generate sufficient support for governmental or (if necessary) international action. The INFACT boycott against the Nestlé Corporation is an example of how publicity mobilized an international public reaction that finally brought about desired changes in Nestlé's policies and led to the development and adoption of international guidelines for the advertising and sale of infant milk substitutes.

Protection payments to those who would do one harm if they were not paid are extortion payments. Such payments are unfair to those forced to pay, and they also encourage the extortionist to extort from others. But since such payments are unfair primarily to those who pay, the payers' acceptance of such harm does not directly affect others. It is clearly a greater evil to demand extortion than to pay it. The harm those who pay extortion do indirectly by supporting the practice can be offset by the good done by making the payment public and so (indirectly) undermining the practice.

In general, large companies are less subject to extortion than small businesses. They are better able to withstand threats and better able to protect themselves, if government is unwilling or unable to protect them. To the extent that they can help shield smaller businesses from harm, they make the atmosphere better for all.

The fight against crime syndicates is properly a function of state power. But where such power is not used or is ineffective, large corporations can help by doing what they can within the limits of the law. Moral imagination comes into play. It is not out of place for corporations to organize small competing businesses to stand up against a syndicate. It is in the self-interest of all to clean out corruption from an industry.

A government should protect businesses and individuals against extortion. It cannot legally allow illegal payments. Publicity will put pressure on the government to take action; and justice will require that it take action not against the person who is subjected to extortion and who honestly reports it, but against the extortionist.

Since corruption breeds corruption, competing with integrity in a corrupt environment is costly. The cost is both external and internal. If a company acts unethically, it should not be surprised if its employees get the message that acting unethically is acceptable. But even if the company acts with integrity, an atmosphere of corruption may adversely influence employees. Corrupt employees may sell company goods and pocket the proceeds; they may get kickbacks, steal or embezzle money, sell trade secrets, or provide keys to warehouses. Clearly, companies are allowed to take needed countermeasures in these instances, while respecting the rights of employees as persons. A corrupt firm will exploit its workers, try to mislead its customers, take advantage of them, provide them with inferior goods, and substitute poorer-quality materials for those originally advertised or promised. The list is endless. An employee with integrity will refuse to take part in such activities or even to work for such an employer. If all employers are corrupt—a highly unlikely scenario, since business would soon grind to a halt if they were—the employee might have to settle for the least bad situation, comparable to the Colombian farmer who plants coca. The solution is to change the system, using joint action, publicity, and any other possible means and strategies.

If a firm's policy or practice threatens serious harm to others, an employee is obliged to do what he or she can to prevent such harm. The employee may be able to do nothing. In a society with investigative media or with an effective government, employees are ethically required to blow the whistle on the firm (that is, go public with the information) if the threatened harm is serious, if the employee has exhausted all internal channels to bring about the change, if the employee has evidence of the threatened harm, and if there is a good chance that going public will diminish the harm.[20] The effectiveness of whistle-blowing is greatly diminished in a corrupt society. The rule still holds, but the conditions that make the rule into an actual obligation are less likely to be met.

Situations of corruption are often situations of quasi-anarchy and sometimes of unrestrained power. The lack of effective legal constraints and other background institutions—such as organized public opinion; consumer, environmental and workers' groups; and investigative media—make ethical guidelines all the more pressing in this area. The absence of adequate regulations and agreements points up the need for an interim set of guidelines, for international agreements, and for actions by multinationals and by nations to help provide structures that will promote ethical actions by multinational corporations.

8

Doing Business in Central and Eastern Europe, the Former USSR, and China

A sealed truck carrying toxic waste crosses the western Polish border. It drives to a small Polish town and dumps its contents in the local landfill. A Western multinational corporation has solved its problem of where and how to dump its toxic waste. The town receives hard currency, which it desperately needs to start up a local industry to provide employment for residents. No laws have been broken, since no laws preclude or regulate the disposal of toxic waste in the community. But the local landfill has no special facilities for handling toxic waste. The waste will seep into the soil and eventually make its way to ground water and rivers. Wittingly or unwittingly, the town is subjecting its population to serious danger. Both the people in the town and the multinational have taken part in a voluntary transaction. Is the transaction ethically defensible?

The breakup of the Communist bloc, the overthrow of Communist regimes in Central and Eastern Europe and the former Soviet Union, and the inclination of China toward privately owned enterprises, whatever its position on democracy and civil rights may be, have led American businesses to turn some of their attention eastward. The North-South business axis has quietly been downgraded to second, third, or fourth place. The countries of South America and Africa are now less attractive markets than are Central and Eastern Europe. The former Soviet Union and China are potentially gigantic markets, desperately in need of goods. They are unable to supply their people with what they need, much less with what they would like to have. The result is not only a shifting of attention, but also a shifting of resources and investments. Multinationals are anxious to take advantage of the opportunities. The situation is ripe for profits and for exploitation. Can a company interested in acting with integrity avoid the pitfalls and ethical disasters that accompanied the entry of multinationals into the LDCs to the South? Will our ethical guidelines and strategies help?

Central and Eastern Europe

Poland, Czechoslovakia, Hungary, former East Germany, Bulgaria, Romania, Albania, and the various states in what used to be Yugoslavia have all thrown off their Communist governments or have at least made the Communist Party just one of the legal parties in their countries. All have reconsidered the Marxist prohibition against private ownership of the means of production. Since the state is no longer the sole owner of the means of production, private ownership is possible. Exactly what that ownership will be like is not yet totally clear and is likely to vary somewhat from country to country.[1] Yet most of those countries will allow foreign firms to establish production and distribution facilities either on their own or as joint ventures with the local government or local entrepreneurs. Some will be anxious to sell enterprises wholly or in part to foreign investors.

For decades Yugoslavia had a mixed economy, with some private ownership of the means of production and with economic experiments in cooperative ownership and economic self-management. Its states thus enter the new period with more free-market experience than do some other countries. But it is also torn by antagonism and differences among its many nationalities. Former East Germany is unique among the former Eastern Bloc countries. Since it has been integrated with the Federal Republic of Germany, it can rely on a set of background institutions developed by West Germany to mitigate prospective abuses to which countries such as Poland and Czechoslovakia are still open. Even so, former East Germany faces many serious problems involving property and property rights, worker entitlements, and other issues that its neighbors also face.

The countries of Central and Eastern Europe all offer multinationals an inexpensive workforce. Their standard of living is well below that of the United States and of Western Europe, and their pay scales are very low in comparison with those in the West. Moreover, the workforces in these countries are already accustomed to industrial productive practices, contain skilled as well as unskilled labor, are reasonably well educated, and are in several ways easier to work with than workers in less developed countries. The former Eastern Bloc countries share a European heritage and culture, have been through the industrial revolution, and are ready to experience the industrial and productive development they were unable to achieve under Communist rule. They will nonetheless need retraining after having lived for forty years in a society that guaranteed employment regardless of the quality of work, tolerated rampant absenteeism, and accepted poor-quality goods.

The countries of Central and Eastern Europe are not industrially less developed countries. But from the perspective of free enterprise, they are in some ways as open to exploitation as an LDC is. They urgently need hard currency, in the form of loans and investment capital, that they can only get from the developed industrial countries—especially Western Europe, the United States, and Japan. Their great need means that they cannot bargain from a position of equality. They are economically feeble and hence vulnerable.

The countries of Central and Eastern Europe also resemble less developed countries in their absence of appropriate background institutions. These countries have the remnants of a vast structure of background institutions that were geared to socialism. All productive property was government-owned. All workers were government employees and had guaranteed jobs. All citizens received medical care, retirement pensions, and social security packages. The government subsidized housing and the everyday staples of life. Although the standard of living was not very high, everyone was guaranteed better-than-subsistence living conditions. Since no one could be fired, however, few incentives existed to impel people to work to their capacity. The law forbade employment (and exploitation) of individuals by other individuals.

The overthrow of Communism as an ideology has opened up the possibility of free enterprise—which envisages private ownership of the means of production, employment of people by other people rather than by the state, disparities in wealth, the loss of job security, the threat of unemployment, the potential loss of social benefits, possible exploitation, and a lack of controls on the inefficiencies of the market, including market failures and market abuses. Even people who claim that the market is self-regulating know that the market always operates in a certain sociopolitical context. It has tendencies toward exploitation of the weak, toward the formation of monopolies, toward unfair practices, and toward failure to internalize pollution costs. Inflation is a worry, as is unemployment and the loss of many of the social securities workers enjoyed under socialism. The countries themselves face problems. Multinationals that operate in these countries must face them as well.

A free-market economy develops best within a democratic framework and through democratic institutions that the countries of Central and Eastern Europe lack. Each country still has to devise a democratic form of government and establish background institutions adequate to manage a free-market economy.[2] In the absence of such institutions, the countries may be subject to the worst abuses of capitalist development,[3] unless multinationals apply ethical restraints and help foster the development of adequate background institutions to make conditions of competition fair.

The story of dumping toxic wastes in Poland illustrates the kind of abuses Eastern Europe may face. Poland has not yet developed restrictions on how private enterprise may handle toxic wastes, and few restrictions existed in the past on how public enterprises handled such waste. Yet importing toxic waste and dumping it into unprotected landfills clearly endangers the health and lives of many people, even if it solves the problem of toxic waste disposal for the Western firms and provides a source of hard currency for the Poles. The Western firms may claim that they are not dumping the waste, but are simply paying to have it disposed of. Yet they know, or should know, that it is being disposed of in a way that harms people; and they cannot escape ethical responsibility for their acts. Poles profiting from the practice may claim that what they are doing is not legally prohibited. But they know, or should know, the dangers to which they are exposing others; and they, too, cannot escape ethical responsibility for their acts. The victims are the innocent people harmed by the toxic waste.

Insofar as the countries of Central and Eastern Europe lack adequate background institutions to temper the abuses to which unrestrained capitalism is prone, they resemble LDCs. The situation is exacerbated by the official corruption that peermeated so much of the Communist bureaucracy and that infected everyday life as well.

When the Communist regimes were overthrown in Eastern Europe, the people in each country reacted against the abuses and corruption of the regimes they overthrew. Throughout the Eastern Bloc the governments were corrupt. Although equality was the official rule, Communist Party and state officials had acquired great privileges and often great wealth. They abused their power and gained their privileges at the expense of the ordinary people, who knew of the abuses before the governments were deposed, although they did not always know how extensive the abuses were. The system led to the corruption of bureaucrats who controlled all important decisions. Bribery became a way of life. People who wished to get things done learned how to get around legal prohibitions, restrictions, rules, and laws. This was true of managers seeking materials they needed to run their factories and of individuals seeking soap or a better cut of meat or whatever they needed that was in short supply.

A dual morality developed: a personal morality that governed family and personal interactions; and a public (and widely ignored) morality that was supposed to govern public life. An acceptable public morality, with concomitant respect for law and public institutions and officials, will take years to develop.[4]

Our discussion of how to operate ethically in a society with a corrupt government is relevant to Central and Eastern European countries that are emerging from a similar background situation. The new governments are still finding their way and are not effectively controlling the negative aspects of free enterprise. They have scarcely had time to pass needed legislation, much less to develop techniques for enforcing it. Remnants of old customs persist: distrust of government, circumvention of regulations, and an underground economy.

These countries lack not only legal background institutions but also the informal and private institutions, customs, and traditions that the developed industrial countries of the West have developed over time. Americans grow up faced with the choice of products that competition has fostered. They are used to comparing products. They know that there are differences in quality; that price does not always represent quality; that in some items the differences are superficial and make little difference, while in others they are important. Choosing among different brands or makes of the same kind of commodity is second nature to Americans. It is completely foreign to most Central and East Europeans. They have grown up in an economy of scarcity. Since all goods were government-made, they tended to be of roughly equal quality. Since goods were most often in short supply, buyers did not do comparison shopping. They bought what was available when it was available.

Not only does this make a difference in the nature of the Central and Eastern European customer, it also means that such things as consumer unions that compare goods and consumer protection groups that represent the interests of consumers have not been developed. Some checks on producers that Americans take for granted and that help keep the marketplace fair do not exist in Central and Eastern Europe. This leaves open opportunities for exploitation of the consumer, for taking unfair advantage of the buyer, and for the worst aspects of capitalism to become rampant.

The same is true in many other areas. Americans have learned to be wary of the dangers of borrowing money. Most Central and Eastern Europeans have not yet learned about the pitfalls of individual credit cards—the excessive interest rates that accompany them if not controlled by state regulation, and the ease with which one's goods can be repossessed for failure to make timely payments.

The switch from government-owned means of production to private ownership is also fraught with problems and potential abuses. One involves the question of justice in acquiring land or factories or businesses. Clear title is often lacking, in which case justice may require weighing competing claims. A second problem involves wages and benefits, and the extent to which former arrangements and expectations should be honored. A third involves the means necessary to keep competition fair and to secure a level playing field for all.

Given this very complex and relatively open situation, what ethical guidelines apply? First, any company that wishes to operate with integrity in Eastern Europe must be conscious that it is entering into an ethically delicate area. The two sides differ enormously in experience and power, and multinationals cannot simply assume that deals will be made on the basis of equal bargaining power and knowledge. In Central and Eastern Europe, a company abuses its power if it knowingly takes advantage of the lack of knowledge and experience of those with whom it deals; it acts unethically if it uses its superior knowledge and power to the detriment of those with whom it negotiates; and it acts as it should not if it cooperates in the exploitation of the people or the country by citizens of that country. One can certainly try to make as good a deal as possible within the limits set by ethical norms. But one cannot ethically make some deals, such as the one involving the dumping of toxic waste.

The first guideline governing multinational corporations in less developed countries, "Do no direct intentional harm," applies to all companies operating anywhere. It thus applies to multinationals operating in Central and Eastern Europe, where it is the key norm.

What of the second guideline, that American multinationals should produce more good than harm for the host country? That norm does not apply across the board to MNCs operating in all countries. It does not apply, for instance, to American MNCs operating in other developed countries. The second guidelines is founded on awareness of the great disparity between developed countries and LDCs and of the dependence of LDCs on developed countries—a situation for which the latter bear some responsible. Neither condition clearly applies in the Central and Eastern European situation. Conditions in general are better in Central and Eastern Europe than in the LDCs, the infrastructure is more developed, the culture more nearly resembles that in the United States, the dependency—if it exists in any sense other than that they are in economic need—is not a result of anything the industrially developed countries have done to them. It is in the long-term interest of the advanced industrialized countries that Central and Eastern Europe develop, that this region produce goods useful to the Western countries, and that its markets be open to Western goods. The second guideline is a special one for special situations and does not clearly apply in the Central and Eastern European context.

The third guideline also applies less forcefully to Central and Eastern European countries than to LDCs, because the former are sufficiently developed that MNCs will not be able to use them simply as sources of raw materials, as MNCs did use the colonies and still use some LDCs.

Guideline four, that the MNCs respect the human rights of their employees, clearly applies and is extremely important.

The fifth guideline requires respect for the local culture. It is not a crucial norm for Central and Eastern Europe because their cultures are more like that of the United States than are, for instance, the cultures of many African nations. Free enterprise does not threaten Central and Eastern European cultures in the same way, since they practiced free enterprise prior to the end of World War II. There is less ethical danger of doing harm in this area, although from an economic point of view remaining conscious of cultural differences is frequently important to business success. The fear of some people in Central and Eastern Europe that title to all their best resources and industries might end up in foreign hands is one that each country must face and regulate—and one that foreign investors should be conscious of—even if such concern does not preclude an individual acquisition or investment.

The rule requiring one to pay one's fair share of taxes applies everywhere. Abuses are less likely to occur here than they did in past dealings with less developed countries. Central and Eastern European countries may give tax incentives to attract MNCs, but they are probably sufficiently aware of the intricacies taxes and tax loopholes to be able to protect their own interests. If they do not currently have such knowledge, they will almost certainly develop it quickly.

Guideline seven is crucial. American multinationals should cooperate with the local government in the development and enforcement of just background institutions. Multinationals with integrity can take the lead by suggesting and helping to develop background institutions, including self-imposed industry-wide rules. They should not oppose unions and consumer groups, and they should not obstruct legislation that keeps competition fair for all. The action of General Motors in developing and implementing the Sulliven Principles in South Africa might serve as a model in this regard. Since multinationals from the developed countries know the ethical pitfalls of unrestricted trade, they should play a leadership role in preventing any repetition of the greatest abuses of unrestrained capitalism.

What approach to free enterprise will the countries of Central and Eastern Europe take? As the final decade of the twentieth century begins to unfold, they seem inclined toward some sort of social democracy, although it will no doubt take a different form in each country. The development of adequate background institutions may depend on how quickly these countries become members of the established trading groups, and whether they adopt wholesale any set of norms and isntitutions developed by those groups or their members.

Ethical norms have a greater rather than a lesser role to play in the period of transition from socialism, no matter what economic, social, and political forms compatible with free enterprise the Eastern European nations eventually develop and adopt.

Property

A distinguishing characteristic of socialism under Communist-type governments is the absence of private property—or more technically, of private ownership of the means of production. Personal property is of course allowed. But prohibited was private or individual ownership of land, factories, buildings, materials, and anything concerned with the production, distribution, and sale of goods. All such property was owned in theory by the people and in fact by the government.

Marxist theory claims that the initial accumulation of capital by the capitalist countries took place primarily through theft or plunder and thereafter through exploitation of workers—by paying them less than the value of what they produced. Communist regimes initially accumulated their capital by expropriating property from those who held it. Rarely was any compensation given. Industries were nationalized, land and buildings were seized, and their former owners were simply removed. All property thereafter was owned and controlled by the state.

The switch from state socialism of this type back to a free-enterprise market economy in which property can be privately held and businesses can be privately owned raises a number of thorny ethical issues. What is the status of property that the state seized without any compensation forty or more years ago from a private owner?[5] Does the original owner have any moral claim to it, and should the law recognize that claim? If such a claim is recognized, is it to the original value of the property, to the present value (whether higher or lower), to the original value plus interest, or to only a portion of the original value? Suppose that the property is a building that for the past forty years has housed a number of families who paid low, government-subsidized rates. Do those families have any claim on the property and any right to remain where they have lived for decades? If the property is returned to the original owner, is anything owed to the tenants, such as the right to live there if the original owner does not return? If such property is not returned to the original owner, who by right owns it? Should it go to the people who lived in it? If it is sold, should the money received go to the people who lived in it, to the state for use as government income, to the people in general according to some pattern of distribution, to the local community, or to some other group or entity?

Similar questions arise with respect to factories, shops, businesses, and enterprises of all kinds. Who owns them, who has a legitimate claim to the proceeds if they are sold, and who has the authority to sell them? Socialist law provided no answers, since the questions could not arise. With the change to a system that allows private ownership, these questions become pressing ones. Each country might handle the problem differently. Some are allowing former owners to claim their property; others are not. Some are considering selling factories to the workers or are giving the workers shares in it; others are selling them to the highest bidder. No matter what solution is adopted, the multinational faces moral pitfalls.

Foreign multinationals cannot decide whom property rightly belongs to in these countries. But multinationals are implicated in the decisions made. Mrs. Johnson's attempt to buy the Gdansk shipyards is a case in point. Since all property in Poland was government-owned, no one knew exactly which enterprise owned which facilities. Although this was not the reason for the eventual failrue of the deal, it was difficult to reach a legal determination of exactly what property constituted the shipyards and who had the authority to sell it. Nor was it clear who should receive the proceeds from such a sale.[6]

In some cases the local factory manager or a local bureaucrat is authorized to sell the factory. That person gets nothing from the transaction and has no incentive to get the best price. Such a seller may also encounter an opportunity to sell it below fair market value to a buyer who is willing to pay a commission or provide a kickback.[7] No firm with integrity would entertain such a deal. But if such deals are available, how does a company with integrity compete? The strategies we saw earlier still apply—publicity, agreement among potential buyers not to engage in such practices, support for laws that forbid such practices, and assistance and advice to those structuring sales to help them do so in a competitively fair way.

Investors want clear title to whatever property they buy. How to ensure that they have clear title is a legal matter and also an issue with ethical implications.

Getting clear title to a business or firm is only the first hurdle. If an MNC buys up a factory, does it have any obligation to the workers? They expected retirement payments or pensions from the state under the old system, sometimes through their place of employment. Who owes workers their retirement plans—the state, the factories, or the new owners? What is fair in such a situation?[8]

Many people in Central and Eastern Europe learned about capitalism from Marxist texts, which portrayed it as exploitative, rapacious, uncaring about people, and interested only in the accumulation of wealth. Absent from such texts were accounts of the restraints on unbridled capitalism that have developed in advanced industrial countries. Firms with integrity will not reinforce the Marxist stereotype, but will help the countries of Central and

Eastern Europe develop conditions in which both firms and workers can flourish, in which creative energy can be constructively channeled, and in which the social ideals championed by socialism can be realized through free enterprise. Firms of integrity are not charitable institutions; but they do act fairly, refuse offers made by unscrupulous middlemen or government agents, and decline to abuse their power by forcing agreements and contracts that damage the country or its people or that violate their human rights.

Advertising

Central and Eastern Europeans will have to adjust to aspects of free enterprise with which they are unfamiliar, just as Western and Japanese enterprises will have to accommodate themselves to idiosyncratic features of the Central and Eastern European market.

The ethical propriety of various practices and issues that have already been discussed and decided in the developed industrial countries may have to be reconsidered in the Central and Eastern European context. Advertising is a case in point.

The ethics of advertising in the United States can only be assessed in an American context, since what constitutes misleading advertising often varies depending on context, audience, and expectations.[9] Advertising aims to convey information and to induce people to buy a particular product made by a particular manufacturer. The advertiser is at least as interested in establishing brand recognition as in articulating any particular message or true statement about the product. Determining what is ethical in advertising involves considering the semantics of advertising, the place of metaphor and imagination, the type of audience addressed, the level of its sophistication, and the likelihood of deception. One must also consider possible misuses to which a product might be put, the need to explain dangers, and the necessity to provide all pertinent information.

Although the intended audience's levels of literacy, sophistication, and education remain pertinent, two other factors have precedence in an ethical appraisal of suitable advertising in Eastern Europe. First, since the people of Eastern European countries have not lived with advertising from their earliest years, as Americans have, they will have to learn how to read and evaluate ads critically. They are not used to competition among products, to the availability of many brands of the same product, and to the subtle differences that distinguish one brand from another. On the other hand, their cynicism with respect to government propaganda may counteract their lack of familiarity with ads; and their mistrust of what official sources or those in authority tell them may carry over into their reaction to advertising. Therefore, in Central and Eastern Europe, a company with integrity must determine how sophisticated its target audience is about advertising and how likely people are to be misled by something Americans would clearly see as exaggeration or metaphor.

In the United States the Federal Trade Commission and the Federal Communications Commission oversee advertising. Truth-in-advertising laws spell out standards to which ads must adhere. In a sense the government imposes on commercial advertising the amount of paternalistic oversight that the American people want. But no one has yet determined how much paternalism and government control of advertising the people of Central and Eastern Europe will want.

In this situation a firm with integrity must decide for itself what is ethically permissible, what does harm, and what misleads. Outright lying in advertising is unethical, just as it is in any other area of life; so is deception and misleading others intentionally. These are clearly disallowed by ethics. But it is not clear exactly what sorts of puffery (if any) would be recognized as such in any of the countries of Central or Eastern Europe and so would not be deceptive. U.S. authorities prohibit any ad that they believe would mislead or be misinterpreted by as little as 2 percent of the target audience. Is this an ethically mandatory percentage? Clearly not. How unfettered does a society want its advertising to be, and how much state regulation of commercial content does the society desire? Should it permit cigarette ads? Should such ads be restricted to certain kinds of media? Should every cigarette ad include a warning that smoking is dangerous to one's health? The United States and most developed industrial countries have already decided these issues, although not always in the same way. How will they be decided in Eastern Europe?

The line between what deceives and what does not depends not only on the pictures or the stated words but also on how these are perceived, on their semantic context, and on the sophistication and expectations of the target audience.

The ethical rules governing advertising cannot simply be transferred from the United States to Eastern Europe. They must be rethought and reformulated to fit the circumstances in which the advertising is used. The same is true of many other common practices that attend free enterprise, such as writing want-ads that are fair, identifying ingredients in packaged food products, using credit, providing guarantees and warranties, and accepting liability for the harm done by one's products. The basic rules to inflict no harm, to tell the truth, and to respect human rights hold across borders. But specific practices that cause no harm and are ethically permissible within one set of background institutions and popular assumptions may cause harm and therefore be unethical when placed against a different set of background institutions and a different set of assumptions.

Multinationals that wish to act with integrity must tread carefully in what will prove to be exciting and sometimes frustrating opportunities for both sides.

Exploitation

At the heart of the Marxist critique of capitalism is the charge that one individual exploits another. Because exploitation was considered inherent in the hiring of workers by the owners of the means of production, private ownership was banned in Communist countries. The demise of Communism signals the demise of the ban on private ownership and on the hiring of employees by private owners. But many in Central and Eastern Europe still have deeply entrenched feelings against exploitation, and they consciously want to avoid its dangers.

Exactly what constitutes exploitation becomes a key question. In classical Marxism exploitation consists of the owners' paying their workers less than the value of what they produce. By buying the labor power of the worker for a fixed sum, the owners can force them to work more hours than are needed for them to earn (that is, produce equivalent value for) their pay.[10] The additional value they produce by their labor is the fruit of what amounts to unpaid labor. It constitutes surplus value over and above what they are paid, and it is equivalent to the owner's profit. Unless the owner obtained more from the workers than he or she paid them, there would be no economic incentive for ownership and no reason for the owner to employ the workers. Hence, exploitation is a necessary part of wage labor, which is a necessary part of capitalism. By getting rid of private ownership of the means of production, Communist states claimed to ensure that all the wealth produced by the workers would revert to them—either through direct remuneration or through the benefits they received from the government out of the proceeds it gained by selling the products the workers made.

Several Central and Eastern European countries previously allowed small private enterprises, run by family members or by a few workers cooperatively. Today, despite the acceptance of free enterprise, it remains unclear what will be considered exploitation. The hiring of individuals by other individuals or by privately owned firms will certainly be permitted, even on a large scale. Yet some notion of exploitation will likely persist, as will strong cultural feelings against exploitation.

In the West exploitation is not a widely discussed concept; and except among Marxist critics, it is not considered an essential feature of wage labor. Rather, exploitation tends to be equated with paying barely subsistence wages, or with taking advantage of workers through evasion of legal responsibilities, poor working conditions, absence of health or retirement plans, long hours, and other abusive treatment.

Exploitation carries with it a negative ethical connnotation, although scholars debate whether Marx actually condemned exploitation (in his terms) as inherently unethical or unjust. The different points of view and the different traditions with respect to what constitutes exploitation make this a potentially contentious issue in Central and Eastern Europe. The issue in relation to hiring and compensating employees is one of fairness and justice. The problem of exploitation is a prime instance in which determining what is fair should be done by ascertaining what all parties to the practice agree is fair, with each having an equal role in the ultimate determination.

Still unclear is the sort of safety net that the new governments of the Central and Eastern European nations will devise for their people to replace the very large net that protected them under socialist governments. For forty years the workers of these countries have had free education and medical care; they have had state-supplied pension plans, subsidized housing and food, and price controls on most items of everyday necessity. Although goods were generally in short supply, everyone was poor together, and no one starved. How are the expectations of people who were raised under this system to be met? Must business now provide what the state previously provided?

The standard joke among workers in Central and Eastern Europe was that the workers pretended to work and the state pretended to pay them. Yet the workers were used to job security, to liberal sick leave, to time off from work to shop and stand in lines for the scarce necessities of life, to childcare and extended maternity leave and the right to return to a guaranteed job as much as three years later, and to controlled inflation and indexed wages. The demise of socialism brought the demise of many of those benefits. Capitalism does not guarantee full employment and freedom from inflation. Indexing is incompatible with market determination of wages and prices. But is it fair and wise to wipe out all the benefits socialism provided, some of which constitute goals that American workers are hoping someday to achieve?

Medical care is a case in point. Under socialism everyone was entitled to free medical treatment. What health benefits should an MNC offer its workers when it takes over or starts a company in Central and Eastern Europe? Should it provide as few benefits as possible until the law or workers' demands and strikes force it to increase them? Will a company of integrity approach the Central and Eastern European employment market as did the industrial giants of the nineteenth century? Will it repeat the history of sweatshops and unsafe working conditions that stigmatized capitalism in its earlier period? A company of integrity must answer "No." What is appropriate must be negotiated with the countries and the workers in question. But justice requires companies to bargain fairly, even if they are in the more powerful position. And equity between companies argues for some agreement on what any company should provide in the way of minimum benefits.

Precluding gross exploitation is a key part of labor legislation; but even in the absence of such laws, a company of integrity must formulate its compensation policy in light of the needs of its workers, their previous expectations, and their justifiable demands.

Social Democracy

Americans should not assume that the countries of Central and Eastern Europe wish to adopt the American system of free enterprise and social institutions. The United States is not their model—even though its standard of living may be.

Socialists have a long tradition of claiming their system's ethical superiority to capitalism. Typically they compared the ideal of socialism with the realities of capitalism, to the latter's detriment. Socialism stands for equality. It aims to minimize the discrepancy between the rich and the poor, to provide all members of society with social benefits, and to guarantee their welfare. In Central and Eastern Europe socialism was unable to deliver what it promised. It was open to abuses that the theory did not encompass. Yet socialism's ideals remain attractive—considerably more attractive than the image of unbridled and unprincipled individualism, or the possibility of failure, or the specter of unemployment and poverty in an otherwise rich and opulent society.

The socialist countries of Central and Eastern Europe lacked not only goods but also democracy. The price of relative equality was domination by a powerful and centralized Communist Party. Although it was supposed to act in the name of the people and for their good, the Communist Party too often served only its own interests and those of its members. Direct democracy—rule by the people for the good of the people—was a central ideal of socialist theory, but it has been better realized in the Western democracies than in the socialist democratic republics.

Some Central and Eastern Europeans are tending toward a type of social democracy that gives continuity to their values and tradition. They are attempting to realize in fact the best of what they strove for in theory. Their lack of experience in joining those values with a free-market economy poses two dangers for them and places some special responsibility on MNCs that wish to profit from the opportunities present in that part of the world.

The first danger is an unrestricted popular democracy in which an absolute majority can tyrannize the minority. Majority rule has already endangered minority groups in several Central and Eastern European countries. The United States tempers majority rule with guarantees for the rights of minorities. Minorities may still suffer—as the history of various racial minorities in the United States shows—but legal and formal guarantees, such as the Bill of Rights and civil rights legislation, help protect them.

Most Central and Eastern European countries have been so taken with democracy and with the power of the people that they have not yet instituted legislative checks on democracy nor sufficiently guaranteed the rights of minorities. In such a situation, multinationals must respect the human rights of all, even if the local society fails to do so.

Multinationals must tread a fine line between respecting the values of the host countries in which they operate and respecting the rights of all its workers. American businesses generally recognize the right of workers to equal opportunity for employment and for advancement. A company of integrity will adopt the same policy abroad.

The second danger is that the people will demand and legislate more than the economy is able to supply. The present emphasis on social democracy indicates that the countries of Central and Eastern Europe are unwilling to discard the social safety net that socialism provided. But they may find it difficult to finance the net they desire. It is one thing to legislate benefits; it is another to fund them. These countries must raise revenue through taxes, and they will expect the multinationals to bear their fair share. Multinationals will be in a position to drive hard bargains, to seek tax incentives and benefits, and to provide as little as they can in the way of employee benefits. Integrity requires each company to pay its fair share of taxes and to provide benefits compatible with its earning a reasonable return on its investment. Legislating benefits is not necessarily the ideal, but it is one way of guaranteeing a level playing field for all and of ensuring that all companies share the burden of providing appropriately for workers' security.

Competition

Just as the Central and Eastern European countries must learn how to control democracy, they must also learn how to control competition—something with which they have little experience.

Competition promotes efficiency and spurs people on to do their best. A racing competition reveals who is the fastest runner: each contestant must run as fast as possible, and the incentive to beat the others helps each one do this. But the race only works if the conditions are fair for all. If one or more contestants are given an advantage, the race is not fair. In any sport, the rules of the game set equal starting conditions for all. Usually there is only one winner. Although all who take part in the game may benefit somehow from the competition, the possibility of winning also implies the possibility of losing.

Economic competition is similar. There are winners and there may be losers. Ideally all who compete find themselves better off afterward than they would have been without competition. Efficiency is achieved when all do their best and try to outdo their competitors by producing better goods, by producing them at a lower price, by finding new ways to do whatever has to be done, or by satisfying whatever needs have to be satisfied. Two aspects of the game analogy need underlining. The first is that, just as a race determines the fastest runner only if the conditions of competition are fair, so a market is efficient only if the conditions of competition are fair. The rules of the game governing any sport are set out in advance. The rules of economic competition similarly need to be preset. Otherwise, unregulated competition can lead to practices that may make the "winner" very rich, but at great cost to the general social good and to other competitors.[11]

The aim of economic competition is not to create individual fortunes, even if that prospect motivates some competitors. The aim of competition within an economic system is to help the society achieve more of what it wants. The rules determining what is and is not allowed set the conditions for fair competition, and they should be structured so that the society benefits. Unbridled competition is not necessarily beneficial to a society, even if some individuals benefit greatly from it.

The second aspect involves a fundamental difference between competition in the economic realm and competition in sports: sports is a game and economics is not. Losing a game does not mean having one's life fall apart. We cannot choose to enter the economic realm or not to enter it; in effect, we are already in it, simply by existing. A just society ensures that those who cannot compete are otherwise taken care of—not simply ignored and abandoned to die. Unlike losing in a game, failing in the economic realm can have disastrous consequences in all the other aspects of one's life. Failure is built into a competitive economic system; therefore, a just system provides some sort of safety net for those who fail economically.

Multinationals are masters at the art of competition. They have the resources to play by whatever rules are set down and to do well when no rules exist. Their expertise in competition and in producing and marketing their products or services can serve as models for Central and Eastern Europe. Where few or no rules currently govern competition, multinationals can introduce the worst aspects of capitalist development, or they can lead the way in helping develop rules that make competition fair.

A company with integrity emphasizes the positive rather than the negative aspects of competition. It competes by striving to produce high-quality goods—a phenomenon little known in much of Central and Eastern Europe, where state monopolies typically produced shoddy goods. It competes by providing attentive and responsive customer service—a new concept in Central and Eastern Europe, where service has tended to be grudging and surly. It competes by developing employee loyalty through its offer of meaningful work in decent and pleasant conditions—ideals that socialism enunciated but rarely achieved. It competes by making serious commitments to preserve and protect the environment, to recycle wherever possible and cost-effective, to modernize and improve the efficiency of its productive processes, and to develop new products that serve human needs. The countries of Central and Eastern Europe have overthrown socialized central planning and a command economy to benefit from these aspects of competition and of the free market. Companies with integrity can demonstrate how the free-market system at its best works for the benefit of workers, consumers, investors, and society as a whole. In this way multinationals can compete successfully and with integrity at the same time. Competition need not and should not be negative and destructive.

A company with integrity does not try to gain a monopoly or to use monopoly power to the disadvantage of customers and employees, even if no law prohibits it from doing so. It welcomes and promote fair competition and works to help keep it fair. It supports regulations that level the playing field, preclude special treatment of or favors to select firms, and defend the rights of workers and consumers to organize and promote their legitimate interests.

Many people in Central and Eastern Europe fear the predatory aspects of capitalism and worry about price gouging. They have little experience with pricing, since centralized planning set prices more-or-less arbitrarily. Nor do they understand profit, which for forty years Marxism told them is theft, or the owners' usurpation of value produced by and rightfully belonging to the workers. They have no practical acquaintance with the capitalist notion of a fair or just rate of profit. Many ordinary people fear that profit rates will now rise to the highest level that the market or demand for scarce goods will bear. Multinationals should be aware that they face this kind of customer; yet their profits may legitimately be proportionate to the risk involved in operating in a largely undefined context. A company with integrity will realize that its long-term interests are not best served by seeking maximum short-term profits immediately. Because of their financial strength, multinationals are in an excellent position to offset fly-by-night predators who may try to charge exorbitant prices for scarce goods, thus fueling the worst fears of consumers.

Neither unrestrained democracy nor unrestrained competition will last long in Central and Eastern Europe. The negative effects of both will soon become evident, and restraints will necessarily follow. Multinationals will serve their own interests and those of the host country if they help it develop the restraints needed to keep competition fair and to respect the rights of all.

The Former USSR

The breakup of the Soviet Union in 1991 provides opportunities for multinationals similar to those afforded by the emancipation of Central and Eastern Europe. Even before the secession of the Baltic republics, McDonald's set an example: it brought in its own supply lines, rules for serving food, training program, and American ways.[12] No Soviet complaints ensued about the introduction of American customs to Moscow or about the resulting change in the city's way of life. The long lines of Muscovites waiting for a Big Mac proved that the opposite was the case.

Most of the things said earlier about doing business with and in Central and Eastern Europe apply equally to the Soviet Union. How business is conducted will depend on what the former Soviet republics allow in place of or alongside government ownership of the means of production. At the beginning of the 1990s, the economies of Russia and of most of the other republics remained highly structured, bureaucratic, and centrally controlled.

Different background institutions and different expectations in the various republics will necessitate independent evaluation of some similar practices. The ethical issues that arise when firms compete in corrupt locales are likely to give way to concerted pressure by outside companies that object to working under such conditions.

The major difficulty in Central and Eastern Europe is the absence of appropriate background institutions, which will take time to develop. That difficulty is exacerbated in the former Soviet republics, most of which spent more than seventy years under the centralized control of the Communist Party. The people have no tradition of free enterprise; they have an ingrained negative attitude toward capitalism and a deep-rooted resentment of inequality. Unless the republics give up Soviet-type socialism and state control, entrepreneurs will find themselves restricted—probably overly so.

The notion of exploitation may well play an even greater role in the countries of the former Soviet Union than in the countries of Central and Eastern Europe.[13] The desire for egalitarianism, even if it means keeping people at the level of the least well-off, is deeply ingrained in Soviet society. People strongly oppose significant differences in wealth. Those who have profited from cooperatives and other free-market experiments have often suffered at the hands of their fellow citizens. They have found themselves taxed out of business and ostracized by those who have less. Those who succeed are automatically suspected of being either unethical exploiters or former Communist Party officials who continue to wield the corrupt power and influence they formerly had. In neither case are they respected.

This popular reaction is in part substantiated by entrepreneurs who claim that, under the existing circumstances, the only way to build up capital is through exploitation. The claim that the objective and subjective conditions in Russia are such that ethical business practices are impossible—if it is to be believed—makes the future of capitalism in Russia seem bleak indeed.[14] Clearly MNCs of integrity have a positive educative role to play in this regard.

Dealing with the former republics of the Soviet Union will continue to be difficult because of their different economic systems, their lack of hard currency, the existing regulations on both sides that prevent or hinder trade, the lack of adequate precedents and agreements between people who have grown up in an atmosphere of mutual distrust and fear, the history of unsuccessful attempts to do business in the Soviet Union, and the new decentralized situation.

Unforeseeable ethical issues will undoubtedly emerge; but the general guidelines and strategies developed heretofore should help multinationals move toward ethically justifiable negotiation, contracts, and profitable business activity within the various republics that once formed the Soviet Union.

China

Mainland China poses a different set of problems because the Chinese government has continued to take a repressive political position vis-a-vis free enterprise, freedom of political expression, and private entrepreneurs. Its attitude toward Western business has cooled from its cordial peak in 1988, even though it still seeks Western tourist dollars and claims to want more investment from Western and Japanese firms.

Few, if any, Western firms that have tried to do business in China have made a profit. Yet the potential market of over 1 billion Chinese consumers is attractive to many firms that are willing to lose money in the short run to get their foot in the door.

With a repressive regime still in power as of the beginning of 1993, the first ethical issue foreign businesses must consider is comparable to the one businesses faced in South Africa: can a business legitimately operate in China, since it will be allowed to do so only to the extent that it strengthens the entrenched government? No Sullivan Principles or other developed set of ethical guidelines can safeguard a firm from indirectly harming the Chinese people while helping the Chinese rulers. Yet a plausible defense can be made on behalf of such service-oriented firms as McDonald's, Pizza Hut, and Kentucky Fried Chicken, all of which are lauded both by the general population and by the Chinese Communist Party.[15] It is dubious whether any such justification can be made for multinational banks or financial institutions or for many manufacturing firms.

Some readers may consider this judgment to impose Western moral norms on China. But as we have observed, a company that wishes to act with integrity must act in accord with its own inviolable principles; it cannot change them to match different political climates, and it cannot adopt the ethics of repressive regimes as a justification for operating in such countries.

Documentation has shown that China uses forced labor in producing some of the goods it exports.[16] The United States does not allow such goods to enter its borders. Ethically, multinationals can no more purchase, use, or sell such products than can anyone else. To do otherwise condones and reinforces an unethical practice. Fearing to offend the leaders of a large and important country and hoping that someday they may change scarcely justify failing to do what is ethically required or doing what is ethically prohibited. When the leaders change the practice, the problem of importing goods made with forced labor will cease to exist. Meanwhile, multinationals have an obligation to ensure that the Chinese products they purchase (most often through Hong Kong) are not made by forced labor.

How far are firms required to go in determining whether products obtained through Hong Kong were made by forced or slave labor? Can they ever be certain that the goods they receive are not tainted in this way? The answer to the latter question is probably not, until the practice has been eradicated. The answer to the former depends on a wide range of circumstances that determine what is possible. Certainly a firm of integrity will not simply ignore the question on the pretext that the source of the goods it buys is not its concern or is not determinable beyond any shadow of a doubt. It must take available reports seriously and use whatever means it can to ensure that it is not buying tainted goods. It must refuse to buy such goods, even if the price is attractive. In addition, concerned firms can join forces to establish guidelines that address the issue, to pressure Hong Kong transshippers into documenting the sources of their goods, and to encourage U.S., UN, and other national and international action to protest and promote change in the practice of using such labor. What is true with respect to China holds as well for any other country that uses slave or forced labor to generate the goods it produces and sells.[17]

When China does open its doors to business, Western and Japanese firms will have to decide whether China falls under the model of the less developed countries, of South Africa, of Central and Eastern Europe, or of the former republics of the Soviet Union—or whether it poses different and specific ethical issues that necessitate another approach. The decision will depend in part on whether China remains under Communist control and continues to have a centralized planned economy or whether it goes the way of most other formerly Communist countries and turns toward some version of free enterprise and a market economy.

No matter what its political climate may be, China is predominantly an agrarian country. The peasantry form a large portion of its burgeoning population. Although pockets of China are notable for budding (and presently restrained) entrepreneurs, most mainland Chinese have no experience with capitalism, with contemporary Western ways of doing business, with advertising, or with marketing strategies. The care required in order to avoid exploiting their lack of experience, to prevent others from exploiting them, and to avoid destroying an old and important culture exceeds that needed in the case of either Central and Eastern Europe or the former Soviet republics.

The guidelines for operating in a less developed country will almost surely apply, since China is such a country. But because of China's size, its Communist heritage, its resources, and its culture, MNCs operating there may well encounter new and unpredictable ethical issues.

Our guidelines and strategies were developed in response to actual and foreseeable ethical issues. New and unforeseen ethical issues will require rethinking of, modification of, and additions to these guidelines and strategies. But having once developed them, we have a base on which to build and models from which to start.

China, Central and Eastern Europe, and the republics of the former Soviet Union will enter into greater trade and monetary relations with Western Europe, the United States, Japan, and others. They may join trading groups that will help establish international background institutions for firms within those countries as well as for multinationals entering those countries. In the interim, as in the case of less developed countries, ethics will have a larger rather than a smaller role to play in international business with formerly Communist countries.

9

Doing Business with Japan and the European Community

Buy a Sony TV, a Toshiba computer, or a Nikon camera in the United States, and chances are you will pay less than the manufacturer's list price for the Japanese-made product. You will also pay less than Japanese consumers do, since until recently Japanese retailers uniformly charged the manufacturer's list price.[1] Some Japanese have asked whether the law is fair to them. American consumers should have no reason to complain, since they can get Japanese products at discount. But that law also prevented American discount chains from operating in Japan, which some American companies said restricted trade and was unfair to them. Even with the list-price law rescinded, other restrictions can cause delays of up to ten years in getting approval to operate in Japan.[2] Are such Japanese laws unfair to non-Japanese multinationals, and therefore unethical?

In several European countries, knocking a competitor's product is considered a form of unethical advertising. Given that belief, can an American multinational that believes such advertising is ethically unobjectionable (as it is widely considered to be in the United States) ethically use such ads in the countries in question? If there is no EC rule or law to the contrary, need an American multinational impose on itself a policy of refraining from running negative comparative advertisements throughout the EC? Need it do so only in countries whose populations believe such advertising unethical? Or need it not impose such restraint on itself, but simply operate in accord with its own ethical norms?

Unlike the situation in less developed countries and in countries newly emerging from Communist domination, Japan and the countries of the European Community are economically flourishing nations with well-developed arrays of background institutions that they continue to refine and implement.

The presence of developed background institutions places the advanced industrial countries on a par with one another. Each is capable of dealing with the others from a position of equality. Each country can protect its own interests. Each can control undesirable infiltration by the firms of other countries and can set limits on exploitation or other potentially harmful acts in which businesses might engage.

Obviously, the basic ethical rules apply in all of them, despite some differences in their particular cultures. Although the rule to do no direct intentional harm and the rule to respect the human rights of one's employees apply to multinationals from one developed country that operate in another developed country, other guidelines that we developed for firms operating in LDCs do not apply to the operations of American multinationals in Japan or Western Europe. The multinationals of one industrially developed country need not contribute to further development of the other developed countries in which they operate, nor need they benefit those countries in any special way.

Nonetheless, the business relations of the United States and Japan raise a number of ethical issues, while the integration of the European Community poses some special questions and raises some unique opportunities.

Japan

When the Japanese stock market went down in 1991, both foreign and Japanese investors suffered losses. That is the nature of the stock market. Some large Japanese investors did not have to bear their losses, however, because four brokerage firms reimbursed them for the difference between the investors' buying prices and the lower prices at which they sold.[3] In doing so, the brokerage firms broke no Japanese laws. Japanese laws forbid advance arrangements between a brokerage firm and a client guaranteeing that the client will not lose money. But the law does not preclude a brokerage house from simply giving its best customers money, even if the amount is equivalent to or greater than the client's losses. The generosity of brokerage firms to their best and largest Japanese customers does not necessarily hurt foreign and smaller Japanese investors. After all, the latter would have lost the same amount whether or not the brokerage firms reimbursed the large players. But although the practice is not illegal, is it unethical?

The disclosure of the paybacks was one of a series of scandals that rocked Japanese financial institutions in 1991.[4] Why it was a scandal and how it was handled indicate some of the differences between doing business in Japan and doing business in the United States, and the explanation raises the question of ethics in two very different societies.

Since no laws were broken, no one was brought to trial and no law suits were filed. Yet by way of apology to the Japanese people, Japan's Finance Minister and some of his high-level deputies announced that they were voluntarily taking 10 percent cuts in their salaries by way of atonement for not adequately overseeing the securities industry.[5] The cause for such self-imposed punishment was the Japanese public's indignation at the news that over $1 billion was involved in the paybacks. The clear implication is that, although the action was legal, the general public considered it improper. In the United States it would be viewed as unfair and therefore unethical.

Some Japanese commentators noted that the practice of such paybacks is not unusual in Japan and observed that, since it is not illegal, it had long been quietly accepted. What made the 1991 incident different—angering so many Japanese and feeding the media coverage—was the magnitude of the paybacks. They were so large that they forced many people to question how the brokerage firms operated, how they could afford to make such payments, whether they did so at the expense of smaller and foreign investors, and whether price manipulation and unfair insider trading were going on as well. Ultimately, the Japanese press was little impressed by the gesture of the Finance Minister and his deputies, given that the paybacks were not rescinded, the brokerage houses were not penalized, and the law was not changed.[6]

The fact that paybacks were a general practice in Japan and that their revelation in this instance caused such a furor indicate an important difference between Japanese society and American society. Common to both is a notion of fairness, to use the typically American term. The outrage shows that the Japanese public is not indifferent to being treated unfairly, even though it has tolerated some practices that give special advantages to large corporations. It has accepted the Japanese version of capitalism: the government helps certain large industries but not others, and usually not smaller firms; the country's high savings rate and low interest rates help the large firms rather than the many who save; and Japanese consumers pays more for Japanese products than do consumers in other countries for the same goods. At least until recently most Japanese seemed willing to accept all this.

Such tolerance is a result in part of the homogeneous and consensual nature of Japanese society. The Japanese people are willing to endure a certain amount of internal favoritism and of what to Americans might appear to be injustice or the bending of principle. They see it as the price of social harmony—a price they have traditionally been willing to pay. Public tolerance of such practices is often interpreted as being tantamount to public approval. But the reaction to the paybacks and to other seamy incidents such as the Lockheed bribes to government officials shows that the Japanese public does not accept the propriety of such practices on any large scale, and that public disclosure is a potent weapon in curbing excesses.

People in Japan and in the United States sometimes differ on what they consider ethical, on the work ethic each implicitly or explicitly espouses, on some of the ends to be achieved through taxation, and on various other social issues. Any American multinational operating in Japan must contend with such factors, because they influence the ethical judgments that Americans make about the Japanese and that the Japanese make about Americans. Central among them are issues of perceived fairness or justice. Since this is the case, a reasonable approach to justice would seem to suggest the need for negotiation. Each side has different laws, so individual firms acting alone are not likely to be able to resolve major differences. Broad issues can only be resolved by ethical displacement to the level of intergovernmental negotiation. In such negotiations one side cannot expect that the other to adopt its version of free enterprise. But each can be willing to accept less than that to which its view of justice says it is entitled. As the economies of both countries become more intertwined, each must be willing to change the way it does business somewhat to accommodate the other.

Japan has accused the United States of "Japan bashing" and claims that Americans are often prejudiced against the Japanese. In recent years Americans have similarly felt themselves attacked by Japanese authors and leaders, such as Akio Morita and Shintaro Ishihara in *The Japan That Can Say "No"*.[7] Each side has much to learn about the other and should respect the unfamiliar society in which each wishes to do business.

Although the question of who is number one is a matter of pride for both Americans and Japanese, it is not answerable. The obvious countering question is: number one with respect to what? After World War II the United States was the only major power that had not been devastated by the war. It was dominant in many areas, and in the forty-odd years since the war, it has grown into its role as a world power and a world leader. In the military realm it was the first nation with an atomic bomb. Soon the postwar world was divided between two military superpowers—the United States and the Soviet Union—and that division dominated most other considerations.

The United States was also the financial leader of the world, helping Western Europe and Japan rebuild. Its multinationals carried American business into the less developed countries of the world as well. With American business and influence came some of the better and worse aspects of American culture. English became the international language of business. In many respects one could have said that the United States was number one. That dominance has now been challenged in the economic realm by the Japanese, since the per capita income of Japan is now higher than that of the United States,[8] and since the Japanese have replaced the Americans to a considerable extent as the foremost creditors in the world. Is there an ethical dimension to this new role for Japan vis-a-vis the world and the United States?

The question of who is number one in which areas is not only a matter of national pride. Whether number one or number two in this area or that, being among the financial leaders of the world carries with it obligations as well as cause for pride. Americans and American multinationals were often in the past (and still are to some extent) seen as arrogant and self-serving; yet they are conduits of internationalization and have responsibilities as well as opportunities.

In a celebrated article Milton Friedman once claimed that the business of business was to make a profit, and that a corporation had no further obligations as long as it obeyed the law.[9] His claims have frequently been answered by commentators who argue that corporations have social and ethical responsibilities beyond those set by law.[10] But while many American businesses and multinationals have come to acknowledge social responsibilities beyond the law, Japanese firms have tended to follow the Friedman position. As a result they have received the same kind of criticism that was once reserved for American multinational corporations.

What are the ethical and social responsibilities of American multinationals in Japan or of Japanese multinationals in America? Frequently such multinational enterprises are joint ventures between a Japanese firm and an American firm. Sometimes they are independent companies.

In general the responsibility of any multinational from a developed countries operating in another developed countries is comparable to the responsibilities of domestic firms in that country. The claim of General Motors and others that they are citizens of each of the countries in which they operate is partly true. They are not quite citizens, because they are controlled by their home office and because they are free to leave their host country when conditions demand it. Moreover, as guests, they are usually restricted in the degree to which they can enter into the politics of the host country. Nonetheless, in many ways they are citizens: they pay taxes; they benefit from the educated labor pool and the developed infrastructure of the host country; and they interact with the communities in which they locate. To this extent they bear many of the same responsibilities as local firms.

Japanese firms operating in the United States have been criticized for carrying with them too much Japanese culture and for assimilating too little American culture. In part this is a function of the Japanese firms' carrying with them the Japanese notion of social responsibility, which is different from the American notion of social responsibility. In particular, Japanese firms tend to concentrate on the firm and its welfare, including the welfare of its workers. They do so by requiring great worker devotion to the firm, both during and after working hours. At the same time, they tend to ignore what in the United States are seen as a firm's broader social responsibilities and its proper interaction with the community.

These responsibilities are not legal obligations.[11] They are social responsibilities, and they may become ethical responsibilities, especially in times of crisis. What multinationals owe to the countries and communities in which they locate is similar to what local companies owe to their countries and communities. In the United States communities come to depend on resident firms for taxes. The communities provide housing for workers and may develop facilities—sewers, schools, police and fire departments—for the firms and their employees. Local businesses spring up. In the United States, local businesspeople typically participate in community affairs, join service groups, sponsor local athletics, and in general act as a resource for the community. Moreover, these ties are such that they cannot ethically be broken unilaterally without due regard for the effect that a plant closing, for instance, might have on the local community.

All of this and more is included in what it means to be a good corporate citizen in American terms. What it means to be a good corporate citizen in Japanese terms is often different. But the terms set by each society are the ones that the multinationals operating in these societies are expected to live up to. The obligation of multinationals in developed countries is to act like good corporate citizens and not like outsiders, even though to some extent they remain outsiders.

Being number one has traditionally brought with it special obligations. Those with much have a greater obligation to help the needy than those with little. Generosity is a fitting virtue for rich countries, as well as for rich firms.

The Japanese and Japanese firms are slowly learning what many people in other countries perceive as the obligations that attend success. Until recently, Japanese aid had been closely tied to returns of some sort to Japan. Aid for projects abroad would involve hiring a Japanese firm to carry out the project in the recipient nation. Giving unconditional aid, donating to local charities, and creating educational and cultural foundations for the benefit of the nations in which they operate—all with no strings attached—are relatively new activities for Japan and Japanese firms.[12] Social pressures encourage firms to engage in such activities, and some resentment may ensue if they do not do so. To some extent the Japanese have been living the experience of the "ugly American" after World War II.

The fact that multinationals operating in developed countries do not have the special obligations they have when operating in less developed countries does not mean they have no obligations. Just as guiding one's actions only by the law is insufficient for a local company that wishes to act with integrity, so it is insufficient for a multinational. Moreover, because it is seen as foreign, the multinational will be all the more resented if it does not live up to what is expected of all corporations in the local context. Relevant background institutions include not only laws but customs, expectations, social groups and pressures, and the many intermediary forces that operate in a society between the level of individuals and the level of government regulation and enforcement.

Any claim to being number one in any aspect of international life opens one up to constant scrutiny, raised expectations, envy, and criticism. That is a price of leadership in any area of human endeavor.

Three issues dominate American ethical discussions about Japanese–American business relations. The first is the claimed inaccessibility of Japan to American products and industries. The second is the alleged dumping of products by Japanese firms to seize market share. The third is the so-called buying of America by Japanese investors. These claims made by Americans have ethical import. In their turn the Japanese have criticized various aspects of American business; but until 1992, they typically did not state their criticisms as ethical complaints against the unfairness of American businesses toward them.[13] Rather, they have offered rebuttals to American charges or have criticized America's short-range thinking, the waning of American industriousness and leadership, America's unwillingness to save, and its consumerist mentality.[14]

The charges and criticisms on both sides indicate the need for continuing negotiations. The disagreements underline the fact that, in important respects, each country practices a different type of capitalism—a type related to the local government and to the social traditions in which it is embedded. Different notions of justice are at play, too. Negotiated agreements of a bilateral, multinational, and even global kind are clearly needed.

Closed vs. Open Markets

Because of the countries' many cultural differences and their different ways of doing business, many American firms in Japan rely on go-betweens who are familiar with Japanese ways and have contacts with Japanese corporate or government officials. Some firms employ "cultural brokers" to help guide them through unfamiliar waters. But American companies cannot avoid moral responsibility for their actions by claiming simply to have followed their broker's advice, if such advice led the company to engage in activities that by its own standards are unethical. Nor can it with impunity break such American laws as the Foreign Corrupt Practices Act. Although cultural brokers can be extremely useful in guiding one through important differences between American and Japanese etiquette, no "moral broker" can relieve corporations of moral responsibility for the actions they perform, whether these are done directly or through an agent acting for them. Nonetheless, such brokers might inform a company about what is and what is not considered just and appropriate by the Japanese.

Any discussion of the justness or unjustness of international trade between the United States and Japan takes place against a background of very important differences between the two countries, including differences in the way their economies work and in the way they do business. Both systems are ethically justifiable, taken by themselves.[15] In the United States free enterprise is king. Although the government is a huge employer, it does not enter directly into productive business activity. It is an enormous purchaser of goods, however, and government contracts are often highly prized. Defense industries have been criticized for joining with government to form a military-industrial complex, in which competition is minimal, so that government in effect supports certain large companies, and in which the prices are not set by the market but by the manufacturers.[16] In other areas government is a regulator of business although deregulation took place with a vengeance under the Reagan administration. Its deregulation of banks and savings-and-loan institutions proved to be a disaster, as the government retained liability while relinquishing control, costing taxpayers billions of dollars. On the whole the market plays an extensive and central role.

The relation of government to business in Japan is quite different. Although competition reigns in the lower echelons of Japanese business, the government singles out key firms and helps develop these as major exporting industries. The relation between these firms and government is very close, with the government financing and legislating to advance and protect the growth of these industries and to champion their interests in negotiations with other countries. The market thus plays a less central role.

The government's approach and involvement are different in the two cases. The relation in the United States—apart perhaps from defense and a few other such industries—tends to be one of some distance; and the primary function of the government is to keep competition fair and to serve as a mediator in disputes. Of course, the U.S. government also represents U.S.

interests in trade and other negotiations with other governments. But typically its role is to regulate industry rather than to work directly and openly with particular industries. The latter is the situation in Japan. Yet one is not ethically proper and the other ethically improper. Both are justifiable, even if one might criticize aspects of each arrangement. It is groundless to complain that the Japanese government is unethical because it supports Japanese business enterprises more actively than the American government supports American business enterprises. The claimed collusion of the Japanese government with Japanese business is a fact of the Japanese politico-economic system. If it gives Japanese firms certain advantages that American firms do not have, that does not make competition between them unfair.

Since the market plays a less central role for Japanese business than it does for American business, and since government direction and intervention play a more central role for Japanese business than for American business, the two are not ideally matched. What appears to Americans as unfair Japanese protectionism is the lack of American-style open and free markets. Some Japanese markets can be breached only by government-to-government negotiations. The Japanese are better geared for that than are the Americans, since they have permanent civil servants whose job is to work for Japanese interests. The Americans, more used to relying on the market, employ more-or-less itinerant negotiators who switch between business and government.

Nonetheless, what constitutes fair trading practices for each side is what both sides can agree to as fair.[17] Given the two different approaches, it is not surprising that agreements have been slow in coming. Moreover, since Americans are forced to negotiate rather than to rely on market forces, they are understandably frustrated at playing a relatively unfamiliar game with experts. Part of what they see as necessary to fairness is a change in the Japanese system. It is unlikely that the Japanese will accept any such changes without some compensatory change in the American system. And clearly changes in systems are difficult to achieve.

Japan's lack of openness to foreign goods is the result of four different factors. One is a long tradition among the Japanese of buying domestically made goods. The United States is a pluralistic and open society. Japan is a relatively homogeneous country that was for a long time closed to outside contact. Within Japan a system known as *keiretsu* developed,[18] which consists of groups or families of firms that each hold shares in one another and that work with one another to supply loans, material, and products. Such structures tend to restrict—but not preclude—competition, because they tend to develop trading relations among certain firms, between certain firms and certain suppliers, and between certain banks and certain firms. Such structural differences between the United States and Japan are significant. Yet there is nothing unethical about buying Japanese if you are Japanese, just as there is nothing unethical about pushing the slogan "Buy American" to promote the purchase of American-made goods if you are American. What is unethical is one side's attacking the other in ads, books, or other media in a way that promotes racism, maligns the other's products, or misleads people.

The second factor is that many Japanese believe that their goods are better made or serve their needs better than imported goods. If the belief is true, there is nothing unethical about it. That it is always true is questioned by some American multinationals, who claim that their products have not been given a chance to succeed in Japan.

The third factor is the enormous cost of land and of rent in Japan. By American standards, real estate is vastly overpriced. The total value of land in Japan, which is roughly the size of California, in 1990 was equal to four times the total value of all the land in the United States.[19] The high cost makes it difficult for American multinationals to acquire land and expensive for them to rent space. But land values in Japan are not different for the Japanese than for the Americans, and new Japanese firms must contend with the same prices. American companies face no special or unfair discrimination in this regard, even though Japanese firms do not face the same problem in getting started in the United States.

The fourth factor is the Japanese government's policy that restricts or taxes imports, limits distribution of foreign goods, and inhibits large discount retailers—such as Sears—from entering the Japanese market. The rules against discount retailers are not geared particularly to foreign enterprises, although it does affect them. The purpose of such laws is to protect the small retailers, who would tend to be driven out by large discount firms (much as has happened in the United States). One might claim that the practice has not only prevented some American firms from entering the market but helped Japanese firms sell their goods at premium prices to the disadvantage of the ordinary Japanese consumer. Some strong Japanese voices are raising just such a complaint.[20] U.S. firms cannot challenge the policy's fairness to them if Japanese firms are similarly restricted. They can complain about lack of reciprocity and lack of parallel opportunities. But each country is allowed to set whatever restrictions it chooses and to protect whatever groups it wishes. No government can be faulted ethically by external critics in this regard. But no country can reasonably expect to find open markets for its goods if it keeps its own markets closed to the entry of foreign goods. This is not a question of ethics but of sound business practices and expectations. Sony Chairman Akio Morito was one of the first important Japanese spokesmen to call for important changes in the way Japanese firms do business abroad, arguing that "it is essential that Japanese companies compete according to the same rules as the rest of the world."[21]

Ethics enters through the back door, so to speak—not with respect to any one of the practices mentioned, but with respect to the results produced by them. What is the overall result? Do the practices produce more harm than good for more people? Are the practices unfair cumulatively, even though each country has the right to pass whatever laws it wishes for its own people? If countries were discrete entities that did not interact with, impinge on, or affect one another, there would be no basis for complaint. No one is obligated to open one's doors to others. But once one interacts, to the extent that one's actions affect others, the possibility of charges of unfair practices arises.

I have claimed that each of the developed countries can take care of its own interests. That does not preclude their doing harm to others while pursuing their own interests, nor does it preclude counteractions by others in response. Perceptions of unfairness are as important as validly documented cases. The perceived unfairness of Japan's efforts to gain access to markets abroad, while its own system limits foreign interests, leads some Americans to call for closing American markets to the Japanese unless more Japanese markets are opened to Americans. Such an act (whether characterized as a response in kind, as a negative inducement, or as retaliation) would not be unethical. Whether it would be wise and in the best interests of U.S. firms, however, is debatable.

The large imbalance of trade between the United States and Japan results from the fact that the Japanese sell large quantities of cars, semiconductors, television sets, computers, and other electronic goods to American buyers, who see these products as being of good quality at attractive prices. Neither the American consumers nor the Japanese suppliers act unethically in their purchases and sales. The result may be an imbalance of payments, but there is nothing unfair or unethical about that, and no rule dictates that only balanced trading between any two countries is ethically permissible. Any such rule would render U.S. trade with many countries in which the balance is in favor of the United States unethical, and indeed would preclude much of the world's trade. It would certainly cause more harm than good to all concerned.

Trade negotiations between Japan and the United States have produced interesting complaints and suggestions from each side. The Japanese are credited with long-term thinking, and the Americans are faulted for looking only as far as the next quarter. The Japanese criticize Americans for their consumerist mentality and low savings rate (about 4.5 percent), compared with the high Japanese savings rate (14.5%). Yet many Americans own their own homes, while Japanese typically have to save many years to buy theirs—in some cases taking out mortgages for as long as 100 years. In Japan interest on savings is tax free; while in the United States interest on mortgages is tax deductible. Japan has surpassed the United States in income per capita, but its standard of living is still below that of the United States. The Japanese claim that American executive compensation and bonuses are excessive, that greed plays too large a role in business, and that leveraged buyouts are detrimental to the economy. Americans say that Japanese firms control too much of their workers' lives and leave them too little time for individual development or family life.[22]

By July 1991, the Japanese had agreed to adopt new regulations against price-fixing and collusion to block imports, and they had rescinded their rules requiring that items be sold at their suggested retail price.[23] At least in theory this opened the way for more competition, including competition from U.S. and other foreign firms. Still unclear is how much effect these new rules will have on the way business is actually done—and how strictly the rules will be enforced. Nonetheless, pressure is being placed on the system by the United States, by other countries with which Japan trades, and by Japanese consumers, who stand to gain by the lower retail prices that competition promises to bring.

Many of the charges and countercharges made by the United States and Japan have an ethical dimension and come from different value perspectives. Each side has some valid criticisms of the other and some legitimate concerns about what the other does. What happens in each country affects the other, since interest rates vary and capital crosses borders with relative ease.

Product Dumping?

A number of years ago an American manufacturer had the bright idea of making fire-resistant pajamas for children. The manufacturer produced these just as the news broke that exposure to asbestos, which the manufacturer had woven into the pajama cloth, could cause cancer. U.S. legislation soon banned the use of asbestos and the manufacturer was stuck with its entire stock of fire-resistant children's pajamas. To avoid suffering a total loss, it dumped the pajamas on various African markets, selling them at or below cost and thereby recouping some of its initial investment. Once brought to light, the firm's actions were roundly criticized. It knew full well the dangers of the product it was dumping, and it took advantage of the lack of preventive legislation in the countries where it sold the pajamas and of the lack of knowledge on the part of the people who bought them. Dumping dangerous products and defective goods on the markets of LDCs is unethical because, if dangerous, the products do harm, and if defective, the products do not give the customer proper value for the price.

The Japanese have been accused of dumping products—most notably semiconductors—in the United States. The products are neither dangerous nor defective. If they were, American law would prohibit their importation and sale. Rather, the term *dumping* is being used here to refer to the practice of selling large quantities of a product in a particular market at less than the product's fair market value, and in some cases at less than it costs to make them.[24] Complaints about this type of dumping come not from the purchasers of the product but from other manufacturers.

In the case of semiconductors, American manufacturers claimed that Japan was dumping its semiconductors on the market at low prices in order to grab as large a market share as possible and in order to ruin American semiconductor manufacturers, who could not sell their products at such prices and continue to stay in business. The Japanese were able to sell their products at those prices because their semiconductor operations were being subsidized in the short term by other areas of their giant conglomerates and by the Japanese government. Once they forced the American manufacturers out of business, thereby securing the market and eliminating competition, they would be able to charge profitable prices. The loss of profit they initially suffered from the dumping would then be recouped in the long term.

This technique was not invented by the Japanese, and it is illegal in the United States. It is outlawed by U.S. antitrust legislation because it was used earlier in the twentieth century to eliminate competition and to gain monopolies. Although consumers gain in the short run from the low prices, they pay in the long run, once competition has been eliminated. At that point the monopoly can charge them higher prices than they would have had to pay in a competitive market. Since it costs so much to open new competitive plants once the old ones are closed, reestablishing competition once it has been eliminated is costly and risky. Moreover, once reestablished, the competitive plants may again be forced to close by the same tactic. Because of the harm this practice ultimately does to the consumer, it is unethical; because it harms the consumer and eliminates competition, it is illegal. The United States imposed tariffs on Japanese imports to protect its own semiconductor industry—partly in the name of national security—rather than have all its firms eliminated through such competitive tactics by the Japanese.[25]

Several issues were involved. In 1986 the American government officially complained to the Japanese government that Japanese firms were dumping semiconductors, and the Japanese agreed to look into the complaint. If the Japanese were not selling the semiconductors below fair market value, but were merely selling them at a price that was less than the cost of producing semiconductors in the United States, they could hardly be faulted from an ethical point of view. This would simply have involved competing on price and using their lower costs or more efficient productive techniques to gain a larger market share. Such behavior is not unethical; indeed, it is what competition is all about. The result would be lower cost—both short-term and long-term—to American users. If what took place was indeed dumping of goods below fair market value, however, the practice could be faulted as unfair competition. The American government might also have cause to complain if the Japanese government subsidized the Japanese firms so that they could charge less than the fair price and remain in business.

In reply to the 1986 complaints, the Japanese government agreed to guarantee American firms up to 12 percent of the Japanese market in semiconductors.[26] Japan has never admitted that it has dumped or does dump goods on the American market. Instead, it claims that, as a more efficient producer of the goods, it can sell at prices that are lower than the costs American firms incur to produce comparable goods. If this is so, American consumers benefit from the lower cost, and American manufacturers must simply do better to compete effectively with the Japanese.

Whether or not Japanese firms were dumping semiconductors on the American market, the United States—for defense or other valid reasons—might want to protect its American semiconductor manufacturers and might place tariffs on Japanese semiconductors to do so, raising the price for imports to a level with which American firms could compete. It might also limit the quantity of Japanese semiconductors that can be imported into the United States. Both techniques are legitimate, but each carries its own costs. The primary cost is to the American users of the goods, who have to pay more for them than they otherwise would. Is it fair to make them pay what amounts to a subsidy to firms that cannot compete on their own? If the dumping is the result of Japanese government subsidies, do Americans have any right to demand a change in the Japanese system? Imposing punitive tariffs might legitimately provoke the Japanese government to retaliate by imposing tariffs on certain American products or by limiting the importation of some goods. The dangers of the reciprocal imposition of trade barriers are that it raises the cost of goods to all concerned, cuts trade, and leads to diminished production in both countries.

Each country must weigh the pros and cons of its trade laws and practices. The United States is capable of weighing its own interests and defending itself against unfair practices by foreign multinationals. It is not at their mercy, the way less developed countries might be. Multinationals that seek American markets can reasonably expect the United States to protect its interests as it sees them. Foreign MNCs are not bound to make sure that their operations provide a net benefit to the United States, although they are bound not to engage in unethical practices.

The Selling of America

No general ethical rule prohibits nationals of one country from buying foreign stock or land or foreign companies. Americans and American companies own many foreign assets, and foreign multinationals own many assets in the United States. Yet Americans have been very concerned at the supposed Japanese "buying of America." The facts do not support the concern of those who complain of Japanese investments. In 1990 the British were the largest foreign investors in the United States, owning assets valued at slightly less than twice as much as the total Japanese investment of roughly $70 billion.[27] Yet there has been no complaint about the British buying America. Why the fear and reaction to the Japanese? Is there any ethical basis for the American reaction, or is it (as the Japanese claim) a matter of prejudice against them because they are Asian or because of the image of them that still lingers from World War II?

American multinationals have long invested, bought, and built in countries throughout the world. They have been accused of exploiting less developed countries and of undermining their culture. Yet surely any such charge about the Japanese with respect to the United States would be unfounded. What is true, as we have already seen, is that the cost of real estate in Japan is prohibitive for many American—as well as for many Japanese—firms. As a result, from the Japanese perspective, American real estate appears both cheap and available. This causes an imbalance in the availability of U.S. land to Japanese investors that is not matched by the availability of Japanese land to American investors. Yet that imbalance is not in itself unethical.

Two other aspects of the Japanese investments in the United States have helped fuel American claims of unfairness and American concern about Japanese purchases. One is the buying of American "trophy" or high-visibility properties. A second is the influx of Japanese into Hawaii and the concentration of Japanese purchases in California. Even though the British own more of the United States than do the Japanese, their investments not as obvious or as geographically concentrated, and hence they cause less anxiety—whether justified or not.

Rockefeller Center and Columbia Motion Pictures. Why did these two sales create so much concern and get so much publicity, while other sales have gone unnoticed and provoked no concern? Was the reaction simply misplaced emotion, or was something deeper at issue? Both Rockefeller Center and Columbia Pictures were privately owned. Despite its name, Rockefeller Center did not have to be owned by members of the Rockefeller family.[28] And did most Americans really know who owned Columbia Pictures?[29] The owners not only had the right to sell these enterprises to whomever they chose, but good business dictated that they should get the best price possible. Neither practice is unethical.

What was different—and to some, threatening—in these two cases was the perception that foreign interests were buying American symbols. What if the United States government sold the Statue of Liberty to Japan, or if France sold the Eiffel Tower to the United States? Both are tourist attractions, and a private concern might make money from paid visits and from the sale of subsidiary rights to photos and souvenirs. Yet some might claim that a country that sells its symbols is like Faust selling his soul. Some things are not proper to sell. The symbols of a nation or its culture should not be sold, nor should they be placed under the control of a foreign nation. To do so is to alienate them from their native context, to lose control over them, and to place them under foreign domination. The injunction to respect the culture of the country in which a foreign multinational operates seems to be violated by such purchases, even though London Bridge was sold to an American and moved stone by stone to the United States, with no perceptible harm to Great Britain.

Some critics claim the sales of Rockefeller Center and of Columbia Pictures were more like the sale of the Statue of Liberty and of the Eiffel Tower than like the sale of other stocks, companies, or ordinary pieces of land. In some sense, they claim, Rockefeller Center did not belong only to the Rockefeller family, even though they were the legal owners of the property. Rockefeller Center also belonged to New York City and to the United States. While it is not as important a symbol as the Statue of Liberty, it is nevertheless an internationally known and recognized symbol of America—its Fifth Avenue buildings, its celebrated open-air skating rink and plaza, its Radio City Music Hall. Posters of any part of Rockefeller Center mean America, just as the Louvre and the Arch of Triumph mean France, or the Tower of London means England. Selling Rockefeller Center to any foreign interest is like selling Times Square or Broadway. Selling such symbols to foreign interests changes them. Although the new owners may not replace a brick or change the name, they could. That right goes with the sale. Another country now controls an American symbol. This control diminishes it as an American symbol and cuts away a piece of American culture, history, and pride.

Was the sale unethical? If so, are the sellers more to blame than the buyers? The Japanese buyers initially were reluctant to buy more than a 50 percent interest in Rockefeller Center, and they eventually did so only at the urging of the American owners.[30] The Japanese were worried about U.S. reaction. Hindsight shows their intuitions and sensitivities in the matter were well placed. Although the sellers may not have seen themselves as custodians and shepherds of a piece of American culture, many Americans saw them as such and accused them of betraying an implicit trust. If they had to sell, the critics claimed they should have sold to American interests. There would then have been no public outcry. Custodians of American symbols, argued the critics, have a trust and obligation that others do not have.

What of the foreign buyers? If anything unethical occurred, it was not the buyers' purchase of the property per se. Rather it involved their not following through on their sensitivity to the fact that they were buying an American symbol. If they had made the purchase for that purpose, they would have been guilty of attempting to undermine another culture. Multinationals should respect the cultural symbols of other countries—both developed and less developed. But there is no evidence that the Japanese purchasers had any intention of undermining American culture. The lesson taught by the sale of Rockefeller Center and by popular reaction to it across the country is that those who control a nation's cultural symbols should not sell them to foreign interests, and that prospective foreign purchasers should be careful not to undermine a country's culture. This places some restraint on what any multinational may acquire in other countries. Yet this restraint is not excessive, and the bad will engendered by ignoring it can scarcely be worth whatever advantage an individual firm gains by its purchase.

What of Columbia Pictures? Is Columbia Pictures really an American symbol, and is its sale to Sony of Japan unethical on the basis of the argument developed for Rockefeller Center? Critics argued that Hollywood is a tinsel symbol of America, but a symbol nonetheless. For decades American motion pictures have symbolized America worldwide. Columbia Pictures was one of the early great names in the production of Hollywood movies, and it is still to some extent a name that stands for America. Columbia Pictures' stock routinely changed hands daily. It is not the selling of its stock that caused resentment, but the purchase of controlling interest in the company by Sony. Columbia Pictures will probably not change the kinds of films it produces. Yet critics fear that, since the new owners control the company, they could choose to slant its production toward Japanese interests. Had Sony purchased Columbia Pictures for purposes of undermining American culture, it could be morally faulted. But no evidence supports any such allegation.

The resentment, concern, and fear revolve around the idea that American symbols and American symbol makers—in this case the motion picture industry—are no longer American but are under foreign control. It would surely be too strong to say that the former owners of Columbia Pictures had a trust or were stewards of American culture to such an extent that they had an obligation to protect it from foreign domination. Yet implicit in the reaction to news of the sale was some feeling of the loss of a symbolic piece of America to foreign interests. Had Columbia Pictures bought Sony, the Japanese might have had a similar reaction—that they were losing a symbolic part of Japan to America.

This reaction is an excellent indicator to Americans of what it means for a country to feel it is dominated by another country, and what it means to respect the culture of another country. Two different elements are at play here: the introduction of new cultural forms that compete with and perhaps drive out the old; and the taking over of the old. Introducing sushi restaurants or Toyota or Nissan cars into America does not subvert American culture, even though it changes it somewhat and enriches it. These are not usually seen as threats. They are absorbed and assimilated easily. Exporting products is a normal part of international trade.

But buying and controlling another nation's symbols is different. Multinationals should respect a nation's public feeling and pride in its symbols. McDonald's is an American institution as are Coca-Cola, Pepsi-Cola, and IBM. Sony and Mitsubishi are Japanese symbols, and Mercedes-Benz is a German symbol. Selling any of them to a foreign company would be like selling part of that country's identity to a foreign interest. This puts a special burden on those companies. It makes their takeover by foreign buyers more delicate than the takeover of most other companies, which are not globally synonymous with a particular country.

The United States and most other developed nations can protect their own interests because they all have developed background institutions and deal with each other from positions of relative equality. The U.S. government has not yet chosen to restrict the sale of its commercial symbols, although Major League baseball did temporarily block the sale of the Seattle Mariners to a group whose major investor was Japanese.[31] The government may decide that such legislation is unnecessary or impossible to frame adequately. How could one decide for purposes of legislation which firms are national symbols? This area may best be left to ethical pressures and corporate consciences.

The ethical obligation not to sell national symbols to foreign interests can be generalized: no country should sell its national symbols, nor should the firms or interests of any country buy the symbols of another country. It would be as wrong for DisneyLand to buy the Eiffel Tower as it would be for the French to sell it to American interests. Direct harm is done not to the buyer or seller but to the wider national public that has an interest in the symbols, even though the public has no direct economic right or control over the property in question. The buyer and the country of the buyer suffer indirect harm since the purchase carries with it the resentment of the people who lose their symbols. That resentment makes the price of the purchase much greater than the actual funds paid by the buyer to the seller.

Selling Hawaii. What about Japanese purchases of property in Hawaii? Is that unethical for some reason? Rockefeller Center and Columbia Pictures can arguably be called American symbols. Hawaii presents a different situation. No particular symbol is being purchased; rather individual parcels of land, houses, and businesses are being sold to buyers who happen to be Japanese.

No one can legitimately complain about any individual purchase or sale. Property can be bought and sold freely, and American interests are not so threatened that any legislation has been proposed to limit the sale of real estate to American citizens. Some nations do have such laws. And in some cases the laws were passed because the governments involved feared domination by Americans who were buying up large pieces of their country. But since American interests have holdings in many countries in the world and own land in many countries, why should not foreigners own property in America?

What makes the buying of Hawaiian property by Japanese purchasers somewhat different from the purchase of Beverly Hills mansions by Arab interests, or the buying of Paris apartments by Americans, is the overall proportion of the state that is now owned by Japanese individuals and firms.[32] Certainly the Japanese holdings in Hawaii do not represent very much when they are compared to the total area of the United States. But their holdings are considerable in comparison to the total of all developable land in Hawaii.

A strength of the United States (and a source of pride for its people) has been that it has accepted and integrated many waves of immigration, assimilating elements of cultures from many lands. However, critics claim that the Japanese in Hawaii have no interest in being assimilated; they are absentee landlords, own vacation homes, or want to bring Japanese culture with them to Hawaii to feel at home there. The problem is not with any individual's purchases or intentions. The problem is the overall effect, the perceived threat to local culture, and the loss of control over one's land. This complaint may seem strange coming from Americans, who overran Hawaii's native culture, forcibly changed Japanese culture after World War II, and even wrote the Japanese constitution.

Clearly, the United States and Japan are capable of protecting their own interests. Yet American and Japanese multinationals must consider more than the economic side of their interactions. The larger the company is, the more conscious it should be of the possible negative impact of its purchase; it may be buying bad will along with the economic bargain of a good company or a desirable piece of property at a low price. The concept of *noblesse oblige* is being modified to make a similar claim: that economic power imposes on its possessor certain obligations, including a duty to be concerned about the effects of one's actions on the culture of the country with which one is dealing. The need for sensitivity to the perceptions of one's host is not only good business; it is also an aspect of treating people with respect, which is a moral norm that multinationals should not ignore.

All multinationals operating in foreign countries have an obligation to respect the culture of the country in which they operate. The cultures of developed industrial countries—and in particular those of Japan and the United States—are not as fragile as those of LDCs, and they have already made accommodations to advanced industrialization. Nonetheless, they are different in many ways, and each deserves respect. Separating cultural aspects that must be respected from those that are rightly subject to negotiated change is a delicate task. Multinationals operate in the thick of this cultural interchange and should be sensitive to it. Misunderstandings about some aspects of their different traditions have led to friction between the United States and Japan. The need for continued negotiation is clear. What is just in Japanese–American business interactions is what both sides agree is just, but reaching that agreement is as difficult as it is pressing. Multinationals of both countries play an important role in clarifying the terms and in implementing the agreements.

The European Community

Rules of conduct that apply to American firms operating in Japan and to Japanese firms operating in America apply as well to either of them operating in the European Community. Yet the values and ethical views of most countries in Western Europe are closer to American than to Japanese values, since those who came from the Old to the New World brought their values and traditions with them. American firms have had a long-standing presence in Europe, and the "American go home" signs have long since disappeared.

The Opportunity for New International Agreements

The five hundredth anniversary of the discovery of the New World marked the beginning of the new European Community (EC), in which the economic and political borders dividing European nations began to fall. Tariffs and trade barriers within the European Community are disappearing, and workers—as well as goods and money—travel freely from country to country. To position themselves for commerce in the new Europe, American firms have been buying some European firms and entering into joint ventures with others. The meaning of multinationals may well change as so many nations interact commercially and financially without barriers and as common laws governing economic activities within the Community are passed. If the EC develops as envisaged, it will no longer be proper to speak of a German multinational operating in Italy but rather of a European firm with operations in two nations, much like a United States firm with operations in more than one American state.

National and cultural differences will continue to exist, and local expectations will still vary; consequentlyparticular locales.
But the emergence of the EC offers a unique opportunity to develop common background institutions that embody the highest standards of conduct present within Europe, rather than the least ethical practices.

Some European nations have been waiting for European Community regulations to help them correct injustices in their own countries and to provide uniform rules that local bickering has prevented them from adopting. The pressure of other nations can help some nations change inadequate pollution control or discriminatory practices that resisted domestic reform. The development of common codes necessarily involves public discussion of ethical norms and values. The opportunity for developing and implementing ethical international norms is unparalleled. The United Nations has been working for over ten years to develop guidelines for multinationals. But their work has not been hastened by the pressures of having to arrive at guidelines by a firm deadline. The European Community must come up with common guidelines as soon as possible; thus it has the opportunity to develop international norms that can serve as guidelines for nations outside the EC as well.

Developing common guidelines will require a great deal of negotiation, since what is fair will sometimes appear different to different parties, depending on their perspective. In the end, those practices will be just that are recognized as being just by all concerned and affected. If the codes, norms, and rules concerning business, trade, employment, and multinational corporations do reflect the best of the ethical norms present in Europe, they can become a benchmark for others. As other European nations seek entry into the EC, they will be motivated to accept the established norms or to negotiate changes acceptable to all.

The United States shares with Great Britain and with much of Western Europe a common heritage, a common ancestry, and the Judeo-Christian and Greco-Roman traditions. The common outlook on many issues makes for similar ethical judgments. Building multinational norms together will be less difficult here than in cooperation with nations that have very different backgrounds, histories, and values. Nonetheless, negotiations with these other nations or trading blocs will be facilitated by negotiated agreements already reached. Thus the realization of the European Community can offer an impetus and a motivation for developing just background institutions that will help make and keep international trade and competition fair on a global level.

As norms and institutions develop, due care must be accorded to those that free enterprise tends to ignore: to the less developed countries, and to those unable to compete at the level of the developed countries. The ethical responsibility to share wealth and resources with the needy and to develop fair means for reallocating such assets can become easier as economic and political barriers fall—not only in the European Community, but more broadly as well.

Three areas exemplify the kinds of issues that might be addressed and resolved: advertising, foreign workers and migration, and industrial espionage.

Advertising

The case presented at the beginning of this chapter poses no serious problem. American firms should respect the culture and the moral views of the countries in which they do business. If the people of a country believe that advertising that explicitly attacks a competitor's product is unethical, an American company that wishes to operate with integrity should respect that view. This is not only what ethics requires; it is also common business sense. To engage in an advertising practice that the target audience considers unethical or otherwise offensive is clearly not a very effective way to win customers or to sell a product.

The European Community is discussing bloc-wide guidelines for advertising, but some countries have traditionally adopted stricter guidelines than others. In the United States some commentators have suggested that American advertisers and ad agencies should lobby for American norms. But why they should do so is not clear. The rules adopted by the FTC or any other regulatory agency do not define what is ethical; they only define what is legal in the United States. A good deal of controversy has surfaced in the United States about ads for cigarettes and alcoholic beverages, about TV ads aimed at children, and about ads for guns, among other things.

Greece forbids TV ads for toys; other European countries forbid advertising for tobacco and alcoholic products; Denmark forbids magazine ads for pharmaceutical products.[33] American multinationals that wish to sell such goods in the European Community can expect to be governed by the same rules that govern their competitors. If advertising a particular item is considered unethical in some countries, and if rules prohibiting such advertisements are adopted by the EC, American companies doing business there have no right to follow American practice in preference to the rules of the countries in which they sell their goods.

A company with integrity has the right to expect fair treatment. It may lobby for practices in which it wishes to engage. But it should do so only if it can justify those practices on ethical grounds, both to itself and to others. Advertisements addressed to children are calculated to raise the target audience's desire for the advertised products. The argument in favor of such ads is that children are the ones who will actually use the toys and other items their parents buy for them; the ads simply let children know what is available. Since a child's parents must still pay for the products, they make the final decision. The argument against such advertising is that children are easily influenced, are not sophisticated enough to evaluate TV ads, and are manipulated by the ads. In the United States the debate over the ethics of such advertising remains unresolved. An ethical ad agency and an ethical firm that wish to engage in such advertising must at a minimum engage in ethically defensible lobbying and not use tactics based purely on self-interest.

The same sort of approach is applicable to ads for tobacco and alcoholic products. The United States has already banned such ads on TV; and magazine and newspaper ads for cigarettes must carry one of the same Surgeon General's warnings that appear on the packages. If the European Community decides to ban all ads for such products, American multinationals cannot complain about unfairness, since the rules will apply to all manufacturers, regardless of their country of origin. To lobby for laxer regulations is to argue for less governmental paternalism. But each country has a right to determine its own degree of intervention in the public interest, and multinationals of integrity will respect such determinations and the values behind them.

Not all EC regulations proposed or adopted are more stringent than those in the United States. For instance, U.S. regulations on auto pollution levels have for many years been more stringent than those of most European countries. The EC agreed to adopt for 1992 standards that the United States adopted in 1983.[34] During the intervening ten years, should U.S. car manufacturers have made cars for export to Europe that exceeded European regulations and met U.S. standards? Consistency argues that the U.S. car manufacturers in Europe had no obligation to abide by the higher U. S. standards if doing so would make their cars more expensive and less competitive there. Yet they could not completely ignore the harm that car pollution does, and they could not ethically have made cars that produced more pollution if they could have made cars that produced less pollution for the same cost. The same sort of argument applies to advertising regulations abroad that are less stringent than those in the United States. Companies may not do what is unethical, even if it is legally permitted. But within the broad range of what is ethically permitted, different societies may make different decisions about what to prohibit, based on their own judgments about the amount of protection their society needs or wants.

To the extent that higher standards in one country tend eventually to raise the corresponding standards in other countries, a company of integrity might well impose on itself throughout the European Community the highest standards of any of the EC countries. While not ethically demanded, it is an ethically praiseworthy policy that might also turn out to be the most efficient and profitable in the long run.

Foreign Workers

The European Community is now gearing up for a problem that American companies have already had to deal with in the United States and that they will also have to face in the European Community. That is the issue of foreign and undocumented workers.

In the 1960s, several Western European countries faced a shortage of workers and instituted "guest workers" programs under which workers from other countries were allowed entry and were given work permits. Workers came from Yugoslavia, Turkey, and various countries of North Africa, among others. Such workers often took jobs that local workers refused.

In the 1990s, the countries of the European Community, some of which are suffering from high rates of unemployment, no longer want or need such guest workers.[35] Yet many of the workers have remained, and many additional workers without work permits have arrived and continue to arrive. The demise of Communist regimes in Central and Eastern Europe has allowed many people from those countries to leave them for better opportunities in the EC. Germany has agreed to accept "ethnic Germans" from what used to be the German empire. Many people from former French colonies have come to France, and many more wish to come. The same is true of citizens of former British colonies with respect to Great Britain.

The European Community is dropping all border formalities with respect to citizens of other EC countries. Such free movement of people means that anyone entering one of the EC countries illegally has easy access to the others. Italy and Spain have been relatively ineffective in preventing illegal immigration. While some Italians hope that their country will impose tighter controls once common EC rules have been adopted, northern EC countries worry that the Italians cannot be relied on to do so.[36]

These are problems for the EC. Are they problems as well for American multinationals operating there?

In the United States, American firms have had to come to grips with laws mandating equal employment opportunity, a nondiscriminatory workplace, and affirmative action. This is not true of most European firms. Reports and studies done in the EC document racial discrimination, prejudice, and unfair treatment of minorities and non-Europeans—especially people from Africa, the Far East, Arab countries, India, and Pakistan. Racial incidents are growing more frequent in several European countries.[37] It is ironic that, as the world grows closer together, old animosities reappear. In one sense the problem is an EC problem, not a problem for non-EC multinational corporations. But once a multinational begins to operate within the EC, it must face the problems of whom to hire and how to treat workers. A challenge for multinationals is not only to rise above local animosities and the resulting discrimination but also to help break them down where they do reappear. Multinationals can play a large role in promoting equal employment practices, especially since they are ethically required to use equal employment practices anyway—even if some European firms do not do so.

In some European countries guest workers and their children have been accorded second-class status and have been subject to gross exploitation.[38] Whether EC companies discriminate or not, an American multinational operating in an EC country should follow the same antidiscriminatory and equal employment policies there that it does at home. It should not discriminate against nationals from the country in which it locates, and it should not discriminate against nonnationals who are legitimately in the country and are eligible by law to work. To do otherwise is to refuse to recognize the right of every worker to fair and equal treatment. On the other hand, if the company has not discriminated in the past, it has no obligation to engage in affirmative action with respect to any foreign group or disadvantaged class, unless required to do so by law.

Just as it should not practice racism, it should not practice sexism, which means that it should follow equal and equitable practices for both men and women. Women should be given opportunities for initial jobs and for promotions on an equal footing with men. American MNCs might choose to lead the way in practicing affirmative action, since many have profited from such policies at home. But they have no special obligations exceeding those of comparable indigenously owned firms.

The problem of illegal immigration is one that the European Community must cope with as it sees fit. American multinationals have no special obligations with respect to such workers; indeed, their obligations in this area are to obey the legitimate laws of the countries in question and to respect the human right of those with whom they deal. In most instances this will mean refusing to hire undocumented workers and cooperating with local authorities with respect to such workers.

Many European countries provide more in the way of social benefits for their employees than do American companies in the United States. In addition, workers are often represented on a company's board of directors, sometimes by law. American companies in EC countries must of course abide by the laws in such countries concerning workers' rights, benefits, privacy, and representation. But even if such laws are more onerous for American multinationals than are U.S. laws, the firms must still follow principles of nondiscrimination, fairness, and equity in dealing with all workers.

Industrial Espionage

With the passing of the Cold War and of the threat of military confrontation with Soviet forces, the need for governmental espionage has diminished. Reports suggest that the demise of governmental espionage has led to an increase in industrial espionage—sometimes practiced by nations and sometimes by individual firms.[39] What are the obligations of multinational firms in such a milieu?

The incidence of espionage varies with the kind of industry and with the amount of secret data, technology, or other kinds of information on which it depends. Sabotage is clearly unethical, but fortunately it is not a major problem. Theft, too, is unethical. But industrial espionage is frequently linked with permissible industrial intelligence, and drawing the line between ethically permissible information gathering and illegitimate theft in the realm of intelligence is not always easy. Wherever the line is drawn, an argument couched in terms of national defense or security will not work. In some instances of statecraft, national security or defense might override other rights—for example, individual rights to privacy. But no such case can plausibly be made with respect to industrial espionage. Neither American nor French nor any other country's national defense or security is jeopardized when the corporations of some other country come out with a new product or develop a new industrial technique first and so capture early market share. And an individual company has no right to violate the privacy or property rights of competitors, even if a competitor's action might seriously threaten that company. That potential outcome is part of the risk of competition.

What is allowable on the international level is comparable to what is allowable on the national level. In general reverse engineering—taking apart a competitor's product to see how it works—is permissible. Obviously this can only take place legitimately after the item has been produced and made commercially available. Patent laws typically protect any inventions contained within an item that is being analyzed through reverse engineering.

Worldwide agreements on patents, copyrights, and trademarks appropri-

ately govern the forms of intellectual property covered by them. More difficult to assess is the area covered by trade secrecy. In general, trade secrets are
pieces of information, such as a marketing strategy or a design, that a company does not make available to outsiders and that it protects by limited
access. An indication of trade secrecy is the degree and kind of protection a
company uses to prevent disclosure.

A multinational may not ethically violate any law to obtain such information. Yet it is not necessarily precluded from attempting to learn what it can,
as many firms try to do. The use of any published material is of course
permissible. In governmental intelligence the collection of public material
released by the government is the largest single source of intelligence. The
same is true of industrial intelligence.

A second allowable way to obtain confidential information is by piecing
together data that are in various ways public. What is done in public cannot be
private. Surveillance that collects public information, for instance, by following employees or executives, is intelligence that may have some use. The use
of surveillance equipment to enter private premises, to intrude on private
space, or to gain access to telephone conversations is prohibited in most
countries by law and in all countries by ethics. Yet the onus of not disclosing
information publicly is on those who wish to keep the information secret, not
on those who hear it or gather it in public.

The monitoring of airwaves is more controversial. In many countries,
information broadcast over the airwaves is not considered private. Yet many
mobile phones use the airwaves to communicate. Such conversations may be
intended to be private, even if they can be overheard (intentionally or not).
People who discuss secret matters over such phones are risking compromise.
Similarly, in some countries garbage left for collection and disposal is not
considered private or protected, and no one is legally prohibited from picking
up garbage or collecting items from dumps. Where this is the case, a company's garbage becomes fair game. Most companies are aware of this and use
shredders.

Electronic stealing—surreptitiously entering a computer system and copy-
ing another person's data—is a form of outright theft, and so is prohibited like
any other type of stealing.[40]

Perhaps the easiest way to get secrets is from a competitor's employees or
former employees. Buying secrets from an employee is not ethically permitted, since the information is not the employee's to sell. Nor would blackmail
or extortion be ethically justifiable. A more common strategy is to hire away
key employees at substantial increases in pay. Such employees may not divulge what is not theirs to divulge and may not duplicate for their new employer what they learned under conditions of trade secrecy in their former
position. But they may provide information that is not governed by trade
secrecy; and this, when pieced together with other bits of information a company has obtained about a competitor or its plans or products, may prove to
be valuable to the firm. The use of "moles" or infiltrators is impermissible to
the extent that they obtain knowledge in their capacity as employees that does

not belong to them and that they are not free to divulge in their private capacities. Still, there is much that trade secrecy rules do not cover, that employees are not forbidden to discuss or divulge, and that can be revealed with perfect ethical propriety.

The gathering of such intelligence is most prevalent among firms from industrially advanced countries, and it may be a factor in determining whether local nationals are hired for certain positions and whether they are given certain information. For this reason, some companies hire only or predominantly citizens of their own country. Whether such a policy is defensible depends on the country in question, the sensitivity of one's product or research, and the incidence (if any) of industrial espionage.

Multinationals in any country are bound to report and divulge to the government of the country in which they operate a good deal of information that the government may legitimately request in order to implement its governing rules and regulations. Companies often reveal to governments what they do not reveal and are not bound to reveal to others. An understood condition for such revelations is that the government will use the information only for legitimate regulatory purposes. It is ethically precluded from using such information to provide intelligence on the firm to the company's indigenous competitors. One function of government may be to help its own industries, but it may not ethically take advantage of its privileged position to do so.

The neatest solution, as to so many other problems that involve multinationals, is to negotiate governmental agreements not to engage in industrial intelligence gathering and espionage, as well as agreements on what is permitted by firms and what is not. In the absence of such agreements a company of integrity will not act illegally or unethically and will take the necessary steps to protect itself against the unethical intelligence-gathering practices of competitors or foreign governments. It should decide what is proprietary information and what is not, and it should communicate this clearly to employees. It should establish clear, defensible criteria for what it considers its trade secrets, and it should make these criteria known. The strategies for dealing with unethical competitors come into play here.

Not everything a company may want to keep private is therefore a trade secret and unethical to divulge. The line between private and secret sometimes depends on the distinction between personal and corporate rights and personal and corporate ownership. An employee's right to privacy precludes a firm from revealing his or her personal data (such as medical records) to unauthorized people. The firm is obligated to safeguard such information, but it is not a trade secret. A company may not wish the salaries it pays particular employees to be made public. Yet if an employee reveals the salary he or she gets, that does not violate the trade secrets of the company; and in discussing a possible move to another firm, one may clearly and appropriately state one's salary. On the other hand interviewing an employee of another company under false pretenses, just to get that information, would be unethical—not because of the nature of the information received, but because of the deception involved in obtaining it.

A company owns its own data, designs, plans, and whatever else it develops. Employees who come to know such information learn it in their official capacities and have no right to use it in their personal capacities or for their personal gain. Yet the experience they obtain from any position belongs to them and not to the firm; they rightly take that with them, and they can use it for their advantage and advancement. The difference between intellectual property that belongs to the firm and intellectual property that belongs to the employee can be specified in advance to some extent. Trade secrets, clearly so designated, belong exclusively to the firm.

Since there is so much gray in the intelligence area, a company that wishes to act with integrity will think through its policy on competitive intelligence gathering and will set clear guidelines for its employees. Furthermore, it should monitor its policy to see that employees do not exceed ethical limits.

With the emergence of closer ties within the European Community, new rules and regulations are being developed and negotiated. This offers an excellent opportunity to make those rules uniform and fair. Policies that take advantage of the best of the European experience and the best of the American experience could become models for the conduct and governance of multinationals throughout the world.

10

Competing with Integrity

The pharmaceutical firm Merck & Company developed a drug (Mectizan) that helps prevent river blindness (onchocerciasis), a disease that afflicts millions of people in Africa. Once Merck developed it, however, those who needed the drug could not afford to buy it. Merck hoped that some governmental or international agency or group would pay for the drug. When none did, Merck decided to distribute it free of charge. But it found that that was no easy task, because there was no effective distribution system for conveying the drug to the remote parts of Africa where it was needed. Thereupon Merck decided to develop the needed distribution systems at its own expense and ensured that the drug reached those in need. Finally, Merck committed itself to continue distributing the drug free indefinitely into the future.[1]

Was Merck ethically required to do all of this? Clearly not. Merck went well beyond what was ethically required in what is surely a morally exemplary set of actions.

Thus far this book has been concerned with rules, guidelines, and strategies. Yet competing with integrity involves more than obeying rules—even the rules we have listed. The moral minimum requires that companies do no harm. The rules we have enunciated can all be taken to be more specific instantiations of that more general rule. Thus they identify the minimum that is ethically required. A company that acts with integrity will not be satisfied with that; nor will it run its business by seeing how close it can come to violating the rules without actually doing so. That sort of legalistic mentality differs fundamentally from integrity. Integrity indicates a robustness, a confidence in one's actions, a willingness to assume responsibility, and a desire to act not only as is required but as is fitting and in a way of which one can be proud. Absent so far is the notion of an ideal, of a goal to be sought, of an end toward which one might strive and stretch and grow. Individuals are rarely proud of the fact that they have gone through a day, or a week, or a year, or a lifetime doing the minimum that is ethically required—especially if the minimum consists merely of obeying negative injunctions. No one thinks it very praiseworthy to claim credit for having gone a day or a year or a lifetime without murdering anyone.

Perhaps those who believe the Myth of Amoral Business will think it remarkable if any firm is interested in or actually achieves the moral minimum. But those who act with integrity will find it neither remarkable nor ethically adequate.

Beyond the Minimum: Obligations and Ideals

From an ethical point of view, marginal firms on the brink of collapse have no more excuse to act unethically than do profitable firms. All firms are bound by the moral minimum, and the threat of failure does not give any firm the right to exploit others, violate their rights, or in any way injure them. The obligation not to harm remains in force.

Yet there is a sense in which we can distinguish the profitable firm from the marginal one. It is not that a marginal firm may act unethically. Rather, it is that profitable firms can fulfill norms beyond the minimum (and so are expected to do so), whereas marginal ones may be unable to meet them (and so are not required to do so, as long as they remain marginal). In this sense, more is demanded of profitable firms. Two aspects of ethics tend to increase one's effective responsibilities. The first relates to positive acts beyond the moral minimum.[2] The second involves the fulfillment of ideals.[3]

Positive Obligations Beyond the Minimum

The obligation to do no harm is a negative obligation. It applies at all times and to all people. The imperative to do good is much broader and vaguer. No individual can do good to everyone, and any firm is limited in the good it can do. Moreover, firms are established for certain specific economic ends and are organized to meet those ends. Their range of ethical concern is narrower than that of human beings, and their general obligation to do good or to maximize the good is necessarily restricted to actions appropriate to corporations.

Any firm, local or multinational, must analyze its obligation to maximize the good in terms of its own ends. It must be run profitably to remain in business, and its obligations to its shareholders, workers, and other stakeholders have priority over its obligation to help others. Those who run the company are caretakers of the assets of others. An individual may decide to give all he or she has to poor; a corporate executive would violate his or her fiduciary responsibilities by giving all the company's assets to the poor, even if it would produce the greatest amount of good on the whole.

Another of a firm's general responsibilities that goes beyond the minimum is its obligation to be charitable, or to help the needy, either at home or abroad. Each person and each firm has this positive obligation; but each also has a certain amount of discretion in determining how to fulfill that obligation. Those who have an abundance of wealth are obliged to help those less fortunate. But this general obligation does not specify whom they should help or how. Consequently, they may fulfill the obligation in a variety of ways that benefit different individuals.

The general obligation to be charitable is generally acknowledged as an ethical demand that applies to individuals. It applies to firms as well, insofar as firms are part of the social fabric and benefit from society in various ways. As part of the social fabric, they are appropriately expected to make certain returns, even when not obliged to do so by law. Often those actions are referred to as being a "good citizen" or a good member of the community. What and how a firm gives are matters for each firm to determine. But just as poor individuals are not usually expected to give money to other poor individuals, so marginal firms are not expected to go into bankruptcy to give to the needy.

Individuals who act with integrity take seriously their obligation to help others. The help they give is most praiseworthy when they give disinterestedly—that is, when they expect nothing back in return. Their help is most appreciated when it involves a gift of themselves, and not just a gift of their money. The same thing is true of firms. A firm may choose whom to help and how to do it. Disinterestedness does not mean that they do not draw on their expertise or central concerns. For instance, firms connected with the print media sometimes participate in literacy programs. Those in the computer industry may lend their experts to teach computer science at a neighboring college or school. The most important contribution a firm may make is not necessarily money, but part of itself—the time and talents of its employees and executives. GE Plastics exemplified this when it substituted for its annual team-building sports event the renovating of run-down community facilities.[4]

Multinationals sometimes fulfill their obligation to help the societies in which they operate by directly contributing to neighborhoods in which they are located. Sometimes they set up charitable foundations that distribute grants to applicants under specified conditions. Sometimes a firm takes upon itself the task of helping rebuild an inner-city area that has deteriorated. The needs are many and diverse, and the general obligation can be met in innumerable ways, limited only by the fertility of one's moral imagination.

Critics sometimes confuse the general obligation to help with particular instances of helping. They claim that corporations have an obligation to help correct illiteracy in the countries in which they operate or to help rebuild decaying cities or to do certain other good works. Unless the firm had a hand in causing the ills described and so is justly obligated to help correct it, such a claim is more specific than the general rule demands. Firms can be faulted for doing nothing along these lines, but not for failing to do some specific act.

Moreover, given their limited ends and their structures, firms are not established to set up or implement public policy and should not attempt to do so. Since the leaders of a firm have not been elected by the general population and are not responsible to them (as are elected public officials), they have no right to attempt by their actions to set or to implement public policy unless directly or indirectly requested to do so by elected officials or by the public.

Those who argue against corporate involvement in public affairs are correct if this is what they mean.[5]

Marginal firms may not have the time, planning resources, and money to do anything beyond providing jobs, producing goods, and paying taxes. But a firm that acts with integrity will be conscious of obligations beyond the minimum and will seek to fulfill them.

Ethical Ideals

Ideals go beyond positive obligations. Ethical ideals inform the goals toward which a firm of integrity aims. A company can be ethically faulted for not living up to its obligations, but not for falling short of its ideals. From an ethical point of view, it deserves blame for not fulfilling its obligations; it deserves no blame for not fulfilling its ideals. While a company merits no special ethical praise for fulfilling its obligations, it does merit special ethical praise for going beyond them and striving toward its ethical ideals. The distinction between obligations and ideals is clearly articulated in the American Bar Association's Code of Professional Responsibility, in which violations of one's obligations (Disciplinary Rules) are censurable, while failure to achieve the ideals (Ethical Considerations) is not. A company's corporate code might usefully distinguish what the company holds itself to as obligatory from what it proposes for itself as ideals toward which it strives.

Ethical ideals are positive norms. They may be related to the degree to which one fulfills one's general positive obligations. A very generous firm, for instance, gives more than the minimum to charity or to worthy causes. The ideals may involve the internal or the external actions of the firm. Generosity and magnanimity are ideals that a firm may pursue with respect to those not connected to the firm, while balancing its generosity against the valid claims of its stakeholders; alternatively, they are ideals that it might pursue internally—for instance, in the wages and bonuses it gives to its employees at all levels, and not just to its top executives. The ideals may be general, such as dedication to excellence in the firm's products; or specific, such as the goal of not closing down plants unless absolutely necessary, even in periods of slow productive demand or economic recession.

The distinction between rules and ideals can be made in various ways. It is exemplified by the difference between the primary prohibitory rules of the Ten Commandments and the positive injunction to love your neighbor. The latter is a demand to commit oneself to an active pattern of conduct, not simply to abstain from certain negative types of conduct. It states an ideal which we can never adequately fulfill. It is a call to perfection; but it does not treat falling short of perfection as a moral fault.

Consider the rule not to violate the human rights of the workers of a firm, no matter what country they are from or where they reside. That negative rule states the minimum that a company—national or international—must do. The rule requires that one pay at least subsistence wages and as much beyond that as is commensurate with the general standard of living in the country or area in which the workers live. That minimum is far from an ideal. A company of integrity that strives toward some ethical ideal would not focus on the minimum that it was ethically required to pay its employees. It would consider its employees valued members of the firm and would treat them accordingly. Some companies commit themselves to continuous employment once an employee has been with the firm a certain minimum amount of time, in effect guaranteeing that a worker who performs well will not be discharged in hard times. Some companies share their profits with their employees and provide benefits for them that go beyond those demanded by law.

A company of integrity will stand by its products. Not only will it ensure that they do no harm, but it will make them as good as possible, sell them at a reasonable price, and replace or repair them if they are defective. Striving for quality is an ideal that goes beyond the required minimum.

Ideals vary with the field of endeavor, as well as with the company and its history. They may emphasize a company's treatment of employees, customers, competitors, shareholders, and creditors; they may focus on excellence in the goods produced; they may involve care and concern for the general community in which the firm operates. AT&T paid special attention to the reliability of its products; Maytag stresses its low frequency of required repair; Johnson & Johnson emphasizes concern for its customers. Whatever the particular ideals, they must then be supported by the necessary means to achieve (or at least approach) them. The structures of the company must be such that the goals are kept in view and that striving toward them is a central mission of the company and of the individual workers. If the ideals are simply slogans that do not inform the practices or structures or activities of individuals in the firm, they do not form part of the corporate culture and will not offer any basis for a reputation for integrity.

A Company of Integrity

Ultimately, integrity depends not on what a company says but on what it does. Small companies may instinctively act with integrity because of the people who own and operate them. A company of any size or complexity is unlikely to act with integrity automatically or reflexively unless some force within it, especially it leaders, commits the company to so acting and articulates and inculcates that commitment.

Rarely would a firm be judged a company of integrity if those within it did not consider it to be one. However, the reverse is not always the case. A company may believe itself to be a company of integrity and yet (correctly) fail to be so perceived from the outside. This discrepancy between internal assessment and external perception typically stems from inconsistencies in one or more of three areas.

The first area involves a discrepancy between what the firm believes it should be and do and what it actually should be and do, viewed from a broader social and ethical perspective. Managers or boards that believe that their obligation is exclusively one of value enhancement for shareholders within the letter of the law may feel that their firm possesses a full measure of integrity because it is profitable and avoids illegal improprieties. Such a firm may not be perceived as having integrity by the general public, who expect more than profitability and legal compliance. Absence of concern for workers, consumers, or the environment may be compatible with legality while falling short of even the ethical minimum. A firm that circumscribes its obligations and its ideals very narrowly may believe that, in fulfilling them, it acts with integrity; but in fact it fails to do so, in many ways.

The test of integrity remains action. But the scale that a firm uses to measure itself must be one that is ethically defensible, that takes into account all who are affected by the firm's actions, that respects human rights, that fosters human development, and that goes beyond the moral minimum. To prevent gaps between a firm's aims and the requirements of integrity, the firm must adopt an objective stance and a broad perspective, which means that it must scrutinize its goals from an ethical point of view.

The second area of inconsistency occurs as a result of a mismatch between what a firm believes and what it actually does. A firm's top management may want the firm to act with integrity and may set out guidelines to help it and its employees do so. It may explicitly commit itself to acting ethically as well as legally, and it may adopt a worthy set of ideals toward which it wishes to strive. Yet what it actually does may fall short on both counts.

This can happen for many reasons. The firm's goals and ideals may be inadequately communicated or transferred; they may be articulated but not inculcated; or they may represent management's views that subordinates consider to have been imposed on them. A company may simultaneously give its employees conflicting messages on what is expected of them, with profit-making or cost-cutting exhortations having preeminence over everything else. Good managerial intentions may be poorly implemented on lower levels. Middle managers or trenchline workers may perceive those above them as being fundamentally self-interested or as failing to live up to the stated corporate goals themselves.

A company of integrity will make the effort to ensure that its goals and ideals are properly perceived at all levels, are shared by the vast majority of those who make up the company, and are implemented in action. This means taking what might be called the moral temperature of the corporation, from time to time. What do employees at all levels believe the corporation's true values and ideals are, and how closely do they feel those ideals match reality? Where are there discrepancies, and how can those discrepancies be diminished or eliminated so that the company as a whole acts as those within it think it should? How can the company convey its ideals and values to all parts of the corporation—to those abroad as well as to those at the home office? What is it doing to implement the ideals, to motivate its employees to live by them, and to monitor the extent to which they do? Only if a corporation asks such questions and follows through on the answers will it be perceived as a company of integrity.

The third area of inconsistency involves differences between what a company commits itself to and implements and what other companies of integrity do. In its own estimation a company may have admirable goals and ideals and may be meeting them very well. Yet they may be perceived from the outside as falling short in comparison to what other firms of integrity are doing and to what the public perceives as constituting integrity. Public expectations about what companies should do and be have risen. When the public sees one company of integrity act beyond the moral minimum in an exemplary manner, it expects more of all companies. The case of Merck provides a benchmark against which firms may ask themselves whether their goals and ideals are as high as they thought. The benchmark keeps moving upward as public expectations rise. What was previously perceived as exceeding the socially accepted minimum becomes the required legally imposed norm.

Companies that wish to be perceived as progressive—as meeting more than the moral and social minimum—should reevaluate their performance and ideals in light of other companies' actions and of changing social expectations. Being a company of integrity is a continuing process, not a static result of decisions once made or ideals once adopted and seldom if ever reevaluated.

Corporate Culture

To strive toward ethical goals, a company must coordinate the actions of its many members so that they may move in the same direction. It must state its goals, motivate its employees to seek them, structure the firm so that many do, and reward those who do. Corporate culture encompasses the firm's ideals or its lack thereof. Firms that excel often have a strong and positive corporate culture that encompasses everyone within the firm, from the chairman of the board to the night-shift cleaning crew.

A corporate code can embody a corporate culture and can transmit a company's ideals to its employees, influencing their attitudes toward the firm and toward those with whom they come in contact.

Corporate codes and cultures—and so, corporate ideals—have encountered three hurdles in recent years. First, takeovers and the threat of takeovers, characteristic of much of the 1980s, tended to undermine employees' allegiance to their firms. One cannot have deep (or well-placed) allegiance to a firm that may tomorrow be swallowed up, sold off, or dismantled, and from which one may be let go as redundant in the event of a takeover. Employees of firms that were taken over and employees of threatened firms suffered the same syndrome of alienation from their firms.

A corporate culture cannot easily be transferred. If a firm is taken over, its old culture is no longer operative, and all the employees and managers who stay on must adjust to the new owners and the new situation. Meanwhile, the acquiring firm cannot easily transfer its own culture to the acquired firm, nor can it simply continue with its own culture as if the addition made no difference. Even raiders who claimed at least a theoretical interest in efficiency seldom worried about the loss of corporate culture. Corporate culture is intangible: it does not appear on asset or liability sheets; it cannot be sold, but it can be destroyed. A company that acts with integrity must have a sense of self-identity. It must identify with certain ideals. And it must look beyond the financial bottom line in forming its policies and planning its actions.

Internationalization presents the second threat to a corporation's culture. As national firms, companies develop an identity, a culture, and a set of ideals. Just as corporate culture does not translate easily across firms, it does not transfer easily across borders. The transnational cultivation of a company's culture and the pursuit of its ideals require conscious planning and effort.

The difficulty with transferring corporate culture across borders stems from the structure of many multinationals, from the different national cultures in which the firm locates, and from the difficulty of developing the same kind of control or producing the same kind of ambiance when the foreign subsidiary is removed both psychologically and geographically from the parent company. Each of these difficulties can be overcome, but each requires thought, care, planning, and conscious effort. To the extent that the basic goals and ideals are transferred, they must be nourished in each locale and reinforced by the general culture of the local setting.

The third hurdle is the structure of many multinational corporations. They have incorporated the international division of labor into the firm itself. An American multinational gathers its raw material in one part of the world; manufactures its goods in a second, where labor is cheap; markets its products in the developed countries; and manages the whole from its headquarters in the United States. The firm is spread out, and each part of it in each country performs a different task. Since each subsidiary is not simply a copy or recapitulation of the parent company, it is difficult to encourage the same culture to inform all parts of the company. It is difficult for many of the parts to see their relation to the whole, and to identify with the whole and its values.

The challenge for a company of integrity is to unify its many geographically distinct parts, infuse them with the same ideals, and develop in each of them the same corporate culture. This may require moving many of its people, especially at the managerial level, among its different locations, much as the army does to maintain its culture. At each of its locations the company must use similar codes, materials, and training programs that emphasize the company's ideals and carry its culture. It must use sensitivity in translating general goals and ideals into a consistent voice in diverse cultural settings. It must use monitoring, positive reinforcement, and effective and frequent communication. All of these steps are difficult and expensive, yet they are necessary if the company's culture is to permeate its many branches.

Corporate Virtue

Corporate ethical ideals can sometimes be translated into the language of virtue.[6] Human virtues are excellences appropriate to human beings; corporate virtues are excellences appropriate to corporations. Efficiency is a highly prized corporate virtue, but hardly the only one. Just as individuals develop their reputations, for better or for worse, so corporations develop their reputations, also for better or for worse. A corporation may be known as an excellent firm to work for, as a reliable company, as a trustworthy supplier, or as a customer-oriented operation. Each of these is a type of corporate virtue. The *New York Times* motto, "All the news that's fit to print," expresses the publisher's dual ideal of comprehensiveness and of good taste, eschewing the gaudy and titillating. Over time the newspaper has become identified with its motto, and its employees feel part of an important tradition, which guides their conduct. The slogan that, if you send a Hallmark Card, you "care enough to send the very best" similarly holds up an ideal of excellence in quality and taste, a theme that the firm and its employees try to carry through in the firm's various operations—in its ads, in the TV programs it sponsors, and in the projects it adopts worldwide.

The two virtues of moral courage and moral imagination are necessary whatever other ideals one chooses to emphasize and work toward. A blending of one's personal values with the corporate values of the firm for which one works should yield a combination in which each positively reinforces the other.

Just as a corporation can be said to have ideals, virtues, and a character, it can be said also have a conscience.[7] For a company to have a conscience, its employees must have a conscience, and the firm as a whole must respond positively to matters of conscience raised by its employees. Continuing the analogy with human beings, the corporation's conscience may be located centrally, but it must be informed by all its parts. Conscience is like a switch that is always present in the background and that lights up when faced either with the unethical or with needs or opportunities that call for a positive response. A corporation that acts with integrity nurtures its conscience and, in striving toward its ideals, consciously works to develop the virtues appropriate to it. It works hard to get the reputation it desires and to keep that reputation unsullied.

Background Institutions

Background institutions are essential to corporate integrity. Corporations are institutions, and they necessarily operate within institutional frameworks. Multinational corporations have developed faster than have adequate international background institutions that can limit abuses and create fair conditions of competition. As a result, unscrupulous companies can exploit peoples and nations with relative impunity, increase profits at the expense of others, and externalize costs (for example, by freely discharging wastes into the atmosphere or land or water) so the costs are borne by others rather than by the firm. Companies with integrity do not harm or exploit or take unfair advantage of others. Rather they help develop adequate background institutions to make competition fair. They have a self-interested reason for doing so, as well as a more altruistic, ethical motivation. What does this mean in practice?

Consider, for example, the banking industry. The negative guidelines that should control international banks mark only the beginning of a bank's possible contribution to global progress. International banks are the lifeblood of economic development throughout the world. They have enormous potential for both good and harm. Unregulated and unopposed—and without any equally strong international organization, body, or legislation to counter them—they typically seek their own good and pursue their own interests, often at the expense of others. They are a prime type of institution whose power needs to be offset by international background institutions.

A first step in the development of such institutions could be a model code of international banking. Would such a code allow secret accounts? Would it prevent money laundering? How would it treat capital flight (especially of aid money) from less developed countries?

Since anyone affected by a practice should have a say in the rules governing that practice, an enforceable model code for international banking should not be drawn up only by banks, or only by government representatives, corporations, or academics. It should be drawn up by representatives of each of these as well as of other pertinent groups. But an initial code might be developed and suggested by any of them, or by some group representing several of them. A multinational bank interested in acting with integrity might well take the lead in calling together the appropriate group or might develop such a draft code on its own. Bankers must participate in drafting the code because they know best the myriad ways in which funds can be transferred, hidden, accounted for, lost, covered up, reported, used, and abused. They know the costs of accountability, the shady practices, and the loopholes that need filling.

Once developed, the proposed code should be publicized, circulated, discussed, debated, amended, and finally tentatively adopted. An individual bank that adopts a model code tailors its own internal code to conform with the model code, and thenceforth follows the practices stated in the code. A code, like the American Bar Association Code of Professional Responsibility, might both impose rules or prohibitions and state ideals. Individual codes are clearly internal guides and are self-enforced. To be effective, the model code not only must be widely adopted, but must have some sort of enforcement mechanism attached to it.

It may seem too much to ask banks to write self-restricting codes or to recommend laws that limit their activities. But it is not too much to ask banks with integrity to participate in presenting a code of ideals as well as a code of enforceable minimum standards. Since any bank, no matter how ethical, is also self-interested, others—such as government representatives, customers, and other financial institutions—should also take part in formulating the model code. A bank with integrity will not object to fair rules that govern all banking institutions, itself included.

A model code is a first step. It encourages voluntary compliance by all banks and sets up criteria by which governments and the public can evaluate the behavior of individual banks. It permits specialized parties, groups, or oversight firms to rate international banks and their adherence to or deviance from the norms stated in the model code. Such information can be used by investors, stockholders, and other interested parties.

A model code lays the groundwork for regulatory codes—whether voluntary or mandatory—and for model legislation. Initially such legislation will be national in scope. Model legislation may be developed by representatives from the various interested groups, by some firm that takes the lead, or by some legislature. National legislation can then form the basis for bilateral, multinational, or international agreements and norms, enforced by reciprocal agreement. Eventually an international board with punitive power might be established, and appropriate punishments—be they fines or exclusion from trading—might be worked out.

Each of these steps yields background institutions that together create a system adequate to the international scope of the multinational banks. Similar codes for other industries are also in order—especially for the pharmaceutical and chemical industries, and for other industries that have been severely criticized for their practices.

International model codes are only one type of background institution. We can envisage controls on the international level comparable to each level of control on the national level: labor syndicates; consumer unions; environmental protection groups; international media with investigative reporters; church groups; and other mediating, spontaneous, and private organizations. Just as fax machines and TV played a vital role in spreading information about Eastern Europe and China and helped move the masses in those countries, so publicity and grass-roots movements can help create controls on abuses by multinational corporations and financial institutions, and can help channel their energies in ways that are productive for the firms and beneficial for the people.

Conclusion

National or international business can be no more ethical than the persons who run the firms. This is the first theme that emerges from our discussions about competing with integrity. Companies that act with integrity are largely a function of individuals within the firms who act with integrity. This is essential. Among those in the firm who act with integrity, the top managers are the crucial players. Unless they exemplify integrity, demand it of their employees, and support it throughout the firm, the company cannot—and so will not—act with integrity. However, personal integrity is not enough.

The second theme to emerge is that of ethical displacement. Ethical issues and dilemmas cannot always be resolved at the level at which they appear. For this reason corporate structures and policies are vitally important. Ethical individuals are constrained by the organization, structures, and policies of the companies for which they work. These may either reinforce ethical behavior or thwart it. The same is true at each level. Firms that wish to act with integrity either may feel impelled to follow unfair industry practices or may find their actions constrained by them. The same story can be repeated at the industry, the national, and finally the global level. Solutions must be sought at the appropriate level, which often differs from the level at which a problem appears.

The third theme is the urgent need for adequate background institutions to counteract the tendencies toward unfairness of the market, of the free-enterprise system, and of perceived self-interest on all levels. Such social, political, and economic institutions promote fair conditions of competition wherever they exist and will offset the otherwise unbridled power of multinational corporations and banks worldwide.

In any society business is allowed to operate because people as a whole benefit from its activities. It is not the good of business that is most important, but the good of society. Business is a means to achieve the good of people, and they appropriately act to restrict and channel it. As we have seen, the major difficulty with international business is its lack of restraints and constraints to ensure that it is socially beneficial. If it does not benefit society, people have no valid reason to tolerate it. The business of business is surely business; but ultimately it is not up to each business to decide what that means, but up to the societies and the global community that allow businesses to operate.

Currently, the power and scope of international business have outstripped the power and scope of international background institutions. The need for ethical norms and guidelines is greater on the level of international business than on the national level—at least in industrially developed countries, where adequate background institutions generally already exist. Ethical norms provide guidance in acting and also touchstones for evaluating multinational practices, for marshaling public reaction, and for applying moral sanctions.

During the long history of business in the United States, many corporations zealously fought proposed legislation that sought to restrict or control their operations in any way, whether in the area of worker benefits, of safety, or of consumer protection. That history is being repeated today on the international level. Firms with integrity can learn from history and can promote rather than hinder the necessary and (we may hope) inevitable emergence of controls and beneficial restrictions.

Leadership and courage are required. Negotiation is essential. A network developed on many levels, across many fields, and intersecting at many points will form the basis for sharing information, model codes, new structures, and imaginative approaches to ethical international business practices.

Competing with integrity in international business means having the courage, the resolve, and the imagination to foster the background institutions and organize the myriad social forces that will create conditions of competition fair for all. In such a situation the best will succeed. Not all firms with integrity will be well run, and some therefore may not be successful. But those that fail will not fail because they have integrity. On the other hand, those that succeed may well succeed because they do. It is possible to compete successfully with integrity; it is imperative that more firms have the courage and the imagination to do so.

Notes

Chapter 1

1. See, for instance, John S. R. Shad, "Business's Bottom Line: Ethics," *New York Times*, July 27, 1987, p. A19; and Felix Rohatyn, "The Blight on Wall Street," *New York Review of Books*, March 12, 1987, p. 21.

2. See James B. Stewart, "Scenes from a Scandal: The Secret World of Michael Milken and Ivan Boesky," *Wall Street Journal*, October 2, 1991, p. B1; and Karen W. Arenson, "How Wall Street Bred Ivan Boesky," *New York Times*, November 26, 1986, p. 8F.

3. *Financial World*, July 27, 1989.

4. For details on these and other corporations, see The Business Roundtable, *Corporate Ethics: A Prime Business Asset: A Report on Policy and Practice in Company Conduct*, February 1988; and Susan J. Harrington, "What Corporate America Is Teaching About Ethics," *Academy of Management Executive* vol. 5, no. 1 (1991), pp. 21–30.

5. The Conference Board, *Corporate Ethics*, Research Report No. 900, 1987. Although the exact number of firms with corporate codes of ethics is difficult to determine, the percentage of major firms with such codes has tended to increase in recent years: Amanda Bennett, "Ethics Codes Spread Despite Skepticism," *Wall Street Journal*, June 15, 1988, p. 13.

6. The European Business Ethics Network was founded in 1987, following the First European Conference on Business Ethics, which took place in Brussels. For a survey of business ethics in the United Kingdom and Europe, see Jack Mahoney, *Teaching Business Ethics in the UK, Europe and the USA: A Comparative Study* (London: Athlone Press, 1990).

7. For an elaboration of the Myth of Amoral Business in the United States, see Richard T. De George, *Business Ethics*, 3d ed. (New York: Macmillan, 1990), Chapter 1.

8. "Alaska: How Clean Is Clean?" *Newsweek*, August 7, 1989, p. 52; "Alaska After Exxon," *Newsweek*, September 18, 1989, pp. 50–55; "Exxon to Renew Alaska Cleanup; Accord Ends Standoff with State," *New York Times*, February 22, 1990, p. 1.

9. "Alaska After Exxon," *Newsweek,* September 18, 1989, p. 54; "An Oil Slick Trips up Exxon, *Time,* April 24, 1989, p. 46.

10. Although this sphere of actions is commonly acknowledged, some philosophers deny that it exists. Among philosophers who acknowledge them, these actions are sometimes referred to as supererogatory actions. See Chapter 10, note 4; J. O. Urmson, "Saints and Heroes," in *Essays in Moral Philosophy,* ed. by A. I. Melden (Seattle: University of Washington Press, 1958), pp. 198–216.

11. For another discussion of the importance of a company's reputation, see Susan Caminiti, "The Payoff from a Good Reputation," *Fortune,* February 10, 1992, pp. 74–77.

12. Douglas McLeod, "J&J Subsidiary Denied Coverage for Tylenol Recall," *Business Insurance* 20(38) (September 22, 1986): 1, 87; Janet Aschkenasy, "Insurers Score Victory in Tylenol Product-Recall Case, *National Underwriter* (*Property/Casualty*) 90(39) (September 26, 1986): 1, 7.

13. "Business' New Link: Ethics and the Bottom Line," *Industry Week* 223(3) (October 29, 1984): 49–53.

14. The "when in Rome" position is often equated with cultural relativism and with ethical relativism. Cultural relativism asserts that mores and customs differ from country to country and from age to age. It is a descriptive statement for which ample anthropological and historical evidence exists. Ethical relativism claims further that, when two cultures (or two individuals) disagree on the morality of an action, neither is right or wrong. For a discussion of ethical relativism, see De George, op. cit., Chapter 2; Thomas Donaldson, *The Ethics of International Business* (New York: Oxford University Press, 1989), pp. 14–19; and Michael Krausz and Jack W. Meiland, eds., *Relativism: Cognitive and Moral* (Notre Dame: University of Notre Dame Press, 1982).

15. For a utilitarian discussion of the immorality of slavery, see R. M. Hare, "What Is Wrong with Slavery," *Philosophy & Public Affairs* 8 (1989): 103–21.

16. For a discussion of bribery and the Foreign Corrupt Practices Act, see Chapter 6.

17. "Facilitating payments" is the term used by the Amendments to the Foreign Corrupt Practices Act for small acceptable and reportable payments to minor government officials to induce them to do their jobs expeditiously. See Chapter 6.

18. Robert Grunts, "Ethics as a Way of Life," *Ethics and the Multinational Enterprise: Proceedings of the Sixth National Conference on Business Ethics,* ed. by W. Michael Hoffman, Ann E. Lange, and David A. Fedo (New York: University Press of America, 1986), pp. 101–6, recounts how Whirlpool's subsidiary, Thomas International Corporation, successfully worked with other U.S. companies to fight the necessity of paying extortion to Mexican border agents to expedite passage of their trucks across the border.

19. Extortion is the act of obtaining undeserved payment by coercion or threat of harm. Because of the force and harm involved, it is a greater offense against morality than is bribery. The harm increases the culpability of the extortioner, and the coercion mitigates to some extent the culpability of the victim. In the present case, where the demand is unexpected, the harm is imminent, the payment is small, and the alternative is the ruin of several truckloads of butter, the American is arguably choosing the lesser of two evils. For a fuller discussion of the conditions attached to corruption and of techniques for responding to it, see Chapter 7.

20. Arthur L. Kelly, "Case Study—Italian Tax Mores," paper presented at Loyola University of Chicago symposium, "Foundations of Corporate Responsibility to Society," April 1977, and printed in *Ethical Issues in Business* ed. by Thomas Donaldson and Patricia H. Werhane (Englewood Cliffs: Prentice-Hall, 1979), pp. 37–39.

21. The injunction to do no harm is widely recognized. John G. Simon, Charles W. Powers, and Jon P. Gunnemann, *The Ethical Investor: Universities and Corporate Responsibility* (New Haven: Yale University Press, 1972), calls the avoidance and correction of social injury the "moral minimum" required of corporations. The injunction to respect the dignity of the human person is also widely recognized, as the basis for human rights. See De George, op. cit., Chapter 4. On rights, see James W. Nickel, *Making Sense of Human Rights: Philosophical Reflections on the Universal Declaration of Human Rights* (Berkeley: University of California Press, 1987); and Thomas Donaldson, op. cit., Chapter 5.

22. For a defense of the argument "everybody's doing it," see Ronald Green, "When Is 'Everyone's Doing It' a Moral Justification?" *Business Ethics Quarterly* 1 (1991): 75–93. For a critique of that position, see Richard T. De George, "Green and 'Everybody's Doing It'," *Business Ethics Quarterly* 1 (1991): 95–100.

23. The reason why the norms apply no matter which of the basic ethical theories one adopts is that all of these theories attempt to justify these norms, which are pretheoretical.

Chapter 2

1. For a fuller description of abortion and the Soviet Union, see Richard T. De George, "Biomedical Ethics," in *Science and the Soviet Social Order,* ed. by Loren R. Graham (Cambridge, Mass.: Harvard University Press, 1990), pp. 195–224.

2. On the lag of the law behind morality, see Christopher D. Stone, *Where the Law Ends: The Social Control of Corporate Behavior* (Prospect Heights, Ill.: Waveland Press, 1991 [reissued], p. 94.

3. For a fuller discussion of the ethical defensibility of the U.S. economic system, see Richard T. De George, *Business Ethics,* 3d ed. (New York: Macmillan, 1990), Chapter 7.

4. Lack of funds, for instance, precludes the kinds of controls that the FDA imposes in the United States. In some countries, such as those in Central and Eastern Europe, the transition from socialism to a market economy has been so rapid that the legislatures in those countries have not yet had time to pass constraining legislation, nor have they had enough experience with the market to know what laws to pass.

5. For discussions of whether MNCs operate in a Hobbesian state of nature, see Manuel Velasquez, "International Business, Morality, and the Common Good," *Business Ethics Quarterly* 2(1) (January 1992): 27–40; Thomas Donaldson, *The Ethics of International Business* (New York: Oxford University Press, 1989), Chapter 2; Hans J. Morgenthau, *Dilemmas of Politics* (Chicago: Chicago University Press, 1958); Marshall Cohen, "Moral Skepticism and International Relations," *Philosophy & Public Affairs* 13 (Fall 1984): 299–346; and Gregory Kavka, "Hobbes' War of All Against All," *Ethics* 93 (January 1983): 291–310.

6. World Health Organization, *International Code of Marketing of Breast-milk Substitutes* (Geneva: WHO, 1981).

7. United Nations, Economic and Social Control, E/1990/94, 12 June 1990, contains the "Proposed Text of the Draft Code of Conduct on Transnational Corporations." For an overview and discussion of other international codes, see John M. Kline, *International Codes and Multinational Business: Setting Guidelines for International Business Operations* (Westport, Conn.: Quorum Books, 1985).

8. "Guidelines for Multinational Enterprises" is an annex to the 1976 "OECD Declaration," *International Investment and Multinational Enterprises: Revised Edition 1984* (Paris: Organization for Economic Cooperation and Development, 1984), pp. 11–22.

9. The Sullivan Principles were drawn up in 1977 by Leon Sullivan, a black Philadelphia minister and a member of General Motors' board of directors. These principles called for desegregation in the workplace and for deliberate violation of all apartheid laws. The Sullivan Principles were widely adopted by American firms in South Africa, and their violation of the apartheid laws was ignored by the South African government. Sullivan hoped that widespread adoption of the principles would help break down the apartheid system in South Africa. After ten years Sullivan concluded that simply following the principles would not suffice to break down apartheid, and that American companies—even those following the principles—could not justify their continued presence in South Africa. He called for disinvestment by all American companies. Since then, most of the largest U.S. companies have left South Africa, many for economic reasons. Nonetheless, the Sullivan Principles show how an individual company can take the initiative in acting ethically, how it can mobilize other companies to join it, and how they can force a government at least to tolerate their ethical stance, even though it involves violating the government's laws and policies. See Chapter 7.

10. On the general issue, see Georges Enderle, "The Indebtedness of Low-Income Countries as an Ethical Challenge for Industrialized Market Economies," *The International Journal of Applied Philosophy* 4(3) (1989): 31–38.

11. Although widely accepted and followed in practice, this principle might be challenged by those who consider it an instance of "particularism" and who claim that moral principles are properly universal. Nonetheless, one can universalize the obligation to help those closest to one first. Nations are built on the principle that they owe help first to their own citizens, even though this does not preclude helping others as well.

12. On the New International Economic Order, see United Nations General Assembly, A/9556 (Part II) 1 May 1974, *Study of the Problems of Raw Materials and Development: Report of the Ad Hoc Committee of the Sixth Special Session,* which contains the "Declaration on the Establishment of a New International Economic Order." For a discussion of this see, Robert F. Meagher, *An International Redistribution of Wealth and Power: A Study of the Charter of Economic Rights and Duties of States* (New York: Pergamon Press, 1979).

13. Many countries ended their economic sanctions in 1991, when South Africa began to dismantle apartheid. Critics claimed that the sanctions were ended too early and argued that, without continued pressure, the South African government would have little incentive to continue to dispense with apartheid. See, for instance, Alan

Riding, "European Nations to Lift Sanctions on South Africa," *New York Times,* April 16, 1991, p. 1.

14. In the hands of some, this thesis has been developed into what has become known as Dependency Theory. See Fernando Henrique Cardoso and Enzo Faletto, *Dependencia and Development in Latin America* (Berkeley: University of California Press, 1979); see also Theodore H. Moran, *Multinational Corporations and the Politics of Dependence: Copper in Chile* (Princeton, N.J.: Princeton University Press, 1977).

15. In addition to commutative justice, we can also speak of distributive justice (the proper allocation of burdens and benefits, usually by the government), retributive justice (punishment for crimes), and compensatory justice (the making good of injury done). What is substantively required to satisfy each kind of justice is determined by one's theory or concept of justice.

16. Although this is a debatable claim, many American companies nonetheless do give something to charity, and the U.S. government allows corporations to deduct up to 5 percent of earnings for charitable contributions. Japanese firms in the United States have come in for criticism because of their failure to contribute to their local communities or to charities, and have slowly started changing their practices. The obligation to contribute in this way is sometimes called a company's "social responsibility." In a 1992 article ("Why Japan Must Change," *Fortune,* March 9, 1992, pp. 66–67), Akio Morita, the chairman of Sony, noted "The average corporate donation in the U.S. in 1989 was 1.55% of pretax profits, while in Japan it was only 0.33%." On the other hand, Milton Friedman argues against such corporate giving in his famous article, "The Social Responsibility of Business Is to Increase Its Profits," *New York Times Magazine,* September 13, 1970.

17. For a fuller discussion of stakeholder analysis, see R. Edward Freeman, *Strategic Management: A Stakeholder Analysis* (Boston: Pittman, 1984). From an ethical point of view, one shortcoming of stakeholder analysis is that it does not consider the effects of an action on those who are not stakeholders but are nonetheless affected. If the analysis does include all those affected, it is equivalent to a utilitarian analysis.

18. For a fuller description and discussion of utilitarianism, see De George, op. cit., Chapter 3. The classical statements of utilitarianism come from Jeremy Bentham, *An Introduction to the Principles of Morals and Legislation,* first published in 1789, and John Stuart Mill, *Utilitarianism,* first published in 1863. For critical articles, see Samuel Gorovitz, ed., *John Stuart Mill, Utilitarianism, with Critical Essays* (Indianapolis: Bobbs-Merrill, 1971).

19. This is not, strictly speaking, an ethical approach, since it does not consider all parties affected by the action and since it typically considers only factors that are expressible in monetary terms.

20. The literature on rights is extensive. An influential work of the overriding quality of rights is Ronald Dworkin, *Taking Rights Seriously* (Cambridge, Mass.: Harvard University Press, 1977). Also important in the international context is Henry Shue, *Basic Rights* (Princeton: Princeton University Press, 1980).

21. For an alternative discussion of the function of human rights in international business, see Thomas Donaldson, *The Ethics of International Business* (New York: Oxford University Press, 1989).

Chapter 3

1. See, for instance, Theodore H. Moran, "Multinational Corporations and Third World Investment," in *Latin America: Dependency or Interdependence?*, ed. by Michael Novak and Michael P. Jackson (Washington, D.C.: American Enterprise Institute for Public Policy Research, 1985), pp. 15–28.

2. "Guidelines for Multinational Enterprises," an annex to the 1976 "OECD Declaration," in *International Investment and Multinational Enterprises: Revised Edition 1984* (Paris: Organization for Economic Cooperation and Development, 1984), pp. 11–22.

3. United Nations, Economic and Social Council, E/1990/94, 12 June 1990, contains the "Proposed Text of the Draft Code of Conduct on Transnational Corporations."

4. International Labour Office, *Tripartite Declaration of Principles Concerning Multinational Enterprises and Social Policy* (Geneva: ILO, 1977).

5. World Health Organization, *International Code of Marketing of Breast-milk Substitutes* (Geneva: WHO, 1981).

6. For examples of blatant conduct charged against American MNCs, see Richard J. Barnet and Ronald E. Müller, *Global Reach* (New York: Simon & Schuster, 1974); and Pierre Jalée, *The Pillage of the Third World* (New York: Modern Reader Paperbacks, 1968).

7. A rule-utilitarian approach, for instance, clearly yields this rule. In particular cases one can imagine doing direct intentional harm in order to produce some greater good. But this cannot be the general rule, because doing direct intentional harm clearly produces harm and may produce no good at all, much less more good than harm. As a rule, the best way not to produce more harm than good is to avoid producing harm at all.

8. For a discussion of dependency theory, see Fernando Henrique Cardoso and Enzo Faletto, *Dependencia and Development in Latin America* (Berkeley: University of California Press, 1979); Thomas J. Bierksteker, *Distortion or Development: Contending Perspectives on the Multinational Corporation* (Cambridge, Mass.: MIT Press, 1978); and Michael Novak and Michael P. Jackson, eds., *Latin America: Dependency or Interdependence?* (Washington, D.C.: American Enterprise Institute for Public Policy Research, 1985).

9. See Charles Medawar and Barbara Freese, "Drug Multinationals in the Third World," *Business & Society Review* 38 (Summer, 1981): 22–24; Kenneth E. Goodpastor and David E. Whiteside, "Note on the Export of Pesticides from the United States to Developing Nations," in *Ethics and the Multinational Enterprise,* ed. by W. Michael Hoffman, Ann E. Lange, and David A. Fedo (Lanham, Md.: University Press of America, 1986), pp. 305–33.

10. The relation of export crops and local malnutrition is a complicated and much debated one. It is briefly discussed in Frances Moore Lappé and Joseph Collins, *World Hunger: Ten Myths,* 4th ed. (San Francisco: Institute for Food and Development Policy, 1982), under "Myth Six"; and in Richard J. Barnet and Ronald E. Müller, *Global Reach: The Power of Multinational Corporations* (New York: Simon and Schuster, 1974), p. 182. For a case study of the Dolefil Operation in the Philippines, see Lee A. Tavis, ed., *Multinational Managers and Poverty in the Third World* (Notre Dame: University of Notre Dame Press, 1982), Part III.

11. Strictly speaking, this would be a rule-utilitarian analysis, since it argues that as a general rule so acting will produce more good than harm, considering all affected. Nonetheless this guideline can be defended from a variety of ethical perspectives, because, if the people of the host country are not benefited, the company is open to the charge of exploitation either of its resources or of the workers. Treatment of workers that did not exploit them—that paid them fair wages—would benefit them; and extraction of resources for which the country was adequately compensated would benefit it. An analysis based on human rights yields a similar guideline.

12. For a study of Union Carbide in India, see Chapter 5.

13. In 1987, after American companies had followed the Sullivan Principles for ten years, Leon Sullivan decided that American companies could no longer justify their continued presence in South Africa on the grounds that they followed the principles, because that action had not significantly eroded apartheid. He then counseled disinvestment, a strategy that many of the largest U.S. firms in South Africa followed. By 1992, apartheid had significantly diminished as a result of both internal and external pressures.

14. The derivation and defense of this guideline is similar to that for the second: it can be derived in the same ways, using both a rule-utilitarian and a rights-based approach. To fail to promote the development of the less developed country from which one profits is to leave it comparatively worse off. To fail to help such a country develop is to contribute to its continued less developed status. This is a type of exploitation. The transfer of appropriate technology can be considered the payment of a debt to those from whom one benefits, since multinationals would not operate in LDCs unless they did benefit. Those in developed countries who enjoy lower prices because of the lower wages paid to indigenous workers benefit from the poverty and underdevelopment of the LDC, and this is the basis of the obligation to improve their condition rather than to continue it.

15. See the OECD section on "Science and Technology."

16. The OECD's Guidelines' "General Policies" read in part: "Enterprises should: 1. Take fully into account established general policy objectives of the Member countries in which they operate. 2. In particular, give due consideration to those countries' aims and priorities with regard to economic and social progress, including industrial and regional development, the protection of the environment and consumer interests, the creation of employment opportunities, the promotion of innovation and the transfer of technology."

17. On the difference between the development of a country and the development of its people, see Richard T. De George, "Property and Global Justice," *Philosophy in Context* 15 (1985): 34–42.

18. The defense of the requirement to observe the human rights of people in less developed countries is derived from the obligation to observe the human rights of all people. The point of listing it as a specific guideline is to underscore the importance of observing this in connection with conditions in which local firms may regularly violate the human rights of their workers and in which governments may do likewise. For discussions of a human rights approach to international business, see Henry Shue, *Basic Rights: Subsistence, Affluence, and U. S. Foreign Policy* (Princeton: Princeton University Press, 1980); and Thomas Donaldson, *The Ethics of International Business* (New York: Oxford University Press, 1989).

19. See Donaldson, *The Ethics of International Business,* Chapter 5, for a discussion of some of the limitations on interpreting the UN Universal Declaration of Human Rights.

20. The claim that undermining a country's culture does that country harm is not difficult to show, since a culture is the way the people of a country express and identify themselves. It forms part of what they are. Thus the doctrine of respect for persons leads to respecting their personality and their ways of self-expression. The defense of indigenous culture can be taken as a collective exercise of that right. The right to self-expression yields similar results, as does the application of the "Golden Rule." A rule-utilitarian can also argue that respecting indigenous cultures produces more good than harm. Although the full argument requires a good deal of empirical evidence, the intuitive notion of harm is a good starting point.

21. The derivation of this guideline from the general obligation of justice should be clear and should need no elaborate discussion here. The argument assumes that taxation in general is justifiable and that the taxes imposed are on the whole fair. Given these assumptions, the fact that one engages in business within the country leads to the obligation to abide by its laws and hence to pay one's fair taxes. The OECD Guidelines, in the section on "Taxation," states this norm in greater detail; and it is the essence of the UN Code of Conduct on Transnational Corporations' section on taxation.

22. Robert Pear, "For Multinationals, a Crackdown on Taxes," *New York Times,* October 30, 1990, p. A14.

23. This is the position cited in the OECD Guidelines under "Taxation" and in the UN Code of Conduct on Transnational Corporations (section 36).

24. This guideline is a specific restatement of the general obligation to promote the good of the country. It can also be taken as deriving from the third guideline. In addition, it can be independently defended both from utilitarian premises and from the perspective of justice, since it seeks to promote good and to extend justice.

25. The Chemical Industry's Responsible Care program and its Guiding Principles are examples. See Chapter 5.

Chapter 4

1. Ruth Norris, ed., *Pills, Pesticides and Profits* (Croton-on-Hudson, N.Y.: North River Press, 1982), p. 13. Cited in Harvard Business School case 9-384-097.

2. David Bull, *A Growing Problem: Pesticides and the Third World Poor* (Oxford: OXFAM, 1982), p. 38; John Davies, et al., *Agromedical Approach to Pesticide Management* (Miami: University of Miami, 1982), p. 88; Marlise Simons, "Concern Rising over Harm from Pesticides in Third World," *New York Times,* May 30, 1989, p. 21.

3. Reported in Bull, op. cit., p. 144.

4. On the Nestlé boycott see, John Dobbing, ed., *Infant Feeding: Anatomy of a Controversy 1973–1984* (London: Springer-Verlag, 1988); Nancy Gaschott, "Babies at Risk: Infant Formula Still Takes Its Toll," *Multinational Monitor* (October, 1986): 11–13; *The Dilemma of Third World Nutrition: Nestlé and the Role of Infant Formula,* 1985 (a report prepared for Nestlé and distributed by it).

5. This did not end the controversy. After Nestlé agreed to abide by the guidelines, critics claimed that it continued to violate some of them. The Action for Corpo-

rate Accountability, which targeted Nestlé and American Home Products Corporation for distributing free formula through maternity wards in Africa, raised a call for a new boycott. Both companies insisted that they were abiding by the WHO code (*New York Times,* October 5, 1988, p. IV, 2). The new boycott was not widely supported, yet Nestlé "promised to support UNICEF's 'Baby Friendly Hospital Initiative'," *Newsweek,* July 6, 1992, p. 58. This case shows the need for continued vigilance, even after norms have been developed and adopted.

6. See Lee A. Tavis, ed., *Multinational Managers and Poverty in the Third World* (Notre Dame: University of Notre Dame Press, 1982); Raymond E. Crist, "Land for the People—A Vital Need Everywhere: In Latin America and the Caribbean, It's Now 'a Prey to Hastening Ills' and Decay," *American Journal of Economics and Sociology* 42(3) (July 1983): 275–90.

7. See Michael Novak and Michael P. Jackson, eds., *Latin America: Dependency or Interdependence?* (Washington, D.C.: American Enterprise Institute for Public Policy Research, 1985).

8. In Costa Rica, Merck Sharp & Dohme have paid $1 million to preserve the jungle in order to "prospect" for pharmaceutically useful plants (*Newsweek,* June 1, 1992, p. 39).

9. See *Newsweek,* June 1, 1992, for various articles dealing with the Rio Conference on the environment and related issues.

10. Peter Passell, "Fighting Cocaine, Coffee, Flowers," *New York Times,* September 20, 1989; "Coffee Impasse Imperils Colombia's Drug Fight," *New York Times,* September 24, 1989, p. 1; "Coffee, Chrysanthemums and Cocaine," *New York Times,* February 20, 1990, p. A20; "High Cost of Fighting Drugs Strains U.S.–Colombia Ties," *New York Times,* June 4, 1990, p. D1.

11. For a summary presentation of the details of the BCCI scandal, see "The Dirtiest Bank of All," *Times International,* July 29, 1991, pp. 18–23.

12. In 1985 the First Bank System, Inc., stopped lending even to private companies in South Africa. Its president commented, "We abhor the apartheid system" (*Wall Street Journal,* August 1, 1985, p. 21). The Chase Manhattan Bank stopped making loans to the South African government or its agencies in 1977. In 1985 it stopped making loans at all in South Africa (*Wall Street Journal,* August 1, 1985, p. 21).

13. Raul L. Madrid, *Over-Exposed: U.S. Banks Confront the Third World Debt Crisis* (Washington: Investor Responsibility Research Center, 1990); World Bank, *World Development Report 1989* (New York: Oxford University Press, 1989); Albert Fishlow, "Coming to Terms with the Latin Debt," *New York Times,* January 4, 1988, p. 17.

14. See, for instance, Roger Thurow, "Third World Hope: Development Bank in Africa Transcends the Region's Despair," *Wall Street Journal,* May 26, 1989, p. 1.

15. Sarah Bartlett, "A Vicious Circle Keeps Latin America in Debt," *New York Times,* January 15, 1989, Sec. 4, p. 3; Barry Herman, "The Outlook for Development," in *Debt Disaster? Banks, Government, and Multilaterals Confront the Crisis,* ed. by John F. Weeks (New York: New York University Press, 1989), pp. 3–19; Chris C. Carvounis, *The Foreign Debt/National Development Conflict: External Adjustment and Internal Disorder in the Developing Nations* (New York: Quorum Books, 1986).

16. See "The Crushing Monster," *Time,* July 27, 1987, pp. 36–38. Other banks traded loans for local currency (Jaclyn Fierman, "Fast Bucks in Latin Loan Swaps," *Fortune,* August 3, 1987, pp. 91–99).

206 <i>Notes: Chapter 5</i>

17. See, for instance, Alberta Piccolino, "Forgive Third World Debt or Expect Apocalypse," <i>National Catholic Reporter,</i> May 8, 1992, p. 15.

18. The U.S. law prompted a similar law in Canada (Stephen Labaton, "Canada Wants Banks to Record Cash Deals," <i>New York Times,</i> March 22, 1990, p. D2).

19. Stephen Labaton, "Group of 7 Asks Money-Laundering Curbs," <i>New York Times,</i> April 20, 1990, p. C1.

20. Alan Riding, "New Rule Reduces Swiss Banking Secrecy," <i>New York Times,</i> May 6, 1991, C1; and "The End of Banking Secrecy in Liechtenstein?" <i>International Living</i> 9 (February 1990): 19.

21. For an overview of the S&L debacle, see Gary Hector, "S&Ls: Where Did All Those Billions Go?" <i>Fortune,</i> September 10, 1990, pp. 84–88.

22. See, for instance, Bruce Babbitt, "The New Improved South America," <i>World Monitor</i> (February 1991): 32–39.

23. For an evaluation of MNCs in extracting industries see, Scott McNall and Sally O. Margolin, "Multinational Corporations in Latin America: The Search for Consumers and Raw Materials," <i>Comparative International Development</i> 12 (Fall, 1977): 65–85. For a study of the change in bargaining strength relative to the host country, see Michael Shafer, "Capturing the Mineral Multinationals: Advantage or Disadvantage?" in <i>Multinational Corporations: The Political Economy of Foreign Direct Investment,</i> ed. by Theodore H. Moran (Lexington, Mass.: Lexington Books, 1985), pp. 25–53.

24. Although the claim is plausible, it comes up against another claim that the goods of the world by right belong to all the people of the earth, and that national boundaries, being artificial, do not justify any exclusive claim of those lucky enough to have natural resources. For a further discussion of these conflicting claims, see Richard T. De George, "Property and Global Justice," <i>Philosophy in Context</i> 15 (1985): 34–42.

25. Harry Makler, Alberto Martinelli, and Neil Smelser, eds., <i>The New International Economy</i> (Beverly Hills: Sage Publications, 1982), p. 20. For some studies of OPEC, see <i>OPEC, the United States, and the World Oil Market,</i> ed. by Wilfrid L. Kohl (Baltimore: Johns Hopkins University Press, 1991); Paul Hallwood and Stuart W. Sinclair, <i>Oil, Debt and Development: OPEC in the Third World</i> (London: George Allen & Unwin, 1981).

26. These charges were common in the literature on multinationals of the 1970s. See, for instance, Richard J. Barnet and Ronald E. Müller, <i>Global Reach: The Power of the Multinational Corporations</i> (New York: Simon & Schuster, 1974). On MNCs and culture see, Armand Mattelart, <i>Transnationals and the Third World: The Struggle for Culture</i> (South Hadley, Mass.: Bergin & Garvey, 1983).

27. This is in effect Lenin's thesis in <i>Imperialism: The Highest Stage of Capitalism,</i> which claims that capitalism in the developed countries had avoided collapsing by moving its grossest exploitation to the colonies. The claim has been widely adopted and adapted since Lenin's time.

Chapter 5

1. Details of the tragedy were carried by the media and are available from various sources. The official report of the Indian government has not been made public. The

New York Times published the results of its investigation in a four-part series on January 28, 30, 31, and February 3, 1985. Union Carbide published a preliminary report; but it never published documents substantiating the claim of sabotage (*New York Times*, June 23, 1987, p. 6), which was to be its defense if the case went to trial. Among the several book-length studies of the disaster and its aftermath that appeared, some, such as Larry Everest, *Behind the Poison Cloud: Union Carbide's Bhopal Massacre* (Chicago: Banner Press, 1985), made the case against Union Carbide and found it guilty; others, such as Paul Shrivastava, *Bhopal: Anatomy of a Crisis* (Cambridge, Mass.: Ballinger Publishing, 1987), presented a more balanced account and attempt to understand how and why the disaster took place and how it was handled. My purpose in considering the case is not to place blame, but to see what we can learn from the case and whether it suggests guidelines that might help prevent similar disasters from arising in the future.

2. *New York Times*, February 15, 1989, p. 1. The estimated numbers of dead and injured vary, and there is no way to establish the precise numbers definitively. Up to 500,000 claims have been filed for death or injury, and separating valid from fraudulent claims has been a continuing difficulty for the Indian government.

3. *New York Times*, December 8, 1984, p. 7; *Time*, December 17, 1984, p. 24.

4. *Wall Street Journal*, May 1, 1992, p. B8.

5. From a statement of Warren Anderson, *New York Times*, March 21, 1985, p. 48.

6. Statement by Ron Van Mynen, Vice President of Health Safety and Environmental Affairs, Union Carbide, May 13, 1986; *San Jose Mercury-News*, January 4, 1986, p. 7F.

7. *Wall Street Journal*, September 27, 1985, p. 6; *Wall Street Journal*, December 4, 1985, p. 2. See also Richard I. Kirkland, Jr., "Union Carbide: Coping with Catastrophe," *Fortune*, January 7, 1985, p. 53.

8. Thomas M. Gladwin and Ingo Walter, "Bhopal and the Multinational," *Wall Street Journal*, January 16, 1985, p. 20.

9. *Wall Street Journal*, December 11, 1984, p. 2.

10. Gladwin and Walter, op. cit., p. 20; *New York Times*, March 21, 1985, p. 48.

11. *New York Times*, March 21, 1985, p. 49.

12. *New York Times*, December 10, 1984, p. A6.

13. *New York Times*, January 28, 1985, p. 1.

14. *Time*, December 17, 1984, p. 24.

15. For a fuller discussion of the different kinds of responsibility, see Richard T. De George, *Business Ethics*, 3d ed. (New York: Macmillan, 1990), Chapter 8.

16. See, for example, Ellen K. Silbergeld, "Put Teeth in the Laws on Toxic Leaks," *New York Times*, August 18, 1985, p. F3; and Cathy Trost, "Bhopal Disaster Spurs Debate over Usefulness of Criminal Sanctions in Industrial Accidents," *Wall Street Journal*, January 7, 1985, p. 6.

17. *Wall Street Journal*, August 19, 1985, p. 5; August 21, 1989, p. 8.

18. *New York Times*, December 16, 1984, p. 4E.

19. Gladwin and Walter, op. cit., p. 20.

20. *Fortune*, January 7, 1985, p. 5; *Time*, December 24, 1984, p. 27.

21. Milton Friedman, "The Social Responsibility of Business Is to Increase Its Profits," *New York Times Magazine,* September 13, 1970.

22. See, for example, Peter A. French, *Collective and Corporate Responsibility,* New York, Columbia University Press, 1984.

23. I defend this position in *Business Ethics,* Chapter 5, and in my contribution to the following volume, which presents all of the contending positions: *Shame, Responsibility and the Corporation,* edited by Hugh Curtler (New York: Haven Publishing, 1986).

24. Alec Flamm, Union Carbide's president, first reported to Warren Anderson that there had been an accident at the Bhopal plant (*New York Times,* May 19, 1985, section 3, p. 8). Newspapers and commentators (e.g., Larry Everest) continue to refer to the incident as an accident. Once Union Carbide determined the incident was caused by sabotage, it no longer used the term "accident" but words such as "tragedy" or "disaster."

25. Union Carbide Press Release, June 27, 1985.

26. Union Carbide paid the money to the Indian Red Cross (*Wall Street Journal,* April 3, 1987, p. 6).

27. *New York Times,* March 21, 1985, p. 48.

28. *Wall Street Journal,* April 2, 1985, p. 34.

29. "Why Suits for Damages Such as Bhopal Claims are Very Rare in India," *Wall Street Journal,* January 23, 1985, p. 1.

30. *New York Times,* May 13, 1986, p. 29.

31. *Wall Street Journal,* April 1, 1985, p. 1.

32. Douglas J. Bersharov and Peter Reuter, "Averting a Bhopal Legal Disaster," *Wall Street Journal,* May 16, 1985, p. 26.

33. *Time,* December 17, 1984, p. 25.

34. Union Carbide Corporation, Annual Report 1985, p. 2.

35. *New York Times,* February 15, 1989, p. 1; *Wall Street Journal,* February 15, 1989, p. A3.

36. *New York Times,* January 22, 1990, pp. C1, C8.

37. *New York Times,* October 4, 1991, p. C4.

38. *Wall Street Journal,* May 1, 1992, p. B8.

39. *New York Times,* July 23, 1990, p. 1. Ironically, even the comparatively small payments being made by the Indian government reportedly are creating concern about inflation, corruption, and the inability of the market to absorb the money now available (*New York Times,* September 12, 1990, p. A6).

40. "Compensation for Bhopal Set," *New York Times,* June 22, 1992.

Chapter 6

1. The term *ethical dilemmas* is used in a great many ways in the literature on business ethics and is at the center of a controversy in ethical literature. Sometimes any ethical case or problem—any issue on which there is a choice—is called an ethical

dilemma. This is the broadest use of the term. More narrowly, an ethical dilemma arises in a situation in which one is faced with two equally unacceptable alternatives, or in which the situation has no satisfactory solution. In the former case one attempts to escape the two "horns" of the dilemma. Some ethical theorists deny that there is any such thing as an ethical dilemma, maintaining instead that in every situation there is a correct way of acting. To hold otherwise, they claim, is to hold that it would be one's duty to do what is unethical (which is self-contradictory) or that it would be ethical to act in a morally unacceptable way (which is also self-contradictory). For a brief summary of the arguments and a survey of the literature on ethical dilemmas, see Peter Vallentyne, "Moral Dilemmas and Comparative Conceptions of Morality," *Southern Journal of Philosophy* 30(1) (1992): 117–24.

2. Paul Richter, "Big Business Puts Ethics in Spotlight," *Los Angeles Times,* June 19, 1986, p. 1ff.

3. The 1992 global conference on the environment in Rio was an attempt to get agreement and concerted action on the necessary steps to preserve the environment and achieve sustainable growth. That conference underlined the need for international agreement and acceptable guidelines to which all countries and industries could be held.

4. For a history of bribery, and an argument that it is unethical, see John T. Noonan, Jr., *Bribes* (New York: Macmillan, 1984).

5. The Lockheed case was widely publicized. For two accounts of the case, see Carl A. Kotchian, "The Payoff: Lockheed's 70-Day Mission to Tokyo," *Saturday Review,* July 9, 1977, pp. 7–16; and Robert Shaplen, "Annals of Crime: The Lockheed Incident," *New Yorker* 53 (January 23 & 30, 1978): 48–50 & 74–91. For a broader account of Lockheed's foreign bribery payments, see David Boulton, *The Grease Machine* (New York: Harper & Row, 1978). However, Lockheed's payments were not the only ones that led to the Foreign Corrupt Practices Act. During the period from 1974 to 1976, according to an SEC report, at least 435 corporations made improper payments to foreign officials or political parties (Securities and Exchange Commission, Report to the Senate Committee on Banking, Housing and Urban Affairs. 94th Congress, 2d Session, "Questionable and Illegal Corporate Payments and Practices" (Comm. Print 1976). See also U.S. Congress, Senate, Committee on Banking, Housing and Urban Affairs, "Corrupt Overseas Payments by U.S. Business Enterprises," Report No. 94-1031, 94th Congress, 2d Session. For details of the Japanese reaction, see Edwin O. Reischauer, "The Lessons of the Lockheed Scandal," *Newsweek,* May 10, 1976, pp. 20–21; "Shame by Association," *Time,* March 22, 1976, p. 26; and Jerome Allan Cohen, "Japan's Watergate," *New York Times Magazine,* November 21, 1976, pp. 37, 104–19.

6. Business Accounting and Foreign Trade Simplification Act: Joint Hearings on S. 708 Before the Subcommittee on Securities and the Subcommittee on International Finance and Monetary Policy of the Senate Committee on Banking, Housing and Urban Affairs, 97th Congress, 1st Session 3 (1981).

7. The Foreign Corrupt Practices Act, Pub. L. No. 95-213, 91 Stat. 1464 (1977) codified at 15 U.S.C. §§ 78a, 78m, 78dd–1, 78ff (1982).

8. Foreign Corrupt Practices Act Amendments of 1988 (Pub. L. 100-418-102 Stat. 1107 (Aug. 23. 1988) codified at 15 U.S.C. §78a note). For one reaction to the Amendments, see Bartley A. Brennan, "The Foreign Corrupt Practices Act Amend-

ments of 1988: 'Death' of a Law," *North Carolina Journal of International Law and Commercial Regulation* 15 (1990): 229–47.

9. For a discussion of the original act and the 1988 amendments, see Bill Shaw, "Foreign Corrupt Practices Act Amendments of 1988," *Maryland Journal of International Law and Trade* 14 (1990): 161–74.

10. John Graham, "Foreign Corrupt Practices: A Manager's Guide," *Columbia Journal of World Business* 89 (1983): 93.

11. U.S. General Accounting Office, Report to the Congress: "The Impact of the FCPA on U.S. Business," (March 4, 1981).

12. Paul J. Beck, Michael W. Maher, and Adrian E. Tschoegl, "The Impact of the Foreign Corrupt Practices Act on U.S. Exports," *Managerial and Decision Economics,* 12(4) (August 1991): 295–303.

13. John M. Kline, *International Codes and Multinational Business: Setting Guidelines for International Operations* (Westport, Conn.: Quorum Books, 1985), pp. 61, 92.

14. On stakeholder analysis, see R. Edward Freeman, *Strategic Management: A Stakeholder Approach* (Boston: Pitman, 1984).

15. Some recent attempts have been made to bring some moral heroes of business to light. Some people have made heroes of whistle-blowers; but they are more a negative than a positive model.

16. Quoted from its annual announcement. In addition to its awards, it also makes available case studies of the awardees for business and classroom use.

17. For a discussion of the Sullivan Principles, see Richard T. De George, *Business Ethics,* 3d ed. (New York: Macmillan, 1990), pp. 419–23.

18. For accounts of various whistle-blowers and whistle-blowing cases, see, Myron Peretz Glazer and Penina Migdal Glazer, *The Whistle Blowers* (New York: Basic Books, 1989); Alan F. Westin, ed., *Whistle-Blowing!: Loyalty and Dissent in the Corporation* (New York: McGraw-Hill, 1981); and *Whistle Blowing: The Report of a Conference on Professional Responsibility,* ed. by Ralph Nader, Peter J. Petkas, and Kate Blackwell (New York: Grossman Publishers, 1972).

19. See, Robert M. Anderson, Robert Perrucci, Dan E. Schendel, and Leon E. Trachtman, *Divided Loyalties: Whistle-Blowing at BART* (West Lafayette, Ind.: Purdue University, 1980).

20. Dan Gellert, "Insisting on Safety in the Skies," in Westin, op. cit., pp. 17–30.

21. Frank Camps, "Warning an Auto Company About an Unsafe Design," in Westin, op. cit., pp. 119–29.

22. Among the numerous articles that cite Johnson & Johnson for exemplary behavior in the Tylenol incidents, see Clark H. Johnson, "A Matter of Trust," *Management Accounting* 71(6) (December 1988): 12–13; Allan Cox, "Exercising Vision and Values," *Executive Excellence* 7(12) (December 1990): 7–9; Christopher Power, "At Johnson & Johnson, a Mistake Can Be a Badge of Honor," *Business Week,* September 26, 1988, pp. 126–28. See also Chapter 1, footnote 12.

23. James Brooke, "Threats Terrorize Colombia's Courts," *New York Times,* August 27, 1989, p. 24; Alan Weisman, "Dangerous Days in the Marcarena," *New York Times Magazine,* April 23, 1989, pp. 40–42.

Chapter 7

1. Ford S. Worthy, "When Somebody Wants a Payoff," *Fortune* 120(13) (Pacific Rim, 1989): 118.

2. Pub. L. No. 100-418, § 5003d(1), (d)(2) (A), 102 Stat. 1424 (1988) indicates that the President should negotiate with the OECD to adopt similar legislation.

3. Nonetheless, the United States approved a move by the Colombian government to entice drug traffickers to surrender by promising them lenient treatment and immunity from extradition (Joseph B. Treaster, "Colombia's Move on Drugs Backed," *New York Times,* December 21, 1990, p. A11).

4. For an account of apartheid in South Africa, see Oliver F. Williams, *The Apartheid Crisis: How We Can Do Justice in a Land of Violence* (San Francisco: Harper & Row, 1986); the Sullivan Principles are listed in the book's appendix. For an economic analysis, see *Business in the Shadow of Apartheid: U.S. Firms in South Africa,* ed. by Jonathan Leape, Bo Baskin, and Stefan Underhill (Lexington, Mass.: Lexington Books, 1985).

5. On June 3, 1987, Sullivan called for the withdrawal of U.S. firms within nine months (Barnaby J. Feder, "Sullivan Asks End of Business Links with South Africa," *New York Times,* June 4, 1987, p. 1). Whether the actions by American companies that adopted the Sullivan Principles played any role in the vote of white South Africans to end apartheid and whether withdrawal—to the extent that it took place, since some questions remain about whether many companies left in name only (see, for example, Harrison J. Goldin, "The Divestiture Con Game," *New York Times,* December 16, 1986, p. 27; Dennis Kneale, "Leaving South Africa," *Wall Street Journal,* August 24, 1987, p. 1)—played a significant role are difficult to determine. Almost certainly the pressure placed on South Africa by the sanctions and condemnations of so many states did play an important role. On March 17, 1992, the white minority of South Africa in a referendum voted a strong mandate to President F. W. de Klerk to negotiate an end to apartheid and to form a new nonracial constitution ("A Mandate for Change," *New York Times,* March 20, 1992, p. A1).

6. See Marlise Simons, "New Telephone Line in Milan Shows Gangster Activity in Northern Italy," *New York Times,* July 1, 1991, p. A4.

7. For an account of the drug lords, see Paul Eddy with Hugo Sabogal and Sara Walden, *The Cocaine Wars* (New York: Bantam Books, 1988).

8. By comparison, it is estimated that 20 percent of Colombia's export earnings come from drug trafficking (Joseph B. Treaster, "Colombians Fear for the Economy," *New York Times,* September 11, 1989, p. A5).

9. How far back one traces the Mafia is a disputed issue. For one history of the Mafia, see Gaia Servadio, *Mafioso: A History of the Mafia from Its Origins to the Present Day* (London: Secker & Warburg, 1976).

10. See, for instance, Hernando de Soto, "Property Rights: The Way Out for Coca Growers," *Wall Street Journal,* February 13, 1990, p. A22.

11. Michael S. Serrill, "Fight to the Death: Colombia Takes on the Lords of Cocaine," *Time,* September 4, 1989, pp. 12–17.

12. See, for instance, "Traffickers Said to Buy Contra's Arms," *Washington Post,* September 18, 1990. For some accounts of the violence, see Paul Eddy et al., op. cit.

13. Eddy, *The Cocaine Wars,* claimed that "in America, at least, ether manufacturers have unwritten agreements with the DEA to tip the agency off about 'suspicious' customers" (p. 285). A 1988 CIA report indicated that, since 1983, the importation of chemicals used to manufacture illegal drugs had sharply increased. The Chemical Diversion and Trafficking Act of 1988 required stringent reporting requirements on the sale of chemicals ("U.S. Chemicals Used to Process Illicit Drugs," *Christian Science Monitor,* July 27, 1988, p. 3).

14. Jose de Cordoba, "Colombia's Narcos Find Brute Force Yields Little Entree," *Wall Street Journal,* October 5, 1989, p. A1; "Colombia Drug Lords Buy Land, Gain Acceptance," *New York Times,* December 21, 1988, p. A1.

15. Douglas Jehl and Robin Wright, "New Strategy Held Promising in Drug Battle," *Los Angeles Times,* September 1, 1989, Sec. I, p. 1.

16. Nonetheless, in 1991 the Colombian government offered major drug traffickers a plea-bargaining package that included a guarantee of no extradition to the United States. Pablo Escobar Gaviria, one of the more violent traffickers, surrendered, as did others. James Brooke, "Colombians See Hope in Killing of Drug Baron," *New York Times,* June 21, 1991, p. A5.

17. See the case described in Chapter 1, note 19. Whether the case actually describes contemporaneous Italian tax practices is not clear. But even today many Italian companies complain of the difficulty of following the maze of Italian tax laws and frequently resort to negotiating sessions to determine their taxes, just as frequently using a licensed *commercialista* to act as the company's negotiator.

18. Alan Cowell, "Italy at Risk to be Titled Sick Man of Europe," *New York Times,* June 1, 1992, p. A6.

19. For an example, see Chapter 1, note 18.

20. For a fuller discussion and justification of these conditions for whistle-blowing, see, Richard T. De George, *Business Ethics,* 3d ed. (New York: Macmillan, 1990), pp. 200–216.

Chapter 8

1. For descriptions of some of the plans different countries in Central and Eastern Europe have devised, see Steve Lohr, "Poland to Privatize Industry By Giving Stake to All Adults," *New York Times,* June 28, 1991, p. 1; "Poland, Pioneer of Capitalism," *New York Times,* January 30, 1991, p. A14; Steven Greenhouse, "East Europe's Sale of the Century," *New York Times,* May 22, 1990, p. C1; Steven Greenhouse, "East Europe Finds Pain on Journey to Capitalism," *New York Times,* Nov. 10, 1990, p. 1.

2. For a survey, see Serge Schmemann, "For Eastern Europe Now, a New Disillusion," *New York Times,* November 9, 1990, p. 1.

3. See, for instance, Stephen Engelberg, "Poland's New Climate Yields Bumper Crop of Corruption," *New York Times,* November 12, 1991, p. 1; Barry Newman, "Poland Has Plenty of One Thing: Crooks," *Wall Street Journal,* April 9, 1991, p. A20; Magoroh Maruyama, "Contracts in Cultures," *Human Systems Management* 10(1) (1991): 33–46.

4. Philip Dimitrov, "Freeing the Soul from Communism," *Wall Street Journal,* March 23, 1992, p. A10. For an account of business and ethics in Poland, see Leo V. Ryan, "The New Poland: Major Problems for Ethical Business," *Business Ethics: A European Review* 1(1) (January 1992): 9–15.

5. See, for instance, Clifford J. Levy, "East Europeans in U.S. Reclaiming Lost Estates," *New York Times,* August 13, 1991, p. A7.

6. For other details of that attempted sale, see Steven Greenhouse, "Rescue of Gdansk Shipyard Stalls," *New York Times,* April 9, 1990, p. D1; David Margolick, "Lech's American Angel," *New York Times,* October 8, 1989, section 6, p. 28; "Tough Terms End a Deal in Gdansk," *New York Times,* January 18, 1990. The next day Mrs. Johnson's representatives denied the story of the Gdansk unraveling (*New York Times,* p. A11).

7. For one account, see " 'Shady' Deals Spur New Agency in Hungary," *BLOC: The Soviet Union and Eastern Europe Business Journal* (April/May 1990): 4.

8. On other aspects of workers' benefits, see Celestine Bohlen, "East Europe's Women Struggle With New Rules, and Old Ones," *New York Times,* November 25, 1990, section 4, p. 1.

9. For a discussion of the ethics of advertising in the American context, see Richard T. De George, *Business Ethics,* 3d ed. (New York: Macmillan, 1990), Chapter 11.

10. For a statement of Marx's account of exploitation, see "Wages, Price, and Profit", Karl Marx and Frederick Engels, *Selected Works* (New York: International Publishers, 1984), pp. 186–229.

11. For instance, consider the charges of price gouging and monopolistic practices in Czechoslovakia ("With No Controls and Little Competition, Price Soar in Czechoslovakia," *New York Times,* January 30, 1991, p. A11).

12. Bill Keller, "Of Famous Arches, Beeg Meks and Rubles," *New York Times,* January 28, 1990, section 1, p. 1. By 1992, however, McDonald's was getting most of its supplies from Russian suppliers (Louis Uchitelle, "That's Funny, Those Pickles Don't Look Russian," *New York Times,* February 27, 1992, p. A4).

13. See, for instance, Francis X. Clines, "Fears of Capitalist Exploitation Slow Soviet–Chevron Oil Venture," *New York Times,* August 16, 1991, p. 1.

14. This position was defended, for instance, by Alexander Filatov, a professor of economics at Moscow's Plekhanov Institute of National Economy, in a symposium on "Ethical Issues on Doing Business in Eastern Europe and the European Community" at the Ninth Bentley Conference on Business Ethics, March 30–31, 1992. See also Fred Hiatt, "Capitalism Afloat Has Russia Awhirl," *International Herald Tribune,* May 18, 1992, p. 1, which quotes Grigory Napolov, deputy minister of industry: "Whatever kind of corruption is possible, we have it."

15. The approbation of these firms by the Chinese Communist Party appeared in the party newspaper, *People's Daily,* reported in the *Lawrence Journal World,* June 14, 1992, p. 2A.

16. "The Last Gulag," *Newsweek,* September 23, 1991, pp. 26–28; Hongda Harry Wu, *Laogai: The Chinese Gulag* (Boulder, Colo.: Westview Press, 1992); A. M. Rosenthal, "Sixteen Million Slaves," *New York Times,* June 19, 1992, p. A15.

17. For an article describing slave or forced labor in various countries, see "Slavery," *Newsweek,* May 4, 1992, pp. 30–39.

Chapter 9

1. Yumiko Ono, "Bargain Hunting Catches on in Japan, Boosting the Fortunes of Discount Stores," *Wall Street Journal,* May 19, 1992, p. B1. Only in July 1991 did it become illegal to enforce "suggested retail prices" (David E. Sanger, "Japan Sets Tough Rules on Business," *New York Times,* July 15, 1991, p. C1).

2. Delaying regulations include the law requiring the approval of other retailers in the area before one can open a store with over 5,000 square feet of space (Kathryn Graven, "Toys 'R' Us, Trying to Break into Japan, Becomes a Test Case for Trade Hurdles," *Wall Street Journal,* February 7, 1990, p. B1; "Mosbacher to Press Japan on Opening up Its Markets," *International Herald Tribune,* March 12, 1990, p. 9); David E. Sanger, "Japanese Give in Grudgingly on a New Way of Shopping," *New York Times,* November 12, 1990, p. 1.

3. Clay Chandler, "Japanese Stock Scandal Sends Strong Message: Small Investors Beware," *Wall Street Journal,* June 25, 1992, p. 1; James Sterngold, "Japan's Scandal: No Laws to Break," *New York Times,* July 15, 1991, p. D3.

4. Among others, see Kenichi Ohmae, "The Scandal Behind Japan's Financial Scandals," *Wall Street Journal,* August 6, 1991, p. A14; James Sterngold, "Another Scandal in Japan, This Time Involving Billions," *New York Times,* February 23, 1992, p. E3.

5. David E. Sanger, "Japanese in Ministry Cut Pay," *New York Times,* July 11, 1991, p. C1.

6. Ibid., p. C8.

7. Akio Morita and Shintaro Ishihara, *"No" to ieru Nihon: shin Nichi-Bei kankei no kado* [*The Japan That Can Say "No": The Card for a New US–Japan Relationship* (Tokyo: Kobunsha, 1989). For a review of the book, see Ian Buruma, "Just Say Noh," *New York Review of Books,* December 7, 1989, pp. 19–20. An English edition appeared: Shintaro Ishihara, *The Japan That Can Say NO,* translated by Frank Baldwin (New York: Simon & Schuster, 1991).

8. Alan Murray, "U.S. Economy Leads Japan's—But for How Long?" *Wall Street Journal,* June 13, 1990, p. A8, claims that, despite their higher per capita income, the Japanese enjoy only 75 percent of the Americans' purchasing power.

9. Milton Friedman, "The Social Responsibility of Business Is to Increase Its Profits," *New York Times Magazine,* September 13, 1970.

10. A large body of literature deals with corporate social responsibility. Among others, see Archie B. Carroll, *Business & Society: Managing Corporate Social Performance* (Boston: Little, Brown, 1981); Richard N. Farmer and W. Dickerson Hogue, *Corporate Social Responsibility,* 2d ed. (Lexington, Mass.: Lexington Books, 1985). See also Hugh Curtler, ed., *Shame, Responsibility and the Corporation* (New York: Haven, 1986).

11. Some Japanese firms are aware of this criticism and have taken steps to adapt themselves to American expectations. See David E. Sanger, "Japan to Give Tax Benefits for Charitable Aid in U.S.," *New York Times,* February 22, 1990, p. 1; Richard E. Wokutch, "Corporate Social Responsibility Japanese Style," *Academy of Management Executive* 4(2) (1990): 56–74.

12. At the Earth Summit in Rio in 1992, the Japanese promised $7.7 billion dollars in environmental aid over five years. The United States promised only $150

million to protect forests. Despite the difference, President Bush claimed that the United States was still the leader in environmental issues (*Kansas City Star,* June 14, 1992, p. 1).

13. In June 1992, Japan accused the United States of breaking the rules of fair trade and claimed that the United States had the most unfair trade among industrialized nations. The United States rejected the charges as unfounded. See James Sterngold, "Japan Accuses U.S. of Breaking Rules of Trade Fairness," *New York Times,* June 8, 1992, pp. 1; Keith Bradsher, "As U.S. Urges Free Markets, Its Trade Barriers Are Many," *New York Times,* February 7, 1992, p. 1.

14. Steven R. Weisman, "Trade Talks Fail to Produce Gains for U.S. or Japan," *New York Times,* March 16, 1990, p. 1.

15. For a discussion of the justice of economic systems and of the American system of free enterprise, see Richard T. De George, *Business Ethics,* 3d ed. (New York: Macmillan, 1990), Chapters 6 and 7.

16. The most plausible of this kind of allegation goes back to John Kenneth Galbraith's *Economics and the Public Purpose* (Boston: New American Library, 1973).

17. Both Japan and the United States claim to abide by the General Agreement on Tariffs and Trade, though each accuses the other of violating its provisions. See James Sterngold, loc. cit.

18. Marshall Auerback, "Japan Inc.'s Days Are Numbered," *Wall Street Journal,* September 3, 1991, p. A12; Karel van Wolferen, "An Economic Pearl Harbor?," *New York Times,* December 2, 1991, p. A13.

19. Susan Moffat, "Meet Your New Japanese Landlord," *Fortune,* June 18, 1990, p. 113. On the high cost of land, see also James Sterngold, "While Land Prices Soar, Officials Fight Back with Words," *New York Times,* March 25, 1990, p. 1; Bob Deans, "Japanese Lenders Try Home Mortgages on the 100-Year Plan," *Lawrence Journal World,* April 20, 1990, p. 1c.

20. Yumiko Ono, op. cit., p. B1.

21. "Why Japan Must Change," *Fortune,* March 9, 1992, p. 67.

22. The United States listed 240 idea for Japan; Japan countered with 80 for the United States. See David E. Sanger, "Japan to U.S.: Tighten Up. U.S. to Japan: Loosen Up," *New York Times,* March 27, 1990, p. D1.

23. See Chapter 9, notes 1 and 2.

24. Susan Chira, "Japan Denies 'Dumping,' Says Chip Pact Intact," *New York Times,* March 18, 1987, p. D7; Art Pine, "Japanese Firms Continue to Dump Chips U.S. Says," *Wall Street Journal,* March 20, 1987, p. 21.

25. Susan Chira, "Tokyo Protests Tariffs; Official Sees Retaliation," *New York Times,* March 28, 1987, p. A35; "Chip Sanction Held Effective," *New York Times,* October 7, 1987, p. D7; Andrew Pollack, "Chip Pact Falls Short of Goals," *New York Times,* August 2, 1988, p. D1.

26. By 1990, U.S. firms had 12.9 percent of the Japanese semiconductor market (*Wall Street Journal,* March 7, 1990, p. B8). A new agreement in 1991 set a goal of 20 percent, but by March 31, 1992, non-Japanese firms had only 14.4 percent of the Japanese market in semiconductors ("Foreign-Chip Lag in Japan," *New York Times,* March 31, 1992, p. D5).

27. Martin Tolchin, "Foreign Investors Held $2 Trillion in U.S. in '89," *New York Times,* June 13, 1990, p. C2; "Japanese Still Spending Billions on U.S. Real Estate, Study Says," *Lawrence Journal World,* March 28, 1991, p. 5B.

28. "Japanese Buy New York Cachet with Deal for Rockefeller Center," *New York Times,* October 31, 1989, p. A1; "Family Reaps Rich Rewards from Symbol of Vast Wealth," *New York Times,* February 16, 1992, Sec. 1, p. 34.

29. For a follow-up report, see Nancy J. Perry, "Will Sony Make It in Hollywood?" *Fortune,* September 9, 1990, pp. 158–66.

30. Moffat, op. cit., p. 116.

31. Claire Smith, "Baseball Will Allow Sale of Seattle Team to Japanese Group," *New York Times,* June 10, 1992, p. 1. The agreement on the sale, however, required that Japanese financial interests be less than 50 percent, and that control be 100 percent in the control of an American.

32. The exact proportion is not known, but Robert Lindsay ("Japanese Riding Hawaii's Real Estate Boom," *New York Times,* March 18, 1988, p. A1) reports that Japanese "own virtually all the major beach front hotels as well as most major resorts on other islands in the state." Governor John Waihee "wished that the Japanese would invest more in industry rather than limit their investments to resorts and private homes" (p. A17). See also Douglas Frontz and Catherine Collins, *Selling Out: How We Are Letting Japan Buy Our Land* (Chicago: Contemporary Books, 1989), Chapter 20, "Colonizing Hawaii," which paints an alarmed picture. But by February 21, 1992 ("Under Water: Japanese Purchases of U.S. Real Estate Fall on Hard Times," *Wall Street Journal,* p. A1), Jim Carlton and Neil Barsky reported that Minoru Isutani, who had bought Pebble Beach Golf Links in 1990 for $841 million had resold it for $500 million, and that the Japanese buying frenzy in Hawaii was over.

33. Kim Foltz, "Advertising: Lobbying Is Recommended to Prepare for Europe 1992," *New York Times,* October 3, 1990, p. C19.

34. Steven Prokesch, "Europe Takes on Auto Pollution," *New York Times,* October 2, 1989, p. 25.

35. "Uninvited Guests," *Newsweek,* February 5, 1990, pp. 18–23.

36; Christopher Dickey, "The Porous South," *Newsweek,* February 5, 1990, pp. 26–27.

37. Tony Horwitz and Craig Forman, "Clashing Cultures: Immigrants to Europe From the Third World Face Racial Animosity," *Wall Street Journal,* August 14, 1990, p. 1.

38. Ruth Marshall, "A Lost Generation," *Newsweek,* February 5, 1990, pp. 28–31.

39. Peter Schweizer, "Our Thieving Allies," *New York Times,* June 23, 1992, p. A15; Bob Davis, "Insecure Feeling," *Wall Street Journal,* March 28, 1988, p. 1; William M. Carley, "Corporate Targets: As Cold War Fades, Some Nations' Spies Seek Industrial Secrets," *Wall Street Journal,* June 17, 1991, p. 1; Douglas Waller, "The Open Door: U.S. Firms Face a Wave of Foreign Espionage," *Newsweek,* May 4, 1992, pp. 58–60.

40. For a fuller development of the arguments on which these claims stand, see Richard T. De George, *Business Ethics,* 3d ed. (New York: Macmillan, 1990), Chapters 12 and 14.

Chapter 10

1. For this action, Merck & Company received a Business Enterprise Award in 1990 from the Business Enterprise Trust, which honors exemplary acts of courage, integrity, and social vision in business. A detailed case study is available from the trust, 204 Junipero Serra Blvd., Stanford, CA 94305.

2. In his philosophical writings, Kant distinguishes between perfect and imperfect duties (Immanuel Kant, *Foundations of the Metaphysics of Morals,* trans. by Lewis White Beck, Indianapolis: Bobbs-Merrill, 1980, pp. 39ff.). Perfect duties are what I have called negative injunctions. Imperfect duties go beyond the negative and require positive action but of a somewhat unspecified type. The obligation to give to charity is of this imperfect type. The literature on the difference between perfect and imperfect duties is considerable. See, for instance, Onora O'Neill, "Universal Laws and Ends-in-Themselves," *Monist* 72 (July 1989): 341–61; N. E. G. Harris, "Imperfect Duties and Conflict of Wills," *Kant-Studien* 79 (1988): 33–42; Joel Feinberg, "The Moral and Legal Responsibility of the Bad Samaritan," *Criminal Justice Ethics* 3 (Winter/Spring 1984): 56–68.

3. The notion of ideals is in a sense intuitive. Nonetheless, in the philosophical literature it is a disputed notion. For one version of the distinction, see John W. Hennessey, Jr., and Bernard Gert, "Moral Rules and Moral Ideals: A Useful Distinction in Business and Professional Practice," *Journal of Business Ethics* 4 (1985): 105–15. For some, there can exist no ideal in the sense we are using it, for one is always obliged to do the best one can. Some utilitarians hold this position. Actions that go beyond what is required are sometimes called "supererogatory" actions. Whether there can be such actions is also a disputed issue, and the literature dealing with it is large. For an important defense of supererogation, see J. O. Urmson, "Saints and Heroes," in *Essays in Moral Philosophy,* ed. by A. I. Melden (Seattle: University of Washington Press, 1958, pp. 198–216. Marcia Baron, "Kantian Ethics and Supererogation," *Journal of Philosophy* 84 (May 1987): 237–62, argues that no one can do without supererogation in a Kantian framework. Terrance C. McConnell, "Utilitarianism and Supererogatory Acts, *Ratio* 22 (June 1980): 36–38, argues a similar thesis with respect to utilitarianism. Even the Christian tradition entertains a dispute about whether one can do more than one is required to do or whether we are all called upon to be saints, even though most of us fall short. Despite the disputes and debates, the distinction between what one is required to do (such that one is blamed for failing to do it) and what one does beyond that (such that there is no punishment for failing to do it, while there is praise for doing it) is a common one and is useful for our purposes.

4. For details of this project, see "GE Plastics: 1990 Recipient, The Business Enterprise Award," available from the Business Enterprise Trust (see Chapter 10, note 1).

5. Milton-Friedman's much discussed article, "The Social Responsibility of Business Is to Increase Its Profits," *New York Times Magazine,* September 13, 1970, seems correct on this point.

6. Business ethics texts have typically dealt with ethics from the point of view either of duty and obligation or of good and bad consequences. These two approaches represented the dominant trends in ethical theory in the second half of this century. In the latter half of the 1980s, virtue ethics began to grow in importance, sometimes challenging the other two approaches. Among the important works in virtue ethics are

Alasdair MacIntyre, *After Virtue* (Notre Dame: Notre Dame University Press, 1981); Philippa Foot, *Virtues and Vices* (Berkeley: University of California Press, 1978); James D. Wallace, *Virtues and Vices* (Ithaca: Cornell University Press, 1978); and Edmund L. Pincoffs, *Quandaries and Virtues* (Lawrence: University Press of Kansas, 1986). For an application to business, see Oliver F. Williams and Patrick E. Murphy, "The Ethics of Virtue: A Moral Theory for Marketing," *Journal of Micromarketing* 10 (Spring, 1990): 19–29.

7. See Judge Miles W. Lord, "Plea for Corporate Conscience," *Harper's* (June 1984): 13–14; and Kenneth E. Goodpaster and John B. Matthews, Jr., "Can a Corporation Have a Conscience?" *Harvard Business Review* (January/February 1982): 132–41.

Bibliography

Books

Aiken, William, and La Follett, Hugh, eds. *World Hunger and Moral Obligations* (Englewood Cliffs, N.J.: Prentice-Hall, 1977).

Anderson, Robert M., Perrucci, Robert; Schendel, Dan E., and Trachtman, Leon E. *Divided Loyalties: Whistle-Blowing at BART* (West Lafayette, Ind.: Purdue University, 1980.

Bairoch, Paul. *The Economic Development of the Third World Since 1900,* translated by Lady Cynthia Postan (Berkeley: University of California Press, 1975).

Barnet, Richard J., and Müller, Ronald E. *Global Reach: The Power of the Multinational Corporations* (New York: Simon & Schuster, 1974).

Beitz, Charles R. *Political Theory and International Relations* (Princeton: Princeton University Press, 1979).

Beitz, Charles R.; Cohen, Marshall; Scanlon, Thomas; and Simmons, A. John, eds. *International Ethics* (Princeton: Princeton University Press, 1985).

Benjamin, Martin. *Splitting the Difference: Compromise and Integrity in Ethics and Politics* (Lawrence: University Press of Kansas, 1990).

Bentham, Jeremy. *An Introduction to the Principles of Morals and Legislation,* ed. by J. H. Burns and H. L. A. Hart (London: Athlone Press, 1970).

Bierksteker, Thomas J. *Distortion or Development: Contending Perspectives on the Multinational Corporation* (Cambridge, Mass.: MIT Press, 1978).

Boulton, David. *The Grease Machine* (New York: Harper & Row, 1978).

Brown, Peter G., and Shue, Henry, eds. *Boundaries: National Autonomy and Its Limits,* (Totowa, N.J.: Rowman & Littlefield, 1981).

Brownlie, Ian, ed. *Basic Documents on Human Rights,* 2d ed. (Oxford: Clarendon Press, 1981).

Bull, David. *A Growing Problem: Pesticides and the Third World Poor* (Oxford: OXFAM, 1982).

Business Roundtable. *Corporate Ethics: A Prime Business Asset: A Report on Policy and Practice in Company Conduct* (February 1988).

Cardoso, Fernando Henrique, and Faletto, Enzo. *Dependencia and Development in Latin America* (Berkeley: University of California Press, 1979).

Carroll, Archie B. *Business & Society: Managing Corporate Social Performance* (Boston: Little, Brown, 1981).

Carvounis, Chris C. *The Foreign Debt/National Development Conflict: External Adjustment and Internal Disorder in the Developing Nations* (New York: Quorum Books, 1986).

Conference Board. *Corporate Ethics,* Research Report No. 900, 1987.

Curtler, Hugh, ed. *Shame, Responsibility and the Corporation* (New York: Haven Publishing, 1986).

Davies, John, et al. *Agromedical Approach to Pesticide Management* (Miami: University of Miami, 1982).

De George, Richard T. *Business Ethics,* 3d ed. (New York: Macmillan, 1990).

Dobbing, John, ed. *Infant Feeding: Anatomy of a Controversy 1973–1984* (London: Springer-Verlag, 1988).

Donaldson, Thomas. *The Ethics of International Business* (New York: Oxford University Press, 1989).

Dworkin, Ronald. *Taking Rights Seriously* (Cambridge, Mass.: Harvard University Press, 1977).

Eddy, Paul, with Hugo Sabogal and Sara Walden. *The Cocaine Wars* (New York: Bantam Books, 1988).

Elfstrom, Gerard. *Ethics for a Shrinking World* (New York: St. Martin's Press, 1990).

———. *Moral Issues and Multinational Corporations* (New York: St. Martin's Press, 1991).

Ellis, Anthony, ed. *Ethics and International Relations,* Manchester: Manchester University Press, 1986.

Everest, Larry. *Behind the Poison Cloud: Union Carbide's Bhopal Massacre* (Chicago: Banner Press, 1985).

Ezorsky, Gertrude, ed. *Moral Rights in the Workplace* (Albany: State University of New York Press, 1987).

Falk, Richard; Kim, Samuel S.; and Mendlovitz, Saul H., eds. *Toward a Just World Order,* vol. 1 (Boulder: Westview Press, 1982).

Farmer, Richard N., and Hogue, W. Dickerson. *Corporate Social Responsibility,* 2d ed. (Lexington: Lexington Books, 1985).

Foot, Philippa. *Virtues and Vices* (Berkeley: University of California Press, 1978).

Freeman, R. Edward. *Strategic Management: A Stakeholder Analysis* (Boston: Pittman, 1984).

French, Peter A., ed. *Individual and Collective Responsibility* (Cambridge: Schenkman Publishing, 1972).

French, Peter A. *Collective and Corporate Responsibility* (New York, Columbia University Press, 1984).

Frontz, Douglas, and Collins, Catherine. *Selling Out: How We Are Letting Japan Buy Our Land* (Chicago: Contemporary Books, 1989).

Galbraith, John Kenneth. *Economics and the Public Purpose* (Boston: New American Library, 1973).

Gauthier, David. *Morals by Agreement* (Oxford: Clarendon Press, 1986).

Glazer, Myron Peretz, and Glazer, Penina Migdal. *The Whistle Blowers* (New York: Basic Books, 1989).

Gorovitz, Samuel, ed. *John Stuart Mill, Utilitarianism, with Critical Essays* (Indianapolis: Bobbs-Merrill, 1971.

Hallwood, Paul, and Sinclair, Stuart W. *Oil, Debt and Development: OPEC in the Third World* (London: George Allen & Unwin, 1981).

Harman, Gilbert. *The Nature of Morality* (New York: Oxford University Press, 1977).

Hauerwas, Stanley, and MacIntyre, Alasdair, eds. *Revisions: Changing Perspectives in Moral Philosophy* (Notre Dame, Ind.: University of Notre Dame Press, 1983).

Held, Virginia; Morgenbesser, Sidney; and Nagel, Thomas, eds. *Philosophy, Morality, and International Affairs* (New York: Oxford University Press, 1974).

Hoffman, W. Michael; Lange, Ann E.; Fedo, David A., eds. *Ethics and the Multinational Enterprise: Proceedings of the Sixth National Conference on Business Ethics* (New York: University Press of America, 1986).

Hoffmann, Stanley. *Duties Beyond Borders* (Syracuse: Syracuse University Press, 1981).

International Labour Office. *Tripartite Declaration of Principles Concerning Multinational Enterprises and Social Policy* (Geneva: ILO, 1977).

Ishihara, Shintaro. *The Japan That Can Say NO,* translated by Frank Baldwin (New York: Simon & Schuster, 1991).

Jalée, Pierre. *The Pillage of the Third World,* translated by Mary Klopper (New York: Modern Reader Paperbacks, 1968).

Kant, Immanuel. *Foundations of the Metaphysics of Morals,* trans. by Lewis White Beck (Indianapolis: Bobbs-Merrill, 1980).

Kline, John M. *International Codes and Multinational Business: Setting Guidelines for International Business Operations* (Westport, Conn.: Quorum Books, 1985).

Kohl, Wilfrid L. *OPEC, the United States, and the World Oil Market* (Baltimore: Johns Hopkins University Press, 1991).

Krausz, Michael, and Meiland, Jack W., eds. *Relativism: Cognitive and Moral* (Notre Dame, Ind.: University of Notre Dame Press, 1982).

Lappé, Frances Moore, and Collins, Joseph, *World Hunger: Ten Myths,* 4th ed. (San Francisco: Institute for Food and Development Policy, 1982).

Leape, Jonathan; Baskin, Bo; and Underhill, Stefan, eds. *Business in the Shadow of Apartheid: U. S. Firms in South Africa* (Lexington: Lexington Books, 1985).

Lenin, V. I. *Imperialism: The Highest Stage of Capitalism* (Moscow: Foreign Languages Publishing House, 1947).

MacIntyre, Alasdair. *After Virtue* (Notre Dame, Ind.: Notre Dame University Press, 1981).

Madrid, Raul L. *Over-Exposed: U.S. Banks Confront the Third World Debt Crisis* (Washington: Investor Responsibility Research Center, 1990).

Mahoney, Jack. *Teaching Business Ethics in the UK, Europe and the USA: A Comparative Study* (London: Athlone Press, 1990).

Makler, Harry; Martinelli, Alberto; and Smelser, Neil, eds. *The New International Economy* (Beverly Hills, Calif.: Sage Publications, 1982).

Mattelart, Armand. *Transnationals and the Third World: The Struggle for Culture* (South Hadley, Mass.: Bergin & Garvey, 1983).

May, Larry. *The Morality of Groups* (Notre Dame, Ind.: Notre Dame University Press, 1987).

May, Larry, and Hoffman, Stacey, eds. *Collective Responsibility: Five Decades of Debate in Theoretical and Applied Ethics* (Savage, Md.: Rowman & Littlefield, 1991).

McComas, Maggie; Fookes, Geoffrey; and Taucher, George. *The Dilemma of Third World Nutrition: Nestlé and the Role of Infant Formula* [a report prepared for and published by Nestlé], 1985.

Meagher, Robert F. *An International Redistribution of Wealth and Power: A Study of the Charter of Economic Rights and Duties of States* (New York: Pergamon Press, 1979).

Moran, Theodore H. *Multinational Corporations and the Politics of Dependence: Copper in Chile* (Princeton: Princeton University Press, 1977).

Morgenthau, Hans J. *Dilemmas of Politics* (Chicago: Chicago University Press, 1958).

Nader, Ralph; Petkas, Peter J.; and Blackwell, Kate, eds. *Whistle Blowing: The Report of a Conference on Professional Responsibility* (New York: Grossman Publishers, 1972).

Nash, Laura L. *Good Intentions Aside: A Manager's Guide to Resolving Ethical Problems* (Boston: Harvard Business School Press, 1992).

Nickel, James W. *Making Sense of Human Rights: Philosophical Reflections on the Universal Declaration of Human Rights* (Berkeley: University of California Press, 1987).

Noonan, John T., Jr. *Bribes* (New York: Macmillan, 1984).

Norris, Ruth, ed. *Pills, Pesticides and Profits* (Croton-on-Hudson, N.Y.: North River Press, 1982).

Novak, Michael, and Jackson, Michael P., eds. *Latin America: Dependency or Interdependence?* (Washington, D.C.: American Enterprise Institute for Public Policy Research, 1985).

Nozick, Robert. *Anarchy, State, and Utopia* (New York: Basic Books, 1974).

Olden, Thomas C. *Conscience and Dividends: Churches and the Multinationals* (Washington, D.C.: Ethics and Public Policy Center, 1985).

Pincoffs, Edmund L. *Quandaries and Virtues* (Lawrence: University Press of Kansas, 1986).

Rawls, John. *A Theory of Justice* (Cambridge: Harvard University Press, 1971).

Securities and Exchange Commission, Report to the Senate Committee on Banking, Housing and Urban Affairs. 94th Congress, 2d Session. *Questionable and Illegal Corporate Payments and Practices* (Comm. Print 1976).

Sen, Amartya. *Poverty and Famines: An Essay on Entitlement and Development* (Oxford: Clarendon Press, 1981).

Servadio, Gaia. *Mafioso: A History of the Mafia from Its Origins to the Present Day* (London: Secker & Warburg, 1976).

Shrivastava, Paul. *Bhopal: Anatomy of a Crisis* (Cambridge, Mass.: Ballinger Publishing, 1987).

Shue, Henry. *Basic Rights: Subsistence, Affluence, and U. S. Foreign Policy* (Princeton: Princeton University Press, 1980).

Sikora, R. I., and Barry, Brian, eds. *Obligations to Future Generations* (Philadelphia: Temple University Press, 1978).

Silverman, Milton; Lee, Philip R.; and Lydecker, Mia. *Prescriptions for Death: The Drugging of the Third World* (Berkeley: University of California Press, 1982).

Simon, John G.; Powers, Charles W.; and Gunnemann, Jon P. *The Ethical Investor: Universities and Corporate Responsibility* (New Haven: Yale University Press, 1972).

Stone, Christopher D. *Where the Law Ends: The Social Control of Corporate Behavior* (New York: Harper Torchbooks, 1975).

Tavis, Lee A., ed. *Multinational Managers and Poverty in the Third World* (Notre Dame, Ind.: University of Notre Dame Press, 1982).

United Nations, Economic and Social Council. *Proposed Text of the Draft Code of Conduct on Transnational Corporations,* E/1990/94, 12 June 1990.

U.S. Congress, Senate, Committee on Banking, Housing and Urban Affairs. *Corrupt Overseas Payments by U.S. Business Enterprises,* Report No. 94-1031, 94th Congress, 2d Session (1976).

U.S. General Accounting Office, Report to the Congress. *The Impact of the FCPA on U. S. Business,* March 4, 1981.

Wallace, James D. *Virtues and Vices* (Ithaca, N.Y.: Cornell University Press, 1978).

Werhane, Patricia, and D'Andrade, Kendall, eds. *Profit and Responsibility* (New York: Mellen Press, 1985).

Westin, Alan F. *Whistle-Blowing!: Loyalty and Dissent in the Corporation* (New York: McGraw-Hill, 1981).

Williams, Oliver F. *The Apartheid Crisis: How We Can Do Justice in a Land of Violence* (San Francisco: Harper & Row, 1986).

World Bank. *World Development Report 1989* (New York: Oxford University Press, 1989).

World Health Organization. *International Code of Marketing of Breast-milk Substitutes* (Geneva: WHO, 1981).

Wu, Hongda Harry. *Laogai: The Chinese Gulag* (Boulder, Colo.: Westview Press, 1992).

Articles

Aschkenasy, Janet. "Insurers Score Victory in Tylenol Product-Recall Case, *National Underwriter* (*Property/Casualty*) 90(39) (September 26, 1986): 1, 7.

Babbitt, Bruce. "The New Improved South America," *World Monitor* (February 1991): 32–39.

Baron, Marcia. "Kantian Ethics and Supererogation," *Journal of Philosophy* 84 (May 1987): 237–62.

Barry, Brian. "Do Countries Have Moral Obligations? The Case of World Poverty," in *The Tanner Lectures on Human Values,* Sterling M. McMurrin, ed. (Salt Lake City: University of Utah Press, 1981), pp. 25–44.

Beck, Paul J.; Maher, Michael W.; and Tschoegl, Adrian E. "The Impact of the Foreign Corrupt Practices Act on U.S. Exports," *Managerial and Decision Economics* 12(4) (August 1991): 295–303.

Becker, Helmut, and Fritzsche, David J. "Business Ethics: A Cross-cultural Comparison of Managers' Attitudes," *Journal of Business Ethics* (May 1987): 289–95.

Benson, George C. S. "Codes of Ethics," *Journal of Business Ethics* (May 1989): 303–19.

Brennan, Bartley A. "The Foreign Corrupt Practices Act Amendments of 1988: 'Death' of a Law," *North Carolina Journal of International Law and Commercial Regulation* 15 (1990): 229–47.

Buller, Paul F. "The Challenge of Global Ethics," *Journal of Business Ethics* (October, 1991): 767–75.

Calero, Tom. "Business and the Foreign Corrupt Practices Act," in *Profit and Responsibility,* Patricia Werhane and Kendall D'Andrade, eds. (New York: Mellen Press, 1985), pp. 191–95.

Caminiti, Susan. "The Payoff from a Good Reputation," *Fortune,* February 10, 1992, pp. 74–77.

Cohen, Jerome Allen. "Japan's Watergate," *New York Times Magazine,* November 21, 1976, pp. 37, 104–19.

Cohen, Marshall. "Moral Skepticism and International Relations," *Philosophy & Public Affairs* 13 (Fall 1984): 299–346.

Cox, Allan. "Exercising Vision and Values," *Executive Excellence* 7(12) (December 1990): 7–9.

Crist, Raymond E. "Land for the People—A Vital Need Everywhere: In Latin America and the Caribbean, It's Now 'a Prey to Hastening Ills' and Decay," *American Journal of Economics and Sociology* 42(3) (July 1983): 275–90.

De George, Richard T. "Property and Global Justice," *Philosophy in Context* 15 (1985): 34–42.

———. "Biomedical Ethics," in *Science and the Soviet Social Order,* Loren R. Graham, ed. (Cambridge, Mass.: Harvard University Press, 1990), pp. 195–224.

———. "Green and 'Everybody's Doing It'," *Business Ethics Quarterly* 1 (1991): 95–100.

Dobson, John. "The Role of Ethics in Global Corporate Culture," *Journal of Business Ethics* (June 1990): 481–88.

Enderle, Georges. "The Indebtedness of Low-Income Countries as an Ethical Challenge for Industrialized Market Economies," *International Journal of Applied Philosophy,* 4(3) (1989): 31–38.

English, Parker. "Bribery and the United States Foreign Corrupt Practices Act," *International Journal of Applied Philosophy* (Fall 1989): 13–23.

Feinberg, Joel. "The Moral and Legal Responsibility of the Bad Samaritan," *Criminal Justice Ethics* 3 (Winter/Spring 1984): 56–68.

Fierman, Jaclyn. "Fast Bucks in Latin Loan Swaps," *Fortune,* August 3, 1987, pp. 91–99.

Frederick, William C. "The Moral Authority of Transnational Corporate Codes," *Journal of Business Ethics* (March 1991): 165–77.

Friedman, Milton. "The Social Responsibility of Business Is to Increase Its Profits," *New York Times Magazine*, September 13, 1970.

Gaschott, Nancy. "Babies at Risk: Infant Formula Still Takes Its Toll," *Multinational Monitor*, (October 1986): 11–13.

Getz, Kathleen A. "International Codes of Conduct: An Analysis of Ethical Reasoning," *Journal of Business Ethics* (July 1990): 567–77.

Goodpaster, Kenneth E. "Business Ethics and Stakeholder Analysis," *Business Ethics Quarterly* (January 1991): 53–73.

Goodpaster, Kenneth E., and Matthews, John B., Jr., "Can a Corporation Have a Conscience?" *Harvard Business Review* (January/February 1982): 132–41.

Goodpaster, Kenneth E., and Whiteside, David E. "Note on the Export of Pesticides from the United States to Developing Nations," in *Ethics and the Multinational Enterprise*, W. Michael Hoffman, Ann E. Lange, and David A. Fedo, eds. (Lanham, Md.: University Press of America, 1986), pp. 305–33.

Gowans, Christopher W. "Integrity in the Corporation: The Plight of Corporate Product Advocates," *Journal of Business Ethics* (February 1984): 21–28.

Graham, John. "Foreign Corrupt Practices: A Manager's Guide," *Columbia Journal of World Business* 18 (1983): 89–94.

Green, C. F. "Business Ethics in Banking," *Journal of Business Ethics* (August 1989): 631–34.

Green, Ronald. "When Is 'Everyone's Doing It' a Moral Justification?" *Business Ethics Quarterly* 1 (1991): 75–93.

Grunts, Robert. "Ethics as a Way of Life," in *Ethics and the Multinational Enterprise: Proceedings of the Sixth National Conference on Business Ethics*, W. Michael Hoffman, Ann E. Lange, and David A. Fedo, eds. (New York: University Press of America, 1986), pp. 101–6.

Hare, R. M. "What Is Wrong with Slavery?" *Philosophy and Public Affairs* 8 (1979): 103–21.

Harman, Gilbert. "Moral Relativism Defended," *Philosophical Review* (1975): 3–22.

Harrington, Susan J. "What Corporate America Is Teaching About Ethics," *Academy of Management Executive* 5(1) (1991): 21–30.

Harris, N. E. G. "Imperfect Duties and Conflict of Wills," *Kant-Studien*, 79 (1988): 33–42.

Hector, Gary. "S&Ls: Where Did All Those Billions Go?" *Fortune*, September 10, 1990, pp. 84–88.

Hennessey, John W., Jr., and Gert, Bernard. "Moral Rules and Moral Ideals: A Useful Distinction in Business and Professional Practice," *Journal of Business Ethics* 4 (1985): 105–15.

Herman, Barry. "The Outlook for Development," in *Debt Disaster? Banks, Government, and Multilaterals Confront the Crisis*, John F. Weeks, ed. (New York: New York University Press, 1989), pp. 3–19.

Johnson, Clark H. "A Matter of Trust," *Management Accounting* 71(6) (December 1989): 12–13.

Kavka, Gregory. "Hobbes' War of All Against All," *Ethics* 93 (January 1983): 291–310.

Kelly, Arthur L. "Case Study—Italian Tax Mores," paper presented at Loyola University of Chicago symposium, "Foundations of Corporate Responsibility to Society," April 1977, and printed in *Ethical Issues in Business* Thomas Donaldson and Patricia H. Werhane, eds. (Englewood Cliffs, N.J.: Prentice-Hall, 1979), pp. 37–39.

Kirkland, Richard I., Jr. "Union Carbide: Coping with Catastrophe," *Fortune,* January 7, 1985, pp. 50–53.

Kotchian, Carl A. "The Payoff: Lockheed's 70-Day Mission to Tokyo," *Saturday Review,* July 9, 1977, pp. 7–16.

Lane, Henry W., and Simpson, Donald G. "Bribery in International Business: Whose Problem Is It?" *Journal of Business Ethics,* (February 1984): 35–42.

Lemke, Dwight K. "Ethics in Declining Organizations," *Business Ethics Quarterly* (July 1991): 235–48.

Longenecker, Justin G., et al. "The Ethical Issue of International Bribery: A Study of Attitudes Among U.S. Business Professionals," *Journal of Business Ethics* (May 1988): 341–46.

Lord, Judge Miles W. "Plea for Corporate Conscience," *Harper's* (June 1984): 13–14.

Mahoney, Jack. "An International Look at Business Ethics: Britain," *Journal of Business Ethics* (July 1990): 545–50.

Maruyama, Magoroh. "Contracts in Cultures," *Human Systems Management* 10(1) (1991): 33–46.

Marx, Karl. "Wages, Price and Profit," in Karl Marx and Frederick Engels, *Selected Works* (New York: International Publishers, 1984), pp. 186–229.

McConnell, Terrance C. "Utilitarianism and Supererogatory Acts," *Ratio* 22 (June 1980): 36–38.

McLeod, Douglas. "J&J Subsidiary Denied Coverage for Tylenol Recall," *Business Insurance* 20(38) (September 22, 1986): 1, 87.

McNall, Scott, and Margolin, Sally O. "Multinational Corporations in Latin America: The Search for Consumers and Raw Materials," *Comparative International Development* 12 (Fall 1977): 65–85.

Medawar, Charles, and Freese, Barbara. "Drug Multinationals in the Third World," *Business & Society Review* 38 (Summer 1981): 22–24.

Moffat, Susan. "Meet Your New Japanese Landlord," *Fortune,* June 18, 1990, p. 112–17.

Moran, Theodore H. "Multinational Corporations and Third World Investment," in *Latin America: Dependency or Interdependence?,* Michael Novak and Michael P. Jackson, eds. (Washington, D.C.: American Enterprise Institute for Public Policy Research, 1985), pp. 15–28.

Morita, Akio. "Why Japan Must Change," *Fortune,* March 9, 1992, pp. 66–67.

O'Neill, Onora. "Universal Laws and Ends-in-Themselves," *Monist* 72 (July 1989): 341–61.

Organization for Economic Cooperation and Development, "Guidelines for Multinational Enterprises" annex to the 1976 "OECD Declaration," *International Investment and Multinational Enterprises: Revised Edition 1984* (Paris: Organization for Economic Cooperation and Development, 1984), pp. 11–22.

Paine, Lynn Sharp. "Corporate Policy and the Ethics of Competitor Intelligence Gathering," *Journal of Business Ethics* (June 1991): 423–36.

Pastin, Mark, and Hooker, Michael. "Ethics and the Foreign Corrupt Practices Act," *Business Horizons* 23 (December 1980): 43–47.

Perdomo, Rogelio Perez. "Corruption and Business in Present Day Venezuela," *Journal of Business Ethics* (July 1990): 555–66.

Perry, Nancy J. "Will Sony Make It in Hollywood?" *Fortune*, September 9, 1990, pp. 158–66.

Ryan, Leo V. "The New Poland: Major Problems for Ethical Business," *Business Ethics: A European Review* 1(1) (January 1992): 9–15.

Shafer, Michael. "Capturing the Mineral Multinationals: Advantage or Disadvantage?" in *Multinational Corporations: The Political Economy of Foreign Direct Investment,* Theodore H. Moran, ed. (Lexington: Lexington Books, 1985), pp. 25–53.

Shaplen, Robert. "Annals of Crime: The Lockheed Incident," *New Yorker* 53 (January 23 & 30, 1978): 48–50 & 74–91.

Shaw, Bill. "Foreign Corrupt Practices Act Amendments of 1988," *Maryland Journal of International Law and Trade* 14 (1990): 161–74.

Shue, Henry. "Exporting Hazards," *Ethics* 91 (July 1981): 579–606.

Singer, A. E., and Van der Walt, N. T. "Corporate Conscience and Foreign Divestment Decisions," *Journal of Business Ethics* (October 1987): 543–52.

Singer, Peter. "Famine, Affluence and Morality," *Philosophy & Public Affairs* 2 (Spring 1972): 229–43.

Snoy, Bernard. "Ethical Issues in International Lending," *Journal of Business Ethics* (August 1989): 635–39.

Turow, Scott. "What's Wrong with Bribery?" *Journal of Business Ethics* (August 1985): 249–51.

United Nations General Assembly. "Declaration on the Establishment of a New International Economic Order," *Study of the Problems of Raw Materials and Development: Report of the Ad Hoc Committee of the Sixth Special Session,* A/9556 (Part II), 1 May 1974.

Unnia, Mario. "Business Ethics in Italy: The State of the Art," *Journal of Business Ethics* (July, 1990): 551–54.

Urmson, J. O. "Saints and Heroes," in *Essays in Moral Philosophy,* A. I. Melden, ed. (Seattle: University of Washington Press, 1958), pp. 198–216.

Vallentyne, Peter. "Moral Dilemmas and Comparative Conceptions of Morality," *Southern Journal of Philosophy,* 30(1) (1992): 117–24.

Van Luijk, Henk J. L. "Recent Developments in European Business Ethics," *Journal of Business Ethics* (July 1990): 537–44.

Velasquez, Manuel. "International Business, Morality, and the Common Good," *Business Ethics Quarterly* 2(1) (January 1992): 27–40.

Wellman, Carl. "The Ethical Implications of Relativity," *Journal of Philosophy* 60 (1963): 169–84.

Williams, Oliver F., and Murphy, Patrick E. "The Ethics of Virtue: A Moral Theory for Marketing," *Journal of Micromarketing* 10 (Spring 1990): 19–29.

Wokutch, Richard E. "Corporate Social Responsibility Japanese Style," *Academy of Management Executive* 4(2) (1990): 56–74.

Worthy, Ford S. "When Somebody Wants a Payoff," *Fortune* 120(13) (Pacific Rim, 1989): 117–22.

Index